MODERN MAN
AND RELIGION

T. G. MASARYK

MODERN MAN
AND RELIGION

Translated by
ANN BIBZA AND DR. VÁCLAR BENEŠ

Translation revised by
H. E. KENNEDY
B.A.

With a Preface by
DR. VASIL K. ŠKRACH
*Literary Secretary to the late
President Masaryk*

GREENWOOD PRESS, PUBLISHERS
WESTPORT, CONNECTICUT

Originally published in 1938
by George Allen & Unwin, Ltd., London

Reprinted from an original copy in the collections
of the Brooklyn Public Library

First Greenwood Reprinting 1970

Library of Congress Catalogue Card Number 78-109783

SBN 8371-4273-3

Printed in the United States of America

PREFACE

THE great man of a small nation is always, however great he may be, at a disadvantage compared with the great men of the larger nations; very special and favourable conditions are essential if he is to emerge over the frontiers of his own country and his influence penetrate to the outside world. The great artists of the small nations find it perhaps easiest to do so, for art speaks in the most convincing and most intimate tones of all.

A philosopher and statesman of Masaryk's kind concentrates naturally upon his own nation, and it is only when he has accomplished a great task for his own people that he attracts the attention of the world. That attention is of course more easily secured if his activities have been projected into a world-wide framework over and above the boundaries of nations and states—the framework of the ideology of humanity and democracy.

The great man of a small nation has a more complicated task to perform within his own nation than have other great men: as a rule he fulfils several functions in the life of the nation. In Masaryk's case the many-sidedness and manifold character of his work are particularly striking. At the University he was Professor of Philosophy, Ethics, and Sociology, but his own character and the character of his academic studies necessarily caused him in time to take up a wider activity in the cultural and political spheres. He was the moral, spiritual, and political "awakener" of the Czech nation, the framer of the national programme, and finally the

v

political liberator of his people; but all the time he maintained an uninterrupted contact with the currents of world thought in which, as a philosopher of history and as a sociologist, he sought an orientation of his own, endeavoured, albeit with critical eye, to reconcile himself to the existing trends of the day—religious and artistic, economic and technical, scientific and educational, moral, social, and political—and to find the right path for his nation to follow.

*   *   *   *   *

From his student days Masaryk devoted the closest attention to Western civilization, especially English and Anglo-American civilization, finding in it the most advanced stage of humanity.

It was in reading Buckle's *History of Civilization in England* during his studies at Leipsig in the year 1877 that he came into closer touch with the lady who later became his wife, Miss Charlotte Garrigue, of Brooklyn, an American puritan, with whom, during his sojourn in Vienna as Lecturer at the University, he translated Hume's *Principles of Morals* into German, and with whom, in Prague at a later date, he collaborated when she was translating Mill's *Subjection of Women* into Czech.

English cultural and political life had, by its spirit of humanity and democracy, long made an intimate appeal to Masaryk. The influence of his wife made that appeal still more intimate. He was well acquainted with religious developments in England, and noted their connection with political evolution, the connection between Parliamentarianism and Puritanism and the spirit of the Reformation. He had already studied the influence of Wycliffe upon Huss and the Bohemian Reformation, and he appreciated the reception given to Comenius in England. He perceived the far-reaching influence of the English Revolution upon the French Revolution and on the subsequent evolution of democracy, liberalism, and socialism in Europe.

In philosophy his starting-point was David Hume, and in logic he was a pupil of John Stuart Mill. Locke and Spencer were also his teachers. He loved Shakespeare, and Byron was to him the representative of the Protestant poetical-thinker spirit.

It was with an analysis of Hume's scepticism that he inaugurated his teaching career at the Czech University of Prague in the year 1882. In all his philosophical and educational activities he combated, by drawing attention to English cultural and political phenomena, the one-sided German influence upon his countrymen. English, after Czech and German, was the language he most used, and under his wife's influence it became the second language in his family circle.

In the year 1906, on the occasion of a Vienna inquiry as to the best books, Masaryk gave the majority of his votes to English literature; for out of a wide selection of twenty-two works he named twelve that were English or American: Leigh Hunt's *The Religion of the Heart*; Thomas Paine's *Age of Reason* and *Rights of Man*; David Hume's *Principles of Morals*; Charlotte Brontë's *Villette, Jane Eyre*, and *Shirley*; Shakespeare's *Tempest*; Lord Byron's *Cain, Manfred*, and *Don Juan*; Elizabeth Browning's *Aurora Leigh*. In a narrower selection of ten works he chose five that were English: Hunt, Paine's *Rights of Man*, Brontë's *Villette*, Shakespeare, Mrs. Browning.

He had visited England before the war, and during the war itself he stayed in England as an exile longer than in any other country (from September 1915 to May 1917). He was appointed in this period a Professor at King's College, London, and by his lectures, articles, memoranda, interviews, and extensive personal contacts, he made known to public opinion in England, in the Allied countries and throughout the world, the aims and aspirations of a small people in the midst of the great conflict of nations. In the spirit of Western democracy he endeavoured to give the Allies a programme for the struggle into which they had been drawn, and to prescribe a plan and an aim for the war. What he had commenced in England he continued in Russia, where he brought into being a Czechoslovak army to fight side by side with the Allies, and he concluded the work in America: American democracy meant *finis Austriae*. It is unnecessary here to relate what he has himself so fully, so vividly and effectively described in his books: *The New Europe* (1918) and *The Making of a State* (1925, English edition, 1927[1]).

In his *World Revolution* (the Czech original of *The Making of a State*) Masaryk tells us in detail how, during his sojourn in London, he remembered and renewed acquaintance with his old loves in English literature, both in philosophy and belles-lettres, and how by their aid he penetrated to the heart of the nation. His "Views

[1] George Allen & Unwin Ltd.

Preface

of England" in *The Making of a State* conclude with these words of appreciation: "English culture I hold to be the most progressive and, as I was able to see during the war, the most humane. Not that I think all the English are angels. But in their civilization the Anglo-Saxons—and this is true of America too—have expressed the humanitarian ideals the most carefully in theory, and have practised them in a higher degree than other nations. In English views of the war and in its conduct this was evident . . ."

At the end of November 1918, on his return from America to Europe and home, Masaryk once more saw England, and was welcomed no longer as a Professor but as the President of a new Republic.

In the year 1923 he was the guest of King George V in London, and the University of Oxford conferred on him the honorary degree of D.C.L. For several years he was president of the English World Association for Adult Education. For the *Encyclopaedia Britannica* he approved and completed the monograph on Czechoslovakia.

The English reader can acquaint himself with Masaryk's views through Masaryk's own works, in particular his great book, *The Spirit of Russia*,[1] written just before the Great War, depicting the philosophy of Russian history and Russian ideology as revealed in Russian cultural and political movements; and he has also at his disposal the book already referred to, on the Great War and the rise of the Czechoslovak State: *The Making of a State* (1927). A more intimate picture of Masaryk the man is given

[1] George Allen & Unwin Ltd., 1919.

Preface

in the talks with him which Karel Čapek has recorded in his *President Masaryk Tells His Story*,[1] and the conversations recorded by Emil Ludwig in *The Defender of Democracy*. The biographies by C. J. C. Street (*President Masaryk*) and Lowrie (*Masaryk of Czechoslovakia*) supplement those direct sources of knowledge in English of the great man of a small Slavonic nation in the heart of Europe.

The English public has learnt much about Masaryk from the Press; during his presidency, throughout the period of consolidation for the new small State in Central Europe with the unpronounceable name, they read more than one speech of this typical democrat, philosopher, and statesman in one person, whose outstanding figure, popularity, and moral authority penetrated to the West.

The well-informed English democrat knew that at Prague the President of the Republic was a great man, and he had the feeling of certainty that nothing could happen to compromise this small State while it remained under his direction. Masaryk's Republic had a sound reputation. Seldom was anything that was not handsome heard of it. There was felt, in particular, a confidence that nothing was likely to occur to deflect the Republic from the straight path of democracy.

In the early years after the war English journalists, politicians, and writers frequently came to Bohemia, and they took back with them reports of the vigorous and active young State with its aged President, whose portraits on horseback or book-in-hand were equally popular everywhere. In the views expressed by Masaryk in his

[1] George Allen & Unwin Ltd., 1935.

Preface

talks with these visitors there was always something interesting, firm, self-confident, and stimulating.

Masaryk's death in September 1937 again touched English public opinion. English publishers came forward of their own initiative to inquire about the possibility of presenting more of Masaryk's ideas and thoughts to the English reader.

To this end three works have been selected, one fairly long and two shorter, from a period that may seem somewhat remote—the middle nineties of last century. They constitute, however, the best introductions to the essence of Masaryk's thought, and are the key to the earlier as well as the later Masaryk. The *fin de siècle* was an interesting epoch; from it issued Masaryk's analyses and syntheses of ideas as fingerposts in a time of transition. Are we not to-day still in a period of transition?

The longer work, *Modern Man and Religion*, a collection of articles written in the years 1896–8 and published later in a single volume, introduces the reader to the very heart of Masaryk's philosophical, literary, and religious interests.

The other two works[1] are the short University lecture of 1898, *How to Work*—a discussion of the technique of work and a revelation of his own intellectual processes—and a series of University Extension lectures on *The Ideals of Humanity*, delivered in the year 1901, presenting his own ethical creed based on a critical examination of the main trends of morality.

[1] These appear together in a separate volume entitled *The Ideals of Humanity*. George Allen & Unwin Ltd., 1938.

3

Preface

It is necessary to connect these three works up with the evolution of Masaryk's personality—at least in brief outline.

*　　　*　　　*　　　*　　　*

Masaryk's study of *Modern Man and Religion*, a product of the nineties, links up with his first considerable work from the closing years of the seventies, his sociological and ethical analysis of suicide as a symptom of the inner spiritual emptiness of the modern man and the whole of society. Its third part, on modern Titanism, remained but a torso as compared with the scheme originally indicated in the book. This section was only dealt with and amplified in the third part of Masaryk's later great work, *The Spirit of Russia*, chapters which were practically finished in manuscript as early as 1914, but have only now been prepared for print. In Masaryk's analysis of the Great War we find also the essence of the views formulated in these studies. They are therefore obviously a kind of axis of Masaryk's thought, and the focus of his literary activities, in point both of time and matter.

In his *Suicide* (*Der Selbstmord als sociale Massenerscheinung der modernen Civilisation*, 1881) young Masaryk goes by way of the problem of self-murder to the root of the subjectivism and confusion of ideas in the modern world which he sees in the collapse of a uniform Christian world-outlook and in the decline generally of religious belief. He sent the book to Herbert Spencer who sent him a formal note of thanks.

Masaryk's second considerable work, *The Foundations of Concrete Logic* (1885), is the attempt of a methodical, modern polyhistorian to present, through a revision of

4

Preface

the contemporary state of learning, its classification and organization, the basis of a modern view of the world, and by a methodical upbuilding of sociology to lay the foundations for a reform of society. In its German rendering (*Versuch einer concreten Logik*, 1887) this work attracted the notice of philosophical circles in England, especially that of the author of a critical survey of the modern philosophy of history, R. Flint. In his *Suicide* and *Concrete Logic* the philosophical-historical character of Masaryk's thought comes into prominence.

At the University, Masaryk was a leader of youth, exerting his influence at this time especially through his lectures on practical philosophy. He organized the whole Czech world of philosophy and learning. He founded a critical review, *Athenaeum*, on the model of the London *Athenaeum* (to the London *Athenaeum* he contributed at this period an article dealing with John Huss in German literature), a review that greatly influenced Czech life. In it he began his fight against the Czech analogy to the Ossian poems, the supposed ancient Czech manuscripts romantically "discovered" at the beginning of the nineteenth century.

After some early political activities and election as deputy in the Vienna Parliament and in the Bohemian Diet (1891–3), Masaryk concentrated upon a study of the cultural and political history of the nation, and from this study there soon issued a national, educational, and political programme. From this stage dates his series of writings on the Czech question, which he already formulated as an international question and no mere chance dispute between the Czechs and Vienna. He stood opposed to the Austrian spirit which he already

5

Preface

regarded as a bastion of reaction, and he made efforts, in the spirit of Palacký, so to recast Austria as an empire that each of its separate nationalities could find the necessary conditions for their free existence.

In the later nineties he passed from Czech intellectual and political history to a consideration of human affairs generally. Thus came into being his series of articles on *Modern Man and Religion*, which present, through its philosophy and its poetical and religious traditions, an analysis of the spiritual and intellectual world at the end of the nineteenth century. To-day, after forty years, even the English reader will be captivated by the fineness of Masaryk's analysis—his keen philosophical, psychological, ethical, and literary analysis. As already noted, his study of the literary representatives of the individual national spheres remained uncompleted in these articles. In the introduction to the third part we read that he had meant to deal not only with the German Protestant Goethe and the French Catholic Musset, but also with Byron as representative of the English Protestant spirit, with the Catholic minds of Poland, with Polish Messianism (Mickiewicz and Krasiński), and with the leading minds of the Orthodox East (Dostoyevski and Tolstoy).

From all this he was taken away by other work, especially that on a great volume on the Social Question (Czech 1898, German: *Die philosophischen und soziologischen Grundlagen des Marxismus*, 1899), which was one of the first profound criticisms of Marxism, and of world-wide significance. The Hilsner affair, too, that is, Masaryk's fight against the superstition of ritual murder, took him away from his activities as an author and from his original plan of depicting "Modern Man" as a whole.

Preface

At this period Masaryk was continually moving between the University and the public, between the sphere of learning and the political arena. An example of his activities among the young University generation at this time is his lecture, *How to Work*, in which his method and his posing of a problem clearly stand out. This is one of Masaryk's most popular works, along with, perhaps, his University Extension Lectures of the year 1901 on *The Ideals of Humanity*, in which he presents the essence of his humanitarian programme and deals with currents close to his own as well as with those he opposes.

It would seem that at this time he had it in mind to present the problems of his articles on modern man and religion in a new form—within the framework of some intellectual history of the nineteenth century. He lectured considerably on that theme. He did not complete even his *Handbook of Sociology*, being continually occupied with current political problems, especially those connected with working-class conditions and the struggle for universal franchise rights. At this time he had become the leader of a political party of his own. From 1905 onwards, after the attempted revolution in Russia, he turned more and more to politics. In 1907 he again entered the Reichsrat in Vienna as representative of his party. As a deputy he declared determined war upon Austria-Hungary, especially after the annexation of Bosnia and Hercegovina, when he openly opposed the foreign policy of Austria as conducted by Aehrenthal. He unmasked Austria's Balkan policy against the Yugoslavs.

In 1911 he once again entered Parliament. He no longer lectured at the University, but concentrated his

Preface

efforts upon current politics and upon his great work, *The Spirit of Russia*, in which he once again endeavoured to present the essence of his philosophical views and criticisms of the ideologies which were the governing features of Russian life, and at the same time operating as echoes of Western, especially German, thought.

On the outbreak of the war Masaryk became one of the great figures of that struggle, and a man of world-wide note. His knowledge of pan-Germanism and his knowledge of Russia found equal application in the course of the war. With his exact imagination he had in almost prophetic fashion forecast, as early as the eighties and nineties of last century, the importance of the German and Russian problem.

The English reader is now given an opportunity of becoming more closely acquainted with the core of Masaryk's teaching and his methods, and of noting how his theories led to a definite practice. In the Great War, in the great clash of nations, Masaryk was able to have an effective hand in the development of Europe in the sense of a greater fund of humanity and democracy.

To-day the world continues to need the spiritual reminders that we find in Masaryk's thoughts. The Great War is not yet liquidated. Anti-democratic and anti-humanitarian tendencies are finding application throughout the whole world. The great man of a small nation has still something to say to the world. He speaks to its conscience, and calls it to work for the realization of the still unfulfilled ideals of democracy and humanity.

VASIL K. ŠKRACH,
Literary Secretary to the late President
Th. G. Masaryk.

INTRODUCTION

I CONSIDERED for a long time what title I should give to this study. "Modern Man and Religion" seems to me a little too pompous, and then, too, I rather dislike the word "modern." It is far too often misused. "Modern man"—verily a whole psychological problem is contained in these words. To compare man as he is today with earlier and with ancient man is to tell how that modern man arose out of the ancient one; what has caused him to become modern, what makes him modern. And then, what, in general, is man—for, if I am to make clear what modern man is, I must know what he was before he became modern—in short what man is. This solemn question sounds to me like a reproach to the word "modern" which is so carelessly tossed about in the literature of today.

What, then, is man? Who is he? What does he want? What does he hope for? What does he fear?—What is the meaning of all that is hidden behind the word "life"? And then again, "religion." I do not like that word either, for it, too, is very much misused. But my chief objection to it is that it sets me the same problem as the word "man." "Modern man and Religion," the phrase constitutes for me a tautology; "modern," "man," "religion"—from each of these words I see grinning at me the selfsame triune sphinx.

One thing I know about the religious question: it has always existed and it will always exist. I have never doubted this or questioned it, even for a moment. All my

9

Introduction

life-experience and study has confirmed me in this conviction again and again. It has always, therefore, been inexplicable to me how people can really doubt this and why they have doubted it. In truth they do not doubt it at all. Scepticism is not the only cause of opposition to religion. The question is to comprehend what is the basis of the fight against religion and what is the content of a seemingly irreligious life.

CONTENTS

Contents

Part One

Modern Suicidism—Wearied Souls

Chapter I

Modern Suicidism

I WAS not yet ten years old when, for the first time, I began to think a great deal about suicide. Perhaps I had heard something about it before (I cannot remember), but it was not until two events occurred that my attention was directed to it: in so far, of course, as this is possible for a lad.

I can still see before me that gate leading to the stable, on which a farm-hand from our neighbourhood hanged himself. It happened long before I found out about it, but it made a great impression upon me when a comrade of the deceased, a man who knew him, told me all about the self-murder and showed me the place . . . a place that was familiar to me, for I myself used often to go to the stable and play mischievous pranks there. But from that time forth the gate on which a man had hanged himself— a man real and well known to me—became taboo. I never crossed the threshold of the stable, it was only at a distance that I passed it by, avoiding that place of horror. Yes, it was a place of horror, for, even now, as in my childhood, suicide is to me something horrible, something darkly unnatural, something inconceivable. I feel the same way about it as does a villager from some remote village I regard the act as he does—something terrible, unthinkable, something that pollutes the brain and burdens and darkens the soul.

At that time I chanced to get hold of a book (I no

longer remember the title) in which that naïve feeling of mine was formulated into a scholastic judgment. The unnaturalness of suicide was proved by the following narratives: In some monastery, a monk, who was thought to be dead, was buried in a crypt. After a time, he regained consciousness and horror and mental conflict set in; the crypt was opened only when a brother died, and it was impossible to call loud enough or to knock hard enough to be heard. What, then, was the unfortunate man to do? Was he to wait for a death of starvation and thirst, there in the neighbourhood of his dead brethren? He began to pray—but was not prayer a supplication that God might grant death to one of his healthy brethren? Against such horrible mental and physical agonies (the reader can well complete the picture), our dear monk held out and remained alive—he kept himself alive by eating insects which fell down into the crypt through a small air-hole, and he licked the drops of moisture from the walls. . . . After many years, they found the unfortunate man wrapped in cloaks which he had pulled out of the coffins, and with his white beard reaching to the ground. . . .

In another case, a seemingly dead man upon awakening despaired and took his life in terrible grief and torment he hung himself on his coffin after having written, with a leaden cross on his shroud, his story and a prayer asking God to forgive him for his weakness. . . .

For a long time this casuistical solution of the question prevented me from sleeping quietly, and, even now, it sticks in my brain like a sting in an open wound.

Further experiences rendered the whole problem more

Modern Suicidism

acute for me and enabled me to look down into the very bottom of the modern soul.

I will not explain how I finally came to deal with this subject monographically; I will only give an example of the kind of thing which led to it. I gave a lecture before the Leipzig Philosophical Society; the following day a member of the audience came to me—he had recently been wishing to die. He had once already attempted to shoot himself, but only a large scar across his cheek and forehead told of this, and now again the black thought had come to him. He would have already done the deed, but he read the announcement of the lecture and waited. . . . That is, of course, only the outside story of the case; but let the reader imagine his state of mind: his father had committed suicide and he discovered that insanity had been the cause; he, as he matured, began to fear the burden of heredity and also attempted death. Failure was an indication by fate that he was still to live for a while; so he went on living—he studied medicine and philosophy in order to be able to understand himself. . . . Can the reader imagine how it all went—what kind of discussions we had; can he guess how and what I said to nail Dr. L. (he still lives) down to life? Those discussions about Schopenhauer, those analyses of heredity, our conversations about Faust, about God... My experience with Dr. L. was not the only one of the kind I had, and afterwards I had even more, before the publication of my book.

So here I will refer to that book of mine; in it I believe I gave quite a good analysis of suicidism, and showed that it is a modern social ailment, an ailment of modern civilization. The very fact that the cases are so numerous indicates that it is a real ailment, and this is also shown by the continual increase in numbers.

Not so long ago an English statistician reckoned that there are now about one hundred and eighty thousand suicides yearly. Just ask yourselves what it means when so great a number of people kill themselves year after year, nay, day after day (there are daily about five hundred suicides): every hour—not counting the night hours—about thirty thus voluntarily depart from the life which our century offers them. What an agitation there is today against militarism—but sum up these armies of suicides: what are wars and battles in comparison to this! Battles, wars, of course, are spectacular, but these thousands and thousands die unnoticed, nobody minds it any more, it is as if it had to be. What a great clamour there was about the Armenian massacre, but is it nothing that four thousand yearly take their lives in Austria—on Czech territory about two thousand?

And suicide is not only spreading further and further, but it might be said to be going deeper and deeper. In Europe there are about two thousand minors, among them many children, who are discontented with life. Pray, consider that: children despairing of life and choosing death! When the Boers and the English fight against one another in Africa and when a few hundred people are killed somewhere else, all Europe is stirred—and still, what is that in comparison to one case of a child seven or eight years old abandoning all hope and taking its life. And of such "children" statistics tell us there are very many.

This suicidism is a modern thing. Whether we take it as a purely temporary phenomenon or not, one thing is

Modern Suicidism

certain, that the ailment has developed more particularly in this country. Single cases had always occurred, of course, but it was not until the new age and especially in this century that there was a tremendous increase in the number of cases, greatly out of proportion to the growth in population. Today there is already an epidemic; that is why I speak not so much of suicide as of suicidism. Suicidism manifests itself in the fact that people today comparatively easily, for comparatively slight and even trifling reasons, seek out death. The previous generations were, I would say, more firmly attached to life. Today people throw themselves into death's embrace for every stupid little thing. They seem to be in love with death. That never was before. What a horror there was among older writers of suicide! The Jesuit Mariana tolerates tyrannicide, but he fears to allow a tyrant to be permitted to poison himself. He would, in that case, he says, commit suicide, and that is against all the laws of nature. When Hume defended suicide, it caused a great clamour in England and Europe, and Hume himself was *ashamed* to publish his work—today, after a hundred years, the teachings of the pessimists à la Mainlander scarcely startle anyone.

However, I already hear the question, how and why is suicidism mainly modern, the self-murderer a modern man? Read over statistics and you will see that people are forced into suicide by poverty and want, and what is so strange about that? The struggle for existence we know well is not a game; it takes its toll. That is but natural, according to Darwin's theory. But when somebody commits suicide it is said the self-murderer acted under an emotional strain; he was ill, he was insane; it's a pity that there are so many cases, but it can't be helped! We get nervous about it though we have already been aware of it for a long time.

Evolution and the struggle for existence, misery—can we explain present-day suicidism thus?

Everything is, after all, evolution, and everything that happens, happens in the course of struggle for existence: what, then, is evolving and what is the meaning of this present struggle for existence? Suicidism as it appears today never existed before; more especially it did not exist in the Middle Ages; here and there it had shown itself already in earlier times, but it was not nearly so intensive and general as it is at present. The same happened at the time of the downfall of Greek and of Roman culture, and there were Mainlanders at that time too (Pliny for instance sees that man is superior to the gods in that he can kill himself!), but it was unknown in the Middle Ages. It was not until the new era, and, more particularly, the nineteenth century, that suicidism developed into a mental epidemic and plague. This peculiar historical development, this periodic rise and fall, forces us to admit that suicidism, if we are to consider it, as Darwin does, as a weakness, must be explained by special historical laws, and that in order to understand what that periodical development means, the so-called law of the struggle for existence in which, as Darwin says, the weaker submits to the stronger, is not sufficient. Why did this weakness develop only in the nineteenth century? Are those who take their lives really always the weaker? If so, wherein lies their weakness? Wherein lies the strength of those who, under similar circumstances, in the very same struggle, do not submit?

The formula of evolution and the struggle for existence is obviously hollow; it is only formally valid, and it does not explain modern suicidism.

Neither does so-called historical materialism offer a sufficient explanation. Want, poverty—what do they explain? I know that many statisticians and sociologists have opposed their explanations to mine, saying that unfavourable economic conditions are the source of suicidism.

Historical materialism is seriously considered today, but, according to my judgment, far too abstractly. But here we have a concrete case, and, making it a touchstone, we could and should be able to determine most precisely what economic conditions cause, and to what extent, and in what measure they are to blame for, modern suicidism. That is, statistics must, in this case, give us purely empirical data concerning the causes of and motives for suicide; to which a psychological and sociological analysis of individual cases must be added.

Statistics themselves show that in many cases misery is not the deciding factor. Do not better-off people also commit suicide? But statistics also prove that in a minority of cases the reasons given for suicide are unfortunate economic conditions. The number of such cases will decrease if they are properly specified and analysed; for example, did a banker who suddenly lost his property shoot himself because of fatal economic conditions only? "Loss of fortune" figuring in the statistics of suicide surely covers a whole series of personal and social conditions; we have to take into consideration the causes of the loss, the social position of the loser is a determining factor, whether or not he was ambitious is not irrelevant either, and so on. In the cases mentioned above of the men who were apparently dead, hunger, misery and poverty were also contributing causes—but one succumbed to them; another did not. Then again, need teaches the Dalibors to play the violin—so unfortunate economic conditions cannot always be the final and determining causes—they are only contributory causes, they are circumstances in which a man can prove himself—one in this way, another in that. Every case of suicide the explanation of which is unbearable misery can be outweighed by numerous others in which people went through unbelievable misery, withstood and overcame it. When, then, one yields to misery and the second, and the third, and the fourth man overcome it, it is not misery but the character of the person which is the determining factor. I do not deny the great influence which misery and poverty have, but they have not the last word. I have shown in my book that purely natural, external circumstances (warmth, for example) have a certain influence upon the decision of the suicide; but the final and deciding factor is the man himself, is his will, his character, his soul, but, of course, there is no soul without a body.

But even if it were true that misery is the cause of suicide—what is to be said from a moral and social point of view? That our boasted civilization calmly bears the fact that people are dying from misery and hunger, not only chronically, but also acutely; a self-murderer who has yielded to misery has died from hunger after all. What then, is the moral and social character of our community? That is a question which finally not even the historical materialists can avoid. Who is responsible here? Does pointing to the laws of nature suffice?

By putting down suicide in the usual way to insanity a merely plausible and at most provisional explanation is given. But again another question arises—why are there so many insane people in this new era? The history of medicine, the statistics of psychosis, and history in general show that insanity has increased tremendously in modern times. Why are we so nervous, why is neurasthenia so prevalent nowadays? Why, in general, is there so much insanity in our times? I did not forget to deal in my book with just this very interdependence of the two groups of mass phenomena. On the contrary, I showed that we have here a strange and, to a certain extent, pathological state of modern society, one phase or aspect of this state being suicidism, and the other various kinds and degrees of psychosis. And finally: why is the man of the nineteenth century more nervous and, in general, more psychopathic than the man of the eighteenth century, or of previous centuries?

Statistics of psychosis undeniably prove that the number of psychopaths in Europe is greatly outgrowing the increase in population, that, then, psychosis is developing in a more intensive manner than ever before. Modern psychosis is just as peculiar as modern suicidism. Statistics show that this psychosis is becoming stronger in so-called

23

advanced countries; the principal centres of culture and civilization are also its endemic centres. I think that a reader with ordinary psychological experience, to the question, "is there more psychosis in the cities or in the country?" will answer without much thinking, "Of course, in the cities,"—just as suicidism is more intensive in cities. Why does this answer come so glibly, and what does it signify? This: that in the very centres of modern life there is more psychosis and there are more suicides. Here we have something really new and modern. But then, again, it is not a matter only of the incidence of psychosis, but also of its various stages, of its peculiar times. And we are interested not only in the physiological and pathological but more particularly in the psychological and social aspects of psychosis and mass-psychopathy. Here scientific analysis confirms what we continually hear today from all sides—that people are becoming more nervous, more sensitive and more hypersensitive, more exasperated and more irritable, that they are more or less weak, tired, wearied, unhappy and saddened. . . .

Why?

The reader who has a deeper interest in this subject should provide himself with literature on psychiatry and psychology and should by means of it analyse more precisely the phenomena of modern life. From this point of view he should also analyse systems of philosophy, literature and the creations of art; for where else could real modern man reveal himself more clearly and at the same time more typically than in these departments of spiritual life?

Modern Suicidism

From this standpoint what judgment can we form about modern pessimistic philosophy? The relation between mass-psychosis and suicide must, I believe, force itself upon even a mediocre observer. Looking at this, we see a new social significance not only in pessimism in philosophy and in literature, but also in all those prevailing emotional and emotionalized naturalistic, decadent and symbolistic figments, in the many scientific, philosophical and theological controversies and disputes, in the various social systems which aim at reforming the whole body politic and its component parts. What is it all?

Perhaps some defender of literary and artistic aristocratism will cry: "Are literature, art and philosophy, the very flower of modern thought and feeling, to be thus studied and analysed psychologically and sociologically? Are Schopenhauer, Nietzsche, Zola, Huysmans, Wiertz, Rops, Munchen and the others to be submitted to psychological and sociological dissection? Are philosophy and literature to be studied as the concomitants of psychosis and suicidism . . . are philosophy, literature and art only —symptoms?"

Yes, to me the manifestation of every soul, even though it did not write fine books, did not create a great work of art, is as interesting as the soul of Goethe or of Nietzsche; I pay more attention, however, to Goethe or Nietzsche because they have expressed themselves for me in words, whereas I cannot see into the souls of those numerous sacrifices of modern civilization whose outcries we do not hear. Newspapers and statistics register only numbers: this week ten people drowned themselves, sixteen

25

hanged themselves, and so on—but what went on in their minds before they resolved to do this?

I assure my aristocrat that, after all, his ideal will not be harmed by the study of philosophy and literature as social symptoms—I do not mean to say that they are *only* symptoms. I do not respect great thinkers and creators the less because they are for me the most significant manifestations of modern man, and therefore I take the liberty of saying here that the problem of suicide is *the* principal problem of modern literary creations—I should almost say it is the sole problem.

What is the subject of *Faust* but the development of man endeavouring to reach the highest ideals of human knowledge and power and yet finally determined to leave this, his battle-field of life—he is already reaching for the deadly drink, when he is called back to earth by the Easter bells—such power over him had the recollection of his childhood's faith.

In *Werther*, light is thrown from many sides upon the Faust problem, in *Wahlverwandschaften*, and more particularly in *Wahrheit und Dichtung* ("The Story of the Sword").

Byron deals with the same problem in *Manfred*, in *Cain*, and in other works of his: Krasiński in the *Undivine Comedy*, Tolstoy in *Anna Karenina* and in *Home Tales*, Dostoyevski, finally, in each of his greater novels and also, of course, in his philosophical articles, for instance in *Dnevnik* (the day labourer). The lower officers and the privates depict spiritual struggles similar to those depicted by the generals of modern thought. What else ' does Zola describe in *Work?* What does Strindberg mean by the suicide of Olla, the artist? What does Hauptman intend to convey by the suicide of Dr. Vocker, and how does Bourget's *Disciple* end? What does Garborg's Gram seek? What do we read of in d'Annunzio's *Triumph of Death*? And so on and so forth.

What does this mean? All the latest poet-thinkers, and those just the greatest, deal in their most significant works with suicide. . . .

Chapter II

Wearied Souls

I THINK that, by this, even a beginner in psychology and sociology will have come to agree that we really have here a great problem of our times, and that the blind formula of historical materialism does not explain it adequately. It cannot throw any light on it. Let us take as an example Gram in Garborg's *Wearied Souls.* "And the generation sit by the road and helplessly drop their hands. They look worn and vacant like the insane. There is darkness ahead, darkness behind. Meaninglessly, aimlessly, above endless marshland dance the will-o'-the-wisps of the sciences. . . ."

What can historical or economic materialism do here? Misery—poverty: yes—but of what kind?

Is there a God?—We do not know. Is there a soul?—We do not know. Is there life after death or not?—We do not know. Is there any purpose in life?—We do not know. Why am I living?—We do not know. Am I living, do I really exist?—We do not know. What, then, do we know? Is it possible for us to know anything at all?—We do not know. And this systematic "We do not know" is called science! And people clap their hands above their heads and cry exultantly: "The progress of the human mind is incomprehensible! We no longer need even faith in God, for science has observed that water boiling in a pot lifts the lid, and that rubbed resin attracts straw. . . ."

Wearied Souls

It is no wonder, then, that Gram-Garborg himself rejects historical materialism. "If life is to be endured it must be a little bad. A famishing man is not so ready to kill himself; he constantly hopes that, after all, he will find an opportunity to eat his fill; but the rich man who has lived luxuriously and pleasurably every day makes haste to the devil—boredom on one hand and a reproachful conscience on the other. . . ."

Isn't that the mind of modern man, displayed like a roll on a baker's stall?

Let us, then, study Garborg's Gram symptomatically as I suggested. Let us look more carefully into *Wearied Souls*. The reader must not, of course, harbour any scruples about analysing this fine work of art psychologically, psychiatrically, and sociologically.

In the first place, what is it all about? We have before us a patient. He places himself under the care of a doctor, hence we must have a purely medical opinion as to what illness he is suffering from, what are the symptoms, and what is the cause.

The main, constant symptom is that the patient thinks about suicide, and is afraid of becoming insane. Sometimes he himself tells us his fancy is exclusively occupied with picturing his suicide by hanging; he considers whether or not he will shoot himself. That such delirious suicidism follows upon heavy drinking, alters nothing; on the contrary, the patient's alcoholism is another aggravating symptom. We know from the patient's anamnesis (which is constituted, for the physician and the psychologist, of Garborg's earlier novels) that Gram has been revelling and drinking for a long time already.

Wearied Souls

The patient is an educated modern man; he is a writer, a critic, an analyst and, therefore, he analyses his own condition.

Gram is weary to the very soul and, just for that reason, he is nervous. "But far down, at the very bottom, in the background, in the underground part of my being, there lurks a grievous, dangerous anxiety, a kind of mysterious imprisoned madness which keeps swelling and swelling and tends to burst. It is a bad conscience, some kind of fear, a sense of terrible humiliation, a strange idiotic horror of something, the Lord only knows of what. I have an infinite, morbid desire to throw myself at someone's feet, at a woman's, at a clergyman's, at God's, and to complain, to lament, to confess, to be reprimanded, to be execrated, to be condemned, and to be taken at last into a dear, dependable embrace like a sick child."

"When shall I finally overcome that eternal restlessness, that gnawing discontent, that dryness and inward thirst? I am like an animal in a desert where there is no water, like a captured lion that runs backwards and forwards behind the bars of his cage, seeking liberty. All that is uneasy, persistent, stealthy, yearning, restless, has heaped up its torment in me; it is like a devouring pain in my breast.

"When I go out of the house I am full of the hope that I shall meet with tranquillity in the person of someone young, a woman with full breasts who will put her arms about my neck and whisper endless confessions of love to me. On my way home I hope that she is sitting there waiting for me, quiet and comely, with subdued yearning in her dark eyes.

Wearied Souls

"I sit down in the most comfortable arm-chair, but I cannot rest there; I lie down on the softest couch, but not even there do I find peace. I am continually watching, watching and watching; all my nerves are on edge, all my senses are strained even to the verge of hallucination. . . ."

The patient seeks in vain for an expression which would describe his state precisely; at last he has nothing to say but that his soul has caught cold. His soul has caught cold; he has caught cold in his soul; he is weary, he is tired in soul; he has, psychologically speaking, a bad taste in his mouth. Nothing but distaste, a disgust for everything, *taedium generale*. . . .

In this disquiet Gram seeks peace, but in vain. Comfortable arm-chairs and couches, as we have heard, do not help; mechanical treatment is of no avail; nor does it help to drink, for after drinking suicidal fancies come oftener and even hallucinations; neither does visiting his sweetheart, Matylda, help. "The more I defile myself with licence, the more sentimental I become." He realizes this himself quite well, and it is just because of these visits that he suffers the most hellish agonies. Neither Bacchus nor Venus are of any help. The only alternative, then, is the revolver or morphia, or the church and the clergyman. . . . An old friend of the patient, Dr. Kvaale, well known from Garborg's earlier novels, has already shot himself. "Suicide is, speaking in general, something one can buy," said a beardless youth (who drowned himself) to him. . . . "Every intelligent man should have a phial of morphia in his domestic medicine chest."

The evil, then, has its seat in the depths of the soul. There is no doubt of that. He sought happiness, bliss; he sought it in lofty ideas, in science and in philosophy, but he did not find what he was looking for. As a child, so long as he did not taste of the fruit of knowledge, so long as he had faith, he was happy and full of bliss; only now does he see how the two roads separate and where each one leads. "The road of faith: from lucidity to lucidity, from light to light; from happiness to happiness. The road of knowledge: from lucidity to lucidity, from light to light, from despair to despair."

Then—knowledge offers us lucidity and lofty light, but it makes us unhappy. . . . He had quenched his thirst for ideas, but he had become only the more unhappy!

He had acquired knowledge of all modern—even the most modern—systems of philosophy; he knew more especially German philosophy and the newest French literature; but he did not find the looked-for happiness that way. Scepticism is the sediment remaining after all those mixtures of ideas. "Positivistic scepticism ate away my soul like an acid."

He lost his balance because he lost a spiritual centre. The soul of the modern man disperses itself in all directions, into all the corners of the earth—there is no solid substance to it; it has no kernel, no unity. The modern man has not worked out a unified view of the world—thence all that misery, that nervousness, all that madness, all that longing for death. "The main cause of the nervous sufferings of our time is that we have not a well-ordered view of life. Man lacks . . . God, let us say; thus spiritual life has lost its centre, spiritual life has lost its regulator, if I may call it so, and is running on erratically, without aim or measure. And it usually happens that the spring breaks. . . ."

Gram lost the old, unified, nourishing faith and became a reed shaken by every wind of thought that blew. His illness is dilettantism, half-and-halfness. "A sad generation is this transitory human race. It is not even unconscious enough to be happy; it is not even conscious enough to be able to be resigned, it only sighs and writhes in a kind of mental hysteria."

He wanted to become a god, but he finally admits that he is nothing more than a vain weakling, aping others. "My entire lack of faith arose from the circumstance that I had a very talented and quick-witted friend whom I feared; I was afraid of his ridicule—and the ridicule of the rest of my comrades. . . ." "My old scepticism is just the cocksure sapience of lads in the highest classes of a secondary school—schoolboys are, of course, too clever for God."

Looking at things rationally, Gram's unhealthy state appears to us as dilettante intellectualism—positivistic dilettantism; through this he not only suppressed emotion within himself, but even fantasy; he trusted only in the exactness of Comte's positivism; on the moral side Cram's ailment is an immeasurable selfishness; always I, I, I . . . my book, etc.

Looking back at the history of his disease our invalid regards it as a transitory condition. There has been a period of decline, of decadence; but now, already, he hopes that he will revive "in a new age of fancy, faith, and cordiality." In short, modern man must once again have faith, for: "All really great minds are religious," and therefore the present age, after a period of decadence, will return to the Church.

Thus, then, this decadent of ours determines the treatment for his illness. He has learned that "those old customs are not so stupid, after all," and he has no longer any scruples about going to church. At first he just slips in when he is feeling bad, but finally he decides to attend regularly the sermons of his old friend, the Reverend Mr. Löchen. Another old friend of Gram's, George Jonathan, makes fun of him of course: "this is weakness," says the Mephisto of *Wearied Souls* (Gram, when he spoke with him for the last time, discerned something satanic in his eyes), "it is a dangerous fracture of the spine, it is *fin de siècle*, it is the *agonie de la bourgeoisie.*" But perhaps it is unavoidable: the wearied ones go to the pastor. This latest Mephisto is apparently already a dilettante too.

Gram is no longer ashamed of it: "I have emancipated myself," he says, "I am giving up all the old phrases. I am seeking satisfaction for my soul—where it is possible to find it." "I have bent because I did not wish to break."

Let us summarize and indicate once more the problem of our Faust—Gram.

Scientific and philosophic intellectualism, especially as it is presented in the positivist creed, with its discordant dilettantism, drives one to despair. ("It is not possible to carry on with Comte.") The modern educated man chases happiness, but catches death. He arrives at lucidity, but he loses peace of mind: instead of the complete knowledge he desires he must be satisfied after all with scepticism, with which and by which there comes disquiet, nervousness, insanity, a longing for destruction. . . . Then, *aut* . . . *aut*, to bend or to break. . . . Gram bent.

Before what, before whom?

Before faith and before God, but in the first place, before his healthy-minded physician. Man must have a spiritual centre, purely abstract ideas are not sufficient. ("I must have a god.") Pastor Löchen explains it to Gram thus: "Only something personal can be the 'central point' of the human soul." It may, to a certain extent, be an idea, but that is not sufficient. "Yes, indeed, something personal is needed—a woman or a god! All abstractions are dead," agrees Gram.

Therefore, not so much God as Christ—"the madness of Christ." A return to Christianity, then, and *nota bene:* the Protestant Gram much prefers to slip into the Catholic Church.

Gram is no longer ashamed of superstition and mysticism. But, still he does not expect complete salvation to come from his spiritual friend; he gets more help—from his physician. The latter does not cure him with medicines, but he cures him by his personality, by his healthy, firm, unsceptical mind.

He does not need medicines, but a physician, because he needs to trust someone. And this, the right kind of doctor, is able to inspire him with trust. The pastor no longer ascribes great powers to himself. "Christianity which we clergymen dogmatized out of the world, will be brought in again, cured by physicians."

It is by confidence, that is, by faith, that this temporary

35

decadence will be overcome. The modern, degenerating man must in the first place undergo a mental change; and by this he will be cured and changed in body. The problem, then, is: how to change a will weakened by scepticism, how to change the will at all, how to change that Gram, who is myself, how to inspire a weakling with confidence? Whoever regains confidence has physical regeneration guaranteed. Gram saw that very thing happen to Pastor Löchen; he himself had been a decadent and a degenerating man before, they had spent many a night together revelling and they had revelled away their souls and their health, but Löchen has found himself and come back to life, and Gram sees with amazement that he has "a face almost like new."

In conclusion: No craving and longing to be equal to God, but the old recipe of Rousseau: "After thinking it over thoroughly—does not happiness, which we are all seeking, really lie in simplicity and modesty?"

Chapter III

Symptoms of the Transition Period

I PUBLISHED fifteen years ago just such an analysis of a wearied soul as Garborg gives us when he analyses the soul of his Gram. The similarity of the principal ideas even to the very details is surprising—for every more significant sentence in *Wearied Souls*, the reader will find a parallel in my book. The difference is, of course, in the form. Garborg presented us with an artistic type, I analysed modern suicidism psychologically and sociologically; for example we see how Gram seeks to forget his condition by going out at night to drink—I deal with alchoholism and its relation to suicidism; Gram in moments of despair visits Matylda—I am concerned with the connection between modern suicidism and prostitution, and so forth. In the one case we have a work of art— in the other a piece of scientific work; in the one case again, one modern soul in all its fulness and living reality, in the other the aspects and characteristics of the modern soul progressively analysed, and, finally, comprehended in a unified historical formula.

And this final formula reads as follows: Modern man is losing his unified religious outlook on the world; this loss means intellectual and moral disquietude and anarchy; for it connotes a more or less violent rejection of the old point of view; it is a struggle between the incomplete new outlook and the old one; the modern man is unready, incomplete, inconsistent, half-finished; he is tired, wearied, nervous, irritable from the struggle, he does not get full, fresh enjoyment out of life—hence he falls into despair very easily and voluntarily departs from life. Thus our era, our century, presents itself to our view as a transition period; the old religion of the people is dying out and modern man is trying to find a substitute for it—it may be a new, or at least a renovated, religion.

Speaking more concretely—the outlook on the world which obtained in the Middle Ages, which was established and disseminated by Catholicism, is falling away. In opposition to Catholicism stand modern philosophy and science, and, therefore, the spiritual struggle of modern times and the weariness are so evident among Catholic peoples—typically in French philosophy and literature. This clash between the old and the new is also evident among Orthodox peoples—typically, again, in Russian philosophy and literature. The difference, of course, between the Catholic and the Orthodox world is well marked, because it is the difference between the two medieval forms of Catholicism and their respective ecclesiastical organizations.

Among Protestant peoples there is, again, a different type of that struggle and of modern weariness, answering to their religious and ecclesiastical forms.

The statistics of suicides vary with the spiritual and moral religious atmosphere; *ceteris paribus* suicidism is strongest wherever the old religious life is most undermined. Statistics show a great number of suicides in France and especially, of course, in Paris; suicidism is further quite marked in Austria and quite considerable in the Protestant parts of Germany and Norway, in Petrograd, and so forth. But it is comparatively weak in English countries and in southern Italy, where religion has still a marked influence; that is why there are fewer suicides in Russia and countries like it—among peoples still governed by ancient forms of religion.

The reader will find in my book more detailed proofs that contemporary suicidism is a fruit of our modern civilization, a fruit of the modern process of civilization. Garborg's *Wearied Souls* constitutes a great and quite a new proof that my diagnosis is correct; Gram's development is the résumé in a single person of the whole development of culture in general.

I shall not repeat what I have just deduced from *Wearied Souls.* I wish here to call attention to one point: did not the reader remark that Gram, a Norwegian and *eo ipso* a Protestant, has a great fondness for Catholicism? Garborg with this personal trait casts a very penetrating light upon the whole problem, not only of Gram, but of the times in general: Protestantism has conformed to a certain extent to modern philosophy and science, but just because of this it seems to be rather incomplete and does not supply the needs of modern wearied souls—we shall see in later studies that the Protestant Gram yields to that Catholic renaissance which is characteristic of this century, and which forms one of the main problems connected with the development of modern thought.

I cannot here omit an introductory historical survey, also requisite for Garborg's *Wearied Souls,* which swarms with names like Schopenhauer and Comte. It is indispensable to show briefly how Garborg's Gram could have developed in the modern cultural atmosphere.

39

Symptoms of the Transition Period

A great landmark in the development of the new age is the French Revolution, a continuation of the revolution inaugurated by the Reformation. I have already written about the French Revolution in *Our Times*, and I pointed out its significance for the development of religion. After all, the Revolution was an attempt to do away with Catholicism as a state religion, and to put the cult of the reason in its place. The Revolution was just precisely the child of the rationalism which so exclusively characterizes the eighteenth century: Hume, Voltaire, the Encyclopaedists, Wolf's philosophy of education, Kant, Lessing, Frederick II, the Emperor Joseph, Catherine of Russia—nothing but reason, nay, even "pure reason."

After the Revolution a reaction began all over Europe. It was not only political, but was a reaction proceeding from the depths of the soul. This movement found expression in so-called romanticism. Already Rousseau rejected a civilization based upon science and art, and Rousseau had a sufficiency of followers. Today, to speak against science and philosophy and to repudiate them, or at least to demand restriction upon them, is almost a characteristic of good form; only the socialists are still so naïve as to labour for science, science, and yet more science. Gram has his origins in Rousseau.

In the beginning the romantic reaction was quite superficial; mainly political, and social. People were fleeing back to the old régime, even as far back as possible, to the Middle Ages, for then there was political and social tranquillity, there was unity and reconciliation. Napoleon concluded a concordat with the Pope. Post-Revolutionary romanticism is mainly Catholic; even the Protestants and

Symptoms of the Transition Period

the Orthodox clutched at Catholicism. Byron was, for example, decidedly pro-Catholic; in *Faust* Goethe, too, adheres to it. According to "Chadajev" Dostoyevski was haunted by it his whole life long.

Having themselves been bred by the Revolution, the romantics *de facto* carry on the Revolution, and very often effectively, without knowing it; and involuntarily they oppose their own revolutionary principles to those of the eighteenth century. The rationalistic devil is being exorcized by the emotional Beelzebub. Emotionailsm places itself in opposition to rationalism and intellectualism; emotion, or properly speaking passion, should guide the modern man. And it does. In the eighteenth and in the preceding century reason and only reason held sway—enlightenment was the watchword of philosophic effort. In opposition to this the nineteenth century turned romantically to emotion. How the modern soul became aware of its emotional side is shown not only in literature, but also in philosophy and science. Schleiermacher's theory that religion is based upon emotion corresponds to the view of Chateaubriand and other romantics; they saw, however, not only religion, but the whole man in the feelings and in the will. Schopenhauer in Germany, and already before him Maine de Biran in France, thought thus. In manifestations such as these the spirit of the times is reflected very clearly and distinctly. It must be especially noted that it was not until this time (I mean until the Revolutionary and post-Revolutionary periods) that philosophy and psychology recognized emotion as a particular part and power of the human soul, alongside of the intellect and the will. Before that, according to Greek psychologists, feeling and will were considered as one faculty only. It was only due to Kant's authority that emotion, in abstract theory too, was differentiated from will—so efficaciously was the cause of emotion forwarded, and not only among the romantics. Science, too, is expressive of the times. Because all human activity must, in the end, be reduced to terms of the fundamental activities of man's soul, this new recognition of emotion has a great and decided significance. It is no wonder that today everything is full of emotion just as at the time of Voltaire it was full of reason—true, there was no superfluity of reason then, just as today there is no superfluity of emotion.

But in life there are not only emotion and reason, there are living men, and the life of Revolutionary and post-Revolutionary men was romanticism. How much has been written and in what a foolish manner about the relations between literature and life by Chateaubriand, Musset, Constant, Byron, Baudelaire, and others, who lived and acted romantically. Thence romanticism made its way into literature, and the fact that here and there some poor fellow concocted in his fancy a romantic life for himself is of no material consequence. Even Napoleon was a romantic—there is also the romanticism, and, eventually, the poetry and the fantasy of action; this should at length be comprehended not only by literary critics, but, above all, by the historians of philosophy, science, art, religion and politics. Napoleon was an artist of his kind, just as Byron was an artist in his deeds. That poetry of life may not be, of course, of the finest kind, but that does not concern us now. I want only to say one thing: although the yost-Revolutionary period follows in the path of the Revolution, it would fain escape from its influence. People were fleeing back to the past, they were carrying on a reaction, but that reaction was, after all, only a forced one, and it was being led by people whose nerves had been rattled by the "poesy" of the Revolution.

The Revolutionary terror (just let us picture to ourselves that bloody violence) preceded the reactionary terror; they alternated and mutually penetrated one another. We know quite well from Musset's confession how people lived and felt—just read over for yourselves his description of the disease of his time. Read over Constant's description of the fear which people at that time harboured in the depths of their souls.

Shall we not, then, understand the life of Baudelaire, staggering between the altar and the brothel, between the Madonna and *Venus vulgivaga*? Should we not understand how, continually and until today, people, thinking and fighting, now grasp at naturalism, and soon after, nay, at the same time, flee to Christianity, to symbolism, to occultism, to defiance and revolt; aye, and are restless, uneasy, irritable and weary.

Shall we not understand Stendhal, who, during that same period, delighted in rending his wearied soul?

Do you not understand why in France and in French literature there are so many wearied souls, and why their attempts to cure themselves are so significant? Musset, Baudelaire, Verlaine, Zola, Bourget, Huysmans, Maeterlinck. . . . Are you not reminded here of Przybyszewski and his aversion to Protestantism? Do you understand why Garborg also becomes a Catholic? Do you not yet

43

perceive how Renan and his dilettantism are connected with this?

Not only the weak but the heroes in the fight feel a kind of fear, and deep down in their souls there arises the doubting question: Would it not be better without strife? . . . The fight is carried on between the mass of older people and the great army of the young. The younger folk oppose religion, and, consequently, the whole existing social and political system. The revolt, as usual, is in defiance of the Almighty. It is a fight about God. These modern Titans, like their ancestors in Greek and Semitic mythology, want to storm the heavens and place themselves on the throne of the Almighty. Faust is in the van, but he has weakened—his place has been taken by Manfred and Kain. . . . Gustav Konrad, Jindrich, and Pancracy have united. . . . Ivan Karamazov and Razkolnikov are the leaders of the youngest squadron of the insurgents. . . .

But here already we hear the voice of Aljos who, at the head of his lads, rushed into the battle to drag away his brother Ivan and his co-Titans from the blood and tear-soaked battlefield, and to reconcile them again with the Almighty.

All of us have stood and are still standing under fire. Some of us in the vanguard and some of us in the main army have fought famous battles victoriously, but many a time we have lost, many of us have fled; others have fallen—but we have not retreated. . . . Everyone, be he a private, an officer or a commander, returns with wounds and scars. And now the warriors are tired, they are resting —now again they are not resting, but preparing for the march and further combats. . . . A glorious, a great, a terrible age!

And modern man too staggers between belief and disbelief, between weakness and defiance, revolt and humility, between anarchy and obedience. . . .

The people of our age are restless, uneasy, excitable, and fatigued. Their mood is not a gay one—in philosophy, in Schopenhauer and modern pessimism, in literature and in politics, loud enough expression is given to it. Many fall into despair and determine to take extreme measures. Their hands reeking with crime, some attempt to take the lives of their neighbours, presuming, in their blind endeavour, that life can be gained by death. Others, greater in number, cast themselves of their own will into that *post mortem* darkness. The Titan, in his equality with God, becomes either a tyrant or joins the army of the despairing and the dying. . . . The weaker ones seek solace in Buddhism, spiritualism, symbolism, and in other forms and formalities of the various kinds of occultism.

While passing through these struggles I wrote a book about suicide. This piece of work, written on the battlefield, is itself restless; it has not caught the mood of the time completely, but as a whole I think that I have correctly comprehended the strength and the weakness of our century—the century of the despairing Titan.

The problem is the same everywhere: how to fight out one's own fight with the old order, how to work up to a consistent view of life, and finally how to calm one's own soul. There are thousands upon thousands who know nothing of this fight, for maybe external conditions, maybe a placid disposition, perhaps even bluntness and insensibility form a natural dam against the storm which tosses about the souls of those who cannot be thoughtless and insensitive. These latter are exactly the ones we are concerned with, for there are many thousands who take example by them.

This fight as it was carried on by Goethe, Byron, Mickiewicz, Krasiński, Dostoyevski, Tolstoy and all the rest, is a fight about an outlook on the world. It is a fight to get all our knowledge unified and assembled and to put it into harmony with our social system. Those unquiet, restless, excitable souls want to find finally quiet, rest, reconciliation and new energy for further living, and almost all of them see the spring of the water of life in religion and in its power to calm stormy thought. Modern people want to believe, they want to believe that they can be reconciled with philosophy, or even it may be that they will find a solution opposed to philosophy. Modern man wishes at all costs to rid himself of all chronic discontent—one desires violently, another wishes mildly—each, however, waits as eagerly and impatiently as the other. . . . Despondency or prayer!

That is why modern suicidism is a real and an actual problem. That is why it is the principal and the greatest problem of modern literary thought. All the stronger spiritual warriors have analysed that state of mind in which man decides to take the step into the dark uncertainty. Modern man wants only to live and to live, but it is very often because of this that he takes his life. He who has not yet become aware of this, does not comprehend this, does not know the modern man. In his mad chase after happiness and pleasure death itself has come to mean heavenly joy for him. . . .

My psychological and sociological analysis of suicidism has taught me that the number of suicides is a direct mathematical measure of the real mood of society, that society is deep down in the depths of its soul excited, perturbed, sick. . . .

I do not know to what extent the reader will agree with me that suicidism is modern. I am afraid that at first the idea that suicidism is modern, mainly modern, will startle and scare him. I know that what I have so far tried to convey throws insufficient light on my thought, but I have purposely placed this main problem in this introductory part, making it a focus to which all the rays of further analysis will converge.

Meanwhile I am mainly interested in grasping the real psychological basis of modern suicidism.

Pray, let us think this over well.

Is it not, after all, rather strange that a man's fate can force him to compass his own death? His fate, considered objectively, may be people, code, God, destiny or some other power—why, then, does not every man set up opposition to that objective compelling agent? And note well: most people *de facto* do oppose the hardships of fate and fight against their destinies; but, and here we have come upon the crux of the matter, a great number of people, more particularly modern people, instead of opposing fate, oppose themselves and destroy themselves. Here we have a philosophical *punctum saliens*—he who does not comprehend this paradox in life will not understand modern man, and will not understand his peculiar subjectivity.

Much talking will not help here—each must think the matter out for himself. Maybe the following consideration will help. The statistics of suicide have long since made it clear that there are very few cases in which men killed themselves after having committed a murder. If we think deeply and intensively, we shall see why. A man, when he murders, is not subjective, but objective. Hence there are so few cases in which people first avenged themselves by murder and then killed themselves. Statistics show that in countries in which, relatively speaking, there are more murders (for instance in Italy), there are, comparatively, fewer suicides, and vice versa. It was only in this century that the tendency to suicide developed. That is, man became, if I may say so, subjective, having, before that, been objective.

The modern man, then, is in a peculiar manner, subjective. It may be said that he takes upon his own shoulders the whole guilt of life, he reproaches himself; but it may also be said that his suicide is as it were a delirium of subjectivity, an annihilation of objectivity, as though he were destroying the object that irritated him.

This he does just through subjectivity, and modern subjectivity. Kant said long ago that introspection is dangerous, that it leads to conflict, and Gram comprehended that too. Let us take in what Dr. Kvaale once said to him: "You study yourselves when that is just what you should avoid. When introspective we are at the same time absorbed and void of will; the will is weakened and self-love increases and very soon we may become fools. Let us rather busy ourselves about something else; there are things enough in the world for us to trouble about, outside ourselves." And in another place: "If we want to live we must live externally. A healthy will always acts upon external things, and if our will is not healthy" (he shrugged his shoulders) . . . "we must be cast into the sea, or go and confess to the priest. . . ."

A modern man, if he wants to overcome the tendency to suicide, must become objective, very objective. The great question for a modern, thinking man is: what view of the world will make and keep me objective, will maintain equilibrium between me (the subject) and the matter to be judged (the object)?

Gram might have put the matter thus: "I must get out of myself, or I can't carry on. . . . And I must be dependent—the question is, whether at a rope's end or something else. . . . I must be dependent on something or somebody—I can't be all to myself. . . . So I'll depend upon my pastor and my doctor . . . it's the rope's end or . . . God! . . ."

Philosophers speak frequently eenough of modern subjectivism—and say that modern philosophy is mainly subjective, that it is subjectivism. Descartes it was who mainly initiated the new philosophy. . . . It is not at all strange that suicide is the cumulative result of subjectivism—obviously the modern man, as he thinks and lives subjectively, dies subjectively too, since it can be no otherwise. He who lives in himself and for himself also dies in himself and for himself. . . . Suicide is simply subjective death, ending a subjective life without waiting for the objective, ordinary end. "I" am the one who decrees, "I" am the lord of life and death.

Nota bene! There is another word which must be pronounced : *Suicidism.* We are not merely concerned with the single fact of suicide, we are speaking of the spiritual and moral life which leads to it. We are not concerned with the last, physical deed, but with the motives which caused it, all the arguments, the chain of reasoning the last link in which was the physical fact itself. It is murder and spiritual death, spiritual suicide and self-killing. When speaking of the analogy between murder and suicide we must draw a distinction between acute suicide and chronic suicide—acute suicide is often the last action of chronic suicide. Statisticians say that everybody might live a third as long again if they lived morally and sensibly to the best of their ability—young and old, we waste our own lives and spoil the lives of others . . . (*The Modern Necropolis* might be the title of a biological and social study about mortality and vitality).

As Jesus saw adultery in looking at a woman and desiring her in the heart, so there is also suicide in thought, mental suicide—there are no statistics of those who despaired and cursed their life, but you may guess the number from your own experience! In general the important thing is to understand this spiritual state of being in which a man must be led towards despair, and to understand that this state is the state of the modern community, and that it will increasingly develop in the new age. Modern suicidism and the modern psychopathic condition are like a prelude—the music that follows will be a great host of voluntary deaths.

While thus sociologically analysing suicidism I do

not forget the body and heredity. I have gone into all this very carefully in my book. But it is just because of the body and heredity that I protest against social and, more particularly, against economic materialism. Economic factors have a considerable influence upon the spiritual condition of the community: man is not a soul without a body. But neither is he a body without a soul. The manner and method of production and the whole economic order of a community have a considerable influence upon the initiation and development of a psychopathic state, and of suicidism. I do not maintain that, let us say, capitalism and industry, economic uncertainty and the resulting mercantile and banking competition do not render a psychopathological condition and suicide more prevalent. I do not say that, looking at the masses of townsfolk employed in factories, one is not disposed towards psychosis and suicidism. And yet all that intensive brain-work, those feverish discoveries, that unquiet need for the possession of all technical improvements, that perpetual travelling and trading, education and amusement, that chasing after wealth and happiness, that striving to enjoy various kinds of excitement, such as alcoholism and prostitution, in a word modern life, with all its great and small things, its beauty and its ugliness, its good and its evil, its sublimity and its degradation, its loftiness and its depravity, does not give us peace and quiet—on the contrary, we are never at peace, we are disturbed, nervous, weary, discomposed. And this condition, taken as a whole, this physiological and psychic condition finds its great, its historical cause in the conflict between the new view of the world and the old one.

Part Two

Modern Philosophy and Religion

Chapter I

Modern Science and Philosophy in Favour of Religion

NOT so very long ago in so-called educated circles (and today most people claim to belong to them), religion was not thought about. "The religious question does not exist for the intelligent and progressive man, it is solved, it was cleared up long ago"—so folk said. Today it is beginning to be spoken about differently, it is beginning to be considered whether religion has really only a historical value for our society, or whether, on the other hand, facts justify its continuance.

The general opinion (of the so-called educated groups) was that religion had succumbed to modern philosophy and science: modern philosophy and science had other things to worry about—political, social, national problems; these were problems, but why bother about religion? And to the same extent that philosophy and science seemed to be modern, religion became to people something ancient, obsolete, outlived. It would serve yet for women and for children . . . for old women.

I always comprehend with difficulty how this opinion concerning the anti-religious basis of philosophy and science could have spread so widely. For the exact opposite is true: philosophy and science (by this I mean the modern, the most modern, philosophy and science) are not anti-religious.

Just look into the history of philosophy and you will

see that the greatest thinkers were not against religion—but on the contrary were for religion.

Recall, please, Descartes with his arguments for theism, Leibnitz with his theodicy, Locke with his striving towards a natural religion, and, further, Pascal, Rousseau, Kant, and after Kant, Jacobi, Fichte, Schelling, Hegel—all, all of them devoted their best energies to speculation about religion. . . .

Kant, perhaps, did more for religion in this century than all his theological opponents.

Some philosophers were the direct founders of religion and churches—Comte, for example; and do you think that Nietzsche would have had the influence he had if he had not gone in among the prophets? And how about Schopenhaeur's influence? Was he not influential because of his mysticism which, after all, is directly identified with religion? And Spencer—does he not preach the reconciliation of science and religion?

Religion is the basic content of the spiritual life of man, it is as necessary for life as air is—that is exactly why so many people do not notice it, just as they do not notice the air, and they do not value its life-giving power. (After all in large cities pure air is paid for dearly and there religion too is most energetically sought for!)

"All truly great minds are religious," we read in *Wearied Souls*, and that is true. And still there are many, many people today without religion.

Is there no contradiction here? There is not. Science too, art too, morality too, belong to the spiritual substance of man, and how many people there are without a real scientific education, without art, without morality! Such people only are without religion—or they have it to extra-ordinary, unique degrees.

Religion, religion!—What, do not, then, science and philosophy stand in opposition to the theologians, to the churches, and to their religion? Religion *in abstracto* does not, after all, exist, but there are different religions, positive and official religions. Do modern science and philosophy agree with them? *Hic Rhodus, hic salta*!

True. But are not philosophy and science also the adversaries of philosophy and science? Is not art against art? Are not morals against morals? Is it possible that a thinking man of today, after so many battles, should not have perceived that where officialdom flourishes truth dies? Positive official science, positive official laws, positive official art, positive official religion. . . . Dear Lord!

But this serious obstacle cannot be surmounted so easily by means of these few words and this comparison with other cultural forces. The relation of philosophy to religion and the struggle between philosophy and religion must be spoken of more expansively and looked at from all sides. Meanwhile I would say only this much—that the fight of philosophy and science against positive religion is not a proof that philosophy and science are *eo ipso* anti-religious.

On the contrary from this conflict, from its tenacity and long duration (it is as old as philosophy and religion), we might draw a directly opposite conclusion. Just because religion is not indifferent to philosophy and science there is a conflict between them. So also in other fields (for example in politics) the parties and tendencies close to one another are in the sharpest opposition to one another. Many a philosopher fights religion because he himself is full of it. It has already been stated several times that there are no atheists. Surely the rejection of God is not yet atheism. Real atheism, positive atheism is a rare herb! At any rate I do not know anyone, even the most robust thinker, in all philosophical literature (except the two Mills and perhaps Hume) whom I consider to be an atheist, and even of these I have some doubts. (Please note that I speak of atheism seriously meant, of conscious, positive atheism—and by no means of negation or even of a more radical revolt against God. A hundred ultra-radical rebel-Titans are not a patch on Hume.)

In short—if only we think more carefully, modern philosophy and science will lose that anti-religious function which has up to the present time been ascribed to them.

Neither is modern natural science against religion.

Very often modern natural science is looked upon as an *enfant terrible*, but that also is unjust. Men like Faraday, Thompson and many, many others were not against religion. Not even Darwin—and it is just the Darwinians, for example Haeckel himself, who have recently made concessions to religion. But here it is not a matter of individual names and authorities. I make a further assertion—that natural science in our century has not the significance which is ascribed to it by those who pronounce it to be mainly a modern science, and who see in it the most characteristic phenomenon of our century.

in Favour of Religion

On the whole, natural science is not a stock feature of our period. Those who say it is do not know about the many and various branches of psychological work. How intensively are psychology, sociology, the study of law, political history, the history of literature, of science, and so forth cultivated today—our age might rather be called historical than naturalistic. Let us look at the great amount and at the content of literature and art—even in music specifically philosophical and religious problems are being solved. Of problems concerning modernity and its victory over naturalism, concerning symbolism and the like we need not even speak. The Church and her (clerical) parties are taking an ever greater part in politics, and parallel to this a new spirit of reform is penetrating into the Church; even nationalism, one of the powers of this world, seeks support in religion, as is proved not only by our humanism, but even by Slavophilism, Messianism, and German nationalism (Lagarde and others). And what does the so-called ethical movement mean, despite the fact that it is expressly irreligious? Is not a uniform philosophical education demanded on all sides, and have not the leading specialists (and those just the natural scientists) admitted that without philosophy nothing can be done? Last but not least: how amazingly intensive is the spiritual work of modern theologians. The very fact that in every hamlet there is an educated clergyman, and that the whole great body of the Church is energetically working, is often forgotten. It is more particularly in Protestant countries that theology really competes with philosophy; the main characteristic of this theology is an unusually critical conception of religion and a searching

59

for new religious forms and formulas. Not only theology, but also the Churches themselves have been taking part in the general activity—religious life is growing stronger, Churches are taking part in social questions, and their representatives are stepping down from their altars into the political arena; they are thinking about uniting the Western and the Eastern Churches into one Church which, with her best leaders, should work against other Churches (polemics, comparative symbolism)—and does all that mean that modern man thinks in accordance with the natural sciences?

So little is it like natural science that the most modern branch of natural science, evolutionism, is becoming natural philosophy and mysticism, and Haeckel himself in his evolutionistic monism sees a reconciliation of science and religion, nay, in truth religion itself.

Surely this is not an age of natural science after all, and truly exact natural science is not materialistic.

That what I say here may stand out more clearly, and that it may not seem to be a mere assertion, the relation between modern philosophy and religion must be defined more exactly and in more detail. The reader must not be scared should this exposition be somewhat difficult—the question is a difficult one and cannot be easily disposed of.

I do not wish to give a survey of all modern philosophy. There are histories of philosophy which do that. But I shall pick out a number of thinkers who are, enough for my purpose, characteristic of the development of modern thinking and the present crisis in thought. I assert that Hume, Kant, Comte, Spencer, Smetana are sufficiently representative of the development of the philosophy of the new age; it is certainly possible to select from the work of these thinkers the information we need. Here and there in our exposition we shall bring in other philosophers whenever it may be necessary to emphasize some special tendency of thought. I will again remind the reader that he will have to tackle some questions which are quite difficult. To refer to philosophers or to their works or even summarize problems does not suffice—the reader must himself think over the main problems if the following exposition is to be comparatively short, yet full enough. An exposition of Hume and Kant alone is difficult enough for me, but what's to be done? If we are to philosophize, let us philosophize!

Chapter II

Modern Scepticism: Philosophy is Religion—
David Hume

THE new philosophy from its very beginning took its stand, whether expressly or tacitly, against scholasticism and theology, and consequently against the religion of the Church in so far as the Churches required from their members acknowledgment of the creed. Of course, the main philosophical quarrel was about revelation. For the new philosophy the truth and the whole truth lay in experience—only a few, following the example of Descartes and Leibnitz, recognized inborn ideas. Others, like Locke, were against inborn ideas.

Hume begins with Locke, but comes to different conclusions, and these are especially aimed against theology. Hume's ultra-empiricism may be summed up briefly as follows:

All our knowledge proceeds from the senses: we have only impressions and sensations, there are no inborn ideas, even ideas are only copies of sensations retained in the memory. Mental activity is not exhausted, of course, by sensations. The mind is not entirely passive, it is active, creative too, for we have a memory and an imagination. Of course, this creative power is modest, it consists only in combining the material given by the senses; in every idea, in every concept, in every bit of knowledge, we can, therefore, find an element of sensation—where there is no such element, there the concept is a mere word, without content. The content of all ideas is empirical, sensuous. (Among sensations Hume also reckons the expression of emotion and of will.)

Man trusts his sensations, he believes in them. I see, for example, the sun rising, that is, I am conscious of certain sensations and I believe in their content, that is, that the sun is rising. I believe in sensations because they exist.

So far there are no difficulties whatsoever in it. But why do I believe in not only what already exists, but in what will be? Why do I believe that I shall have certain sensations, why do I expect them? Why, for example, do I believe that on the billiard-table a ball will jump away if I drive another into it? Why do I believe that the sun will rise tomorrow? How can that accord with empiricism? As an empiricist, I believe only in the senses: but tomorrow's sun has not yet risen, that ball has not yet jumped away: why then do I believe in that which has not yet come about, the experience of which I have not yet had, why do I thus anticipate my senses, why do I believe in future experience which is *de facto* still not experienced?

This belief of mine in future experience is a judgment, an inference: why do I believe in judgment, in inferences, since, as an empiricist, I believe only in my senses? The senses, after all, do not infer, do not judge—what grounds have I, therefore, for my belief?

That belief in future facts is, according to common opinion, based on the knowledge of causal nexus—from the cause I infer, I judge the effect, and I expect it because I know the cause and the causal connection of things.

But Hume rises up against this common and ancient

opinion, he asks if it is true that I know the cause and the causal nexus of things? And he answers: It is not true, we have no conception at all of what force is, we have no knowledge of causal connection whatsoever.

But am I not able of my own will, then, by my own force to move, let us say, this finger of mine? Do I not feel and do I not here know directly that my will is the cause of the motion-effect? How then should I not perceive and know the causal connection?

Hume goes on to prove the negative. In the first place we do not know the connection between body and mind at all, we do not know how they affect each other, and therefore we also do not know how the will moves the finger, we do not see how the power of the will is connected with the finger in motion. Secondly: is it not strange that we cannot move all our organs? Why can we not, for example, move our heart? If it were possible to see into the will and perceive its connection with the organs we should not wonder at that, because we should know exactly what the power of the will was. Why do we wish to move a hand which has been injured and which we cannot move? Obviously, we do not know about our will either in this, in any ordinary case. Thirdly: anatomy teaches that the immediate object of the will is not the organ, but nerves, muscles, and heaven knows what else— I do not perceive, then, in my consciousness any causal nexus whatsoever.

And it is just this way that Hume refutes the opinion that we could set in motion our ideas and our mental states according to our will. We do not know how the will guides mental activity. In the first place we absolutely do not understand what the mind is and what ideas are, and how they originate in the mind; secondly: the power of the mind over mental activities is limited, and again, and yet again, I know that only from experience; and finally, in the third place: our power over ourselves is not always the same; in the evening, for example, we do not control our thoughts so well as in the morning—in short, neither outside ourselves nor inside ourselves, nowhere and never, do we perceive and know the causal connection.

That this is really so Hume makes still more clear by referring to the example of the billiard balls. If I see for the first time one ball hit another, why do I not presume that a second ball will in like manner jump away, that is, why can I not infer and conclude that from one case? If I perceived the causal nexus, if I knew what the force is, I should necessarily know how it is connected with the result, for it is because of the result that it is a causal force.

The consequences of this extreme empiricism we can now see very easily. The causal nexus we do not know, we only perceive how things follow one another; we perceive, then, mere succession in time, but no necessary connection whatsoever. If we have seen some succession more often (the bound—the rebound of those billiard balls) we expect that which we have observed until now to follow again in the future. I see now the impact of one ball against another—I expect that it will rebound.

But what is that expectancy? No rational judgment and conclusion, but mere habit—irrationality. A dog having been beaten several times, will also run away from you if you take up a stick, he then also expects to be beaten, but he does not judge and conclude with his reason. What prompts and incites us to expect so-called results after so-called causes is some kind of instinct not reason—reason and empiricism exclude each other.

Then, the so-called cause and the so-called result—are they only *flatus vocis*, as the nominalists of the Middle Ages said? Am I to think of nothing more when I hear the words "cause," "effect," than just of a succession of events? What is their meaning—or are they meaningless?

To this our modern nominalist answers: Certainly there is a difference between this expectation of mine that the sun will rise tomorrow, and a picture of that same sun; I not only imagine that sun, but I believe precisely that tomorrow it will rise. The psychological law of association teaches me why, under similar conditions, a picture arises in my fancy, but it still does not explain that belief of mine; for every idea, every concept must have some kind of meaning, then even the concept "cause" or "effect" has a meaning: when many similar instances appear to us, when thus the same things succeed each other again and again, we form for ourselves a concept of cause and causal connection, and we form this concept because we get a new impression, namely, that of customary connection between an object and its customary consequence. Only in this does the repetition of the same reiterated succession differ from the first experience, and that is why we are unable to judge from the first case what will happen, but we expect it only when we have had more such instances.

Here, then, we have according to Hume a psychological explanation of what is belief and in what it differs from mere imagination or fancy.

Philosophy is Religion

Empiricism, Hume says in conclusion, is blind, we believe in it instinctively; in practice, our expectations, based upon experience, do not, on the whole, deceive us; man can get along in this world somehow with this instinct-guide of his—there is some kind of a queer pre-established harmony, says Hume, quoting Leibnitz. All empirical knowledge, all empirical sciences are uncertain; only mathematics is absolutely certain, its statements are evident, obvious, they can be demonstrated, as the old philosophers used to say. Hume, like Plato before him, Descartes, Spinoza and Leibnitz after him, has a respect for mathematical knowledge. He does not believe in and does not trust any other. He believes in mathematics because its judgments and conclusions come about through comparing ideas, by pure reason: even if the triangle did not exist, the statements which geometers make about it would be valid—the statements proceed from the comparison of the ideas themselves. The so-called causal nexus is also a comparison, but it is an empirical comparison; the relation between cause and effect cannot be deduced from mere ideas, only experience informs one of their regular succession, into their causal connection I cannot see. I imagine it only because I perceive the so-called transition from cause to effect or, conversely, from effect to cause.

That is in brief the content of Hume's brief treatise, which had a great influence upon the further development of philosophy. But, before I speak further about that influence, I beg the reader to reflect well upon Hume's exposition of the impossibility of perceiving the causal nexus.

Modern Scepticism:

I do not think that a fairly reflective person could fail to perceive what Hume with his ultra-empiricism is driving at.

If all knowledge outside of mathematics is uncertain and does not deserve to be trusted in, there is, of course, also and above all, an end to metaphysics, and, obviously, to theology. In all those theoretical studies, and likewise in all his practical dealings, man is not guided by reason but by habit, as has already been stated by Montaigne. And if we do not comprehend the causal nexus, if we do not comprehend causes, we do not perceive the cause called the first, we do not know God. And belief in God is what belief is in general—experience of frequent repetition of one and the same succession of events. . . .

Just as, for example, we infer from watches a watchmaker, when we see the world we guess at the Being who made it; that Being, however, we picture from natural instinct, according to our own image.

This sceptical theory of his Hume unfolds in two works devoted to religion—they are, as has been stated, the logical results of his theory of experience, but they contain, nevertheless, some new formulas, and these we must deal with. For it is just these formulas which have aroused and are arousing the most controversy, even though they are nothing more than the logical result of his theory of knowledge.

In these writings Hume attempts to explain how religion (revealed) came about in an altogether natural manner.

As has already been noted, religion arose out of anthropomorphism.

Philosophy is Religion

Emotions arising out of the needs of life, various hopes, but mainly fear, inspire people to take an anthropomorphic view of life: unknown causes become the constant objects of our hopes and fears. Ideas of those powers upon which we feel dependent create imagination; we transfer our nature to those unknown causes—those myths of ours are for us our gods.

This tendency to believe in unseen powers does not clash with the sense perceptions of primitive, uneducated man who associates those unseen powers with some kind of visible object. Hume calls this anthropomorphic process allegory. He admits, however, that, alongside of allegory, hero-worship prevails, the worship of outstanding individuals; but even this worship of heroes originates from the same cause, namely, from fear and from the seeking for help in the troubles of our life.

The reader must read over Hume's works on religion in order to see with what inexorable logic and ruthlessness he carries his theory through and how he opposes his philosophy to religion. He admits philosophical theism, but he differentiates it from anthropomorphic theism.

Philosophical theism is based upon reason, it rests upon argumentation, anthropomorphic theism upon sensuous fantasy aroused by emotion and mainly by fear; the philosopher believes that the world is regulated only by universal laws, the anthropomorphist that it is regulated by beings like us, for anthropomorphism is ruled by the law that like results prove like causes.

Whether Hume took seriously that rational and philosophical theism of his, and how he understood it—that is another question; certainly not much is left of it if

69

reason has authority only in mathematics. Furthermore, he is not interested in this theism, but in religious theism, he only tolerates the other in order to show the more obstinately that religious theism is nothing more than bare superstition — for anthropomorphism is nothing more than superstition, and rude superstition at that. So also monotheism and Christianity are nothing but superstition, for even religious monotheism developed naturally out of polytheism, and that development was not rational but irrational—purely psychologically, in our fantasy, one idol absorbed other idols, and so on.

The more Hume idealizes philosophical theism, the more effectively he attacks unphilosophical theism, or popular and vulgar theism, opposing to one another genuine and false religion. Genuine or philosophical religion is to him a branch of philosophy, its content is philosophical theism. On the other hand popular religion is false and therefore a superstition; this superstition is for him merely anthropomorphism; it is at the same time idolatry, polytheism, demonism, enthusiasm, "experimental" (read "materialized") theism. And, of course, the same thing holds for Christianity (Hume aims mainly at Catholicism, in this he is a real Scot; but all the arguments hold as well for Protestantism) and *in concreto* for priests and pastors, who are represented to us in Hume as old augurs, either on account of their low mental status, or of their guile. And Hume even though he tends to show that religion developed from human nature in an altogether natural way, still he has in him enough of the deist of his time to look upon them rather as smart fellows, cleverly taking advantage of human stupidity.

Philosophy is Religion

In short: Hume reduces religion to superstition and places it, as unreasonableness, sternly in opposition to philosophy; it is only by the new philosophy, he says, that people free themselves from the spiritual and moral burden of superstition, under which they have groaned for ages. Why, the first real Christian was really Locke! "Ignorance is the mother of piety."

That is about the quintessence of Hume's anti-religious scepticism—the reader must, of course, read over what he says in detail about the fatal influence of religion (read always the Christian religion), upon morals, how he prefers polytheism to monotheism, and so forth. Hume wrote venomously against religion (meaning Christianity). Polytheism, he declares, teaches one to be more tolerant, more manly, more reasonable, more convinced—theism is narrow-minded, intolerant, and leads to a slavish spirit; it spreads unreasonableness; scholastic philosophy is a proof of this and just exactly because of this, it causes scepticism—a theistic religious conviction is always more artificial than sincere, it is an inexplicable state of mind, between unbelief and conviction, always nearer to the former than to the latter. Let those who today see such extraordinary power in Nietzsche's Antichrist just read Hume—in comparison to him Nietzsche is but a child, for he gets angry and boils up, whereas Hume writes with calmness, perfidious calmness.

And it was just this "devilry" that exerted an influence. It is said that the Parisian sceptic and revolutionary gentlemen, when Hume came to see them, were suspicious that he was a dandy. Hume said at Holbach's that up to then he had not known any real atheist; Holbach, obviously offended in his atheism, made known to him the unhappy coincidence that seventeen of them were sitting just then at his table. Diderot himself, the strongest and the most convinced of the French Encyclopaedists, was led by Hume to believe that the English still believed a little in God, whereas the French did not believe in Him at all. . . . Is that not interesting and instructive? Hume remains up to the present day the main stone of offence for philosophy (and even for theology), and the French did not look upon him as a radical! In reality it was he who was radical; the French were in revolt and were preparing for a revolution, they were emotionally radical, but they were not real atheists. Who cares today about Mr. Holbach and his seventeen atheists?

Hume—and here we come to a serious matter—is calm in his scepticism. After all, he considered theism as a possible hypothesis, but it was all the same to him, whereas the gentlemen *à la* Holbach became excited and raised the devil (not to mince words), but in the end they sought refuge again not only in God, but also in the Church. To what extent personal character is the cause of this calm of Hume's, I do not know; to what extent he was a typical philosopher, I shall discuss in the following essay. Here, meanwhile, I would fain briefly indicate how great Hume's influence was and is.

At once the whole Scottish school rose against him; in Germany, Sulzer, Mendelssohn, but chiefly Kant opposed him immediately. After Kant the philosophy of our period continued to oppose him, though there were some who followed him; Fries and Beneke, in France Legerando and some of the mathematicians. Official philosophy as a whole—so-called spiritual philosophy—was in opposition to him. However, Schopenhauer derived much from his reasons against theism, and Comte by his positivism accepts Hume's theory of the unknowableness of the causal connection between things. Among the latest English philosophers, the Mills, Bain and the empiricists in general, and to a certain extent Spencer also, were in agreement with him, whereas Hamilton and others declared against him. In France at that time positivism was debated as it is indirectly also in German philosophy at the present time. Hume's influence is very evident in Stirner and in Nietzsche—Nietzsche especially has more of him than is known to many of his followers.

As can be seen, Hume had a great influence on modern philosophy. Anyone who is concerned to arrive at clear and precise views will learn much from Hume. I realize more and more that when considering the modern period we must begin with him. In German philosophy we are told, of course, that we must go back to Kant; but that is only partly right, it is right insomuch as Kant with his *Critique* refuted Hume. It is, therefore, necessary to know Hume. At least I got along with difficulty with Kant until I got to know Hume; it is only by constant comparison of them that I attained to knowledge which I consider really important in connection with our problem. A thinking man must manage to master Hume, his empiricism and his scepticism,—*hic Rhodus, hic salta.* That, of course, means not only to go over Kant's *Critique*, but to place oneself in the noetic mystery at a certain place, and, if possible, on one's feet.

Modern Scepticism:

But I should not paint dear Hume blacker than he is. Though in theory such an ultra-empiricist and sceptic, he would not be a sceptic in ethics. By his cautious empirical method he comes to the understanding that man has by nature an unselfish, even though weak, sympathy with his fellow-men; and he understands that, because this feeling of sympathy quite obviously forces itself upon us, it is impossible not to have it, and it is impossible not to regard it as justified. Thus Hume, in theory the harshest of the rationalists and intellectualists of the century, comes finally to ethics based upon emotion: the feeling of sympathy (Hume calls it also humanity) together with egoism regulates the mutual relations of people to one another.

And thus, feeling, compassion, sympathy kept the sceptic Hume from complete scepticism and from anarchy —love towards our fellow men, even though Locke and not Jesus was for him the first Christian, and though in general he considered Christianity as superstition.

If we add that Hume argues empirically that politics will become a science (of course in so far as it can be a science at all) we have a complete outline of his outlook on the world and on society, and he was a typical representative of the eighteenth century: a consequent rationalist, that is, a man trusting only in reason and criticizing the whole world from a rational point of view; his ideal is mathematics; but just because he believes only in reason, he knows that that reason is weak and he trusts in it only in so far as it leans upon experience, upon the senses. He has a little faith in emotion, too. He with his rationalism is the last of a line of deists who (in England, but also in

74

Philosophy is Religion

Germany and France) sought a natural religion. And he tells us that there is a natural religion—it is philosophy, sceptical philosophy, of course. He realizes that our reason does not amount to much, but, with all its weakness, he considers it to be better than all metaphysics, theology and religion put together.

Chapter III

Modern Criticism: Religion is Morality— Immanuel Kant

SOMETIMES I like to take a look at Hume's face as it is pictured in an old woodcut, and more than all I always notice how Hume, despite his scepticism, put on weight— a nice double chin and an irreproachable pigtail and wig strangely adorn the mighty rationalist. Of course, if you look at the picture long enough you can see that the mouth is a little curved from constant smiling, the lips are thin, gentle, even though a little fleshy; and those eyes—they smile too and blink somewhat, but are nevertheless wide open, to take in as many impressions as possible. . . .

And is not Hume's philosophy obviously false? This spirit of ours, our whole life and this whole world are impressions, purely sensuous and emotional impressions —mere impressions, I should say absolute impressions, for Hume does not see any certain "ego" whatsoever— the "ego" is nothing more than a handful of ideas, there is no substance in it at all, only our impressions exist, and where did and do these come from? Who knows and who cares about that? Chance, only chance. . . . Let us not wonder then that religions (the popular kind) are sick men's dreams—and what after all are the ideas of the philosopher? . . . It is a good thing, anyhow, that those geometrical figures and arithmetical formulae and equations have some kind of a sure, clear order—nothing else is of much value. It is by a lucky chance that people have a little human feeling and that at least in decent society they do not step on one another's feet (our leisurely gentleman, having served as a diplomat, illustrates human feeling in his ethics by this example).

Isn't it all quite obviously false? So false that it is even —stupid? It is stupid, but at the same time clever, very clever. For twelve years Kant meditated and meditated upon it. Hume's sceptical bomb roused even the Königsberg professor from his dogmatic doze; and no sooner had Adam Smith published his friend's posthumous work in which he formulated his views on religion, than Kant came forward (1781) with his *Critique of Pure Reason*, in order to refute the theoretical bases of this work and in general the whole philosophy of Hume.

It is not an easy task to give a brief and yet comprehensible exposition of Kant's *Critique*; nevertheless I make bold to try to give a correct outline of Kant's effort, of course only because I have given one of Hume's scepticism. If the reader has comprehended Hume well, he will comprehend Kant comparatively easily. In every case he who wishes to understand the course of modern philosophical, scientific, and literary thought must know Kant's views—Kant's philosophy is becoming a modern philosophy, and even the fashion—whether we want to or not we must bite open this hard nut.

At first Kant's philosophy was repulsive to me. But when I had to do with him again and again, seeing that everyone around me referred to him, I reconciled myself to him. Not at all for his teachings, nor for his method; but I learned that his philosophy is the most real attempt to escape Hume's scepticism—and that is a lesson which cannot be paid for too dearly, especially by those who understand that Kant did not escape Hume.

Let us consider once more and as clearly as possible what the whole thing is about.

Our knowledge proceeds from experience, that is, from the senses—real empiricism; our knowledge, our concepts and our judgments are made possible only through experience—experience only makes concepts possible.

Would not the contrary be also possible: our concepts proceed from the reason and render sense experience possible. That is Kant's starting-point. But Kant himself calls attention to the fact that, while taking this opposite point of view, we may assume either of two attitudes to the question, namely that our concepts are only accidental and are not authoritative, or that they are not accidental and are authoritative, universal and necessary. In the first case they would be nothing more than accidental sense-perceptions; but because they are necessary this is out of the question; there is nothing then left but the standpoint of the *Critique of Pure Reason*, which argues that we do not get our necessary concepts from the senses, but from reason, even though we should begin to think in terms of experience. But the fact is that we do not think and we do not arrive at concepts from experience; without any experience whatsoever we could have no concepts, but the whole point is that we do not arrive at them from experience.

Kant, then, as we see, above all sharply differentiates reason from sense-perception—the senses and reason are for him absolute opposites, as they were for the older philosophers and theologians as far back as Plato and still further. Knowledge derived from the senses (empirical knowledge) is absolutely different from knowledge originating in reason, from knowledge in general, from conceptual thinking. The senses give us accidental ideas and knowledge (Hume's dog also "knows"), reason gives us necessary knowledge, i.e. knowledge in the right sense of the word.

According to Hume man is a sensuous being, according to Kant a rational one. Rationality consists precisely in the fact that knowledge and the concepts and judgments of reason are necessary and universal, and therefore also apriori. In truth there is no sense-"knowledge," the senses only give us the material, and this is put into form by apriori kinds of knowledge, that is, by forms of perception (of space and time) and by forms of conception (in the narrower sense of the term) called categories. The material of the knowledge presented by the senses is formed—formed by the reason.

I do not want to unfold here in detail the whole apriori activity of knowing; the reader should look into the *Critique,* and he will soon see that Kant's main interest is concentrated on the problem of how the human mind spontaneously and of its own, its very own, power works up the material which the senses supply it with. Before you get accustomed to the *Critique* you will have the feeling that you are in a mill before a huge, complicated machine; one after the other workmen are spilling grain into the opening at the front and out at the other end there fall beautiful loaves of bread and cakes. After all, even this comparison is inadequate—the thing is to under-

79

stand that Kant places the whole emphasis upon the spontaneity amd independent activity of reason, whereas Hume's man is a basically passive being, for even the creations of our fancy depend, according to him, only on the various combinations of given impressions. According to Kant, the material of our impressions can indeed be combined by sensuous fancy, but it is and will remain only material—it is the mind that works it out and makes real knowledge out of it. According to Hume our mind is like a kaleidoscope, according to Kant it is a creative artist.

The importance of the *Critique* consists in its explanation and analysis of the creative power and independent activity of the reason—synthesis, the synthetic activity of the reason is for Kant the chief concept. Apriori synthesis, of course, apriori forms of perception, apriori categories, and sensuous non-apriori material—these elements are combined in the mind into an organic unity; by means of synthesis the concept of a given thing arises —for example of this or that body, in which sensuous elements (like colour) are combined with forms of spatial extension perceived deductively, categories of substance perceived deductively, and perhaps still other categories.

But synthesis is not exhausted by this. If I say "body" I have not only an image of a body, but I can say something about it. If I say then: all bodies are heavy, I have pronounced a judgment, a statement, and at that an empirical statement. This is empirical knowledge, accidental. I convince myself of the weight by means of my senses. But if I make the statement: in all changes of bodies the quantity of matter remains unchanged—that is not empirical knowledge, but apriori knowledge, hence a universal and necessary, not an accidental truth. In this and in similar statements the synthesis of the subject and the predicate is apriori, therefore it is the principal, nay, the only aim of the *Critique* to show how such judgments, apriori according to Kant, are possible.

How are synthetic apriori judgments possible—this is the problem by the solution of which Kant refuted Hume's scepticism. For the concept (category) of the causal connection, the origin of which Hume sought in vain in the reason, has according to Kant its origin in the reason, and moreover the reason can create apriori judgments, it can deductively connect single elements of knowledge. Hume, Kant goes on to say, erred in thinking that one concept only of the causal connection was in question— there are more (twelve) of such concepts or categories; by the fact that the existence of those fundamental apriori concepts of the human reason is proven, Hume's scepticism is *eo ipso* refuted, first of all because among those twelve concepts (unity, reality, substantiality, possibility, etc.) there is also the concept of causality.

A psychological analysis of Kant's synthetic apriori rational activity is not, evidently, easy. Everyone sees, though only the main points are here presented, that it is a very complicated activity, and still we have not touched upon the main and the fundamental rational activities; we have not yet said a word about pure reason.

Before going on I must insert here a philosophic remark: Kant discriminates between *Verstand* and *Vernunft*, and the critique of pure reason is really a critique of pure *Vernunft*.

Modern Criticism:

What is this pure reason and how can a *Critique* deal with it?

Kant explains thus: The human spirit tends towards the unification of all its concepts, including those arrived at by deduction, and this unification is the function of pure reason. Pure reason derives its concepts from principles, and it seeks the highest form of principle, namely unified and systematic conception. Pure reason perceives how one concept results from the conception of others, and these from yet others, and so forth, and it seeks an unconditioned, an absolute principle.

Of these highest principles there are three: the soul—the world—God. These ideas have an obvious connection and unity: from knowledge of ourselves we advance to knowledge of the world; and by that we come to knowledge of God, of original being, of the most real being (*ens realissimum*).

He who has understanding to understand let him understand.

These ideas are—ideas, that is creations of pure reason; no object of experience whatsoever answers or could answer to these ideas—but these highest principles or ideas have their foundation "in the nature of human reason (*Vernunft*)"; man tends towards them with his whole nature, by means of them he gives all his knowledge, empirical and deductive, a necessary and absolute completeness. This completeness is also, of course, only subjectively elaborated, those ideas are "illusions" but they are necessary "illusions."

Kant emphatically and expressly does not consider these creations, these "illusions" of pure reason as "mere webs spun by the brain" (*Hirngespinnste*): they are not "mere fables" arising by chance. No: they have sprung from the nature of pure reason, they are "sophistications" of pure reason, they are, we repeat, "necessary illusions," but illusions which the wisest man cannot rid himself of. The *Critique* (here then we finally hear what the *Critique* is) explains them, but it cannot destroy or uproot them, nor does it wish to.

Let us take a rest and think over what we have heard from Kant against Hume's scepticism.

There is no doubt that Kant in his *Critique* showed comprehension of the action of the human mind, of that constant searching for the truth, that meditating over and penetrating into ("boring into") a matter. With still greater penetration did he point out the organic character, the completeness and the logical system of that knowledge of ours. Hume contents himself with (besides mathematics) "the skein of ideas." Kant thinks that he is the authorized Copernicus of the theory of knowledge: as Copernicus is said to have reversed the view of astronomical science by showing that it is not the sun which moves around the earth, but the earth which moves round the sun, so Kant proves that knowledge does not regulate itself according to the objects of our experience, but these objects according to our knowledge.

With all respect, there is a mistake here. Kant is not Copernicus, he is only Mohammed, who at first wanted the mountain to come to him, but, when it would not, went to it.

The question always was and is, how does our knowledge originate: by the acting of the object upon the subject? And what then is the object—what the subject? Simple reversal in the manner of Copernicus would be simply to assert that objects are our creation, that the world is our imagination: but whence comes the illusion, how is it that we consider this world as objective, as existing outside ourselves? In every case and always, if we are to explain our knowledge, we must explain the difference between an objective and a subjective, a purely subjective, world.

Let us recall how the leading teachers of Kant, and above all Plato, whose system had a great influence on him, thought about it.

Plato sees a difference between sense knowledge and rational knowledge, between a sensation, a rational judgment and a universal fact to which individual sense-perceptions respond. The difference is that empirical perceptions are changeable, inconstant, by no means perfect, whereas concepts, ideas are constant, immutable, precise, perfect. Therefore he asks how ideas (Kant also has the word and concept from him) originate, and, as is well known, he does not know what else to do but to teach that our soul, before its incarnation, existed in a pure world of ideas and there, being pure, without body, without senses, it learned to know, to perceive objective ideas by pure reason. When it was plunged into a sensuous body it recalled ideas through indirect sense perceptions, which acquired significance just in so far as they referred to the idea.

There is no doubt that here Plato gives us a myth— he himself admits it and renounces his doctrine concerning ideas. But he showed the noetic problem in an extraordinarily bright and beautiful light; which is why he has had such a great influence on the development of thought —greater than anyone who does not know the historical development of philosophy can guess.

Plato then (and in this he had numerous predecessors in Greek philosophy) sets up a decided distinction and contrast between the senses and the reason; the reason is passive, for it perceives (in the realm of ideas) ideas existing objectively, and its cognition is intuition, a looking into—on earth its activity consists in recollecting the world of ideas. Furthermore, Plato has here an emotional motive—the love of ideas. But truth comes to man from the outside, it is objective, and just because of its objectivity it is truth for us. Plato's ideas are those of an ultra-objectivist.

His view about the objective reality of the world as we know it was held all through the Middle Ages. Besides, the Christian philosophy of the Middle Ages had in its God and in eternal life what Plato saw in ideas: above uncertain and imperfect natural knowledge there was placed an absolute and perfect knowledge of the truths of the eternal world of revelation.

In the new philosophy, beginning with Descartes, human reason and its powers begin to be analysed more carefully. The novelty consisted mainly in the fact that man began to analyse himself more deeply, began to differentiate between what the object gives us, and what the subject adds to it and what it creates out of it. Is that subject only a *tabula rasa* upon which the object, the objective world reflects itself, or is it something more? It is the old opposition between subjectivism and objecti-

85

vism, which simultaneously also rises up against empiricism, in other words, against sensualism and rationalism.

It is obvious how this complication originates: the object, the world is not this little bit of it now visible to us, audible to us, and so forth, but we come to know it as a whole, a system, and not as a storehouse of individual things. And this whole—of which we ourselves are a part—we do not conceive through the senses. If only we conceived that world whole and ourselves in it and penetrated it at once and for all!—but we come to know it piecemeal, we put the bits together in our reason and by our reason: what do the senses give, what do they not give, and to what extent does the world which we carry within ourselves respond to that real world? The senses—the reason, the object—the subject, here we have the old problem.

New philosophy dealt with it too. Descartes expressed himself in favour of reason (and inborn ideas), seeing at the same time in theism the ultimate foundation of knowledge and truth. Locke was more for the senses, Descartes, in order to escape scepticism, emphasized the subject, his own inner "ego"—but he did not escape scepticism by doing this; on the contrary he strengthened it, as the further development of philosophy attests; from Descartes to post-Kantian idealism, step by step, subjectivism, scepticism, become stronger. Leibnitz in his opposition to Locke fled back—to Plato, and arrived at the doctrine of pre-established harmony. Between the body and the spirit (the senses and the reason) there is no mutual interaction, there is only an inward development of the individual monads of which the world is composed—but the development in all individual monads corresponds, as do two exact watches going at the same time and pointing to the same hour. The object, then, does not act upon the subject, but the subject develops and to this development corresponds the development of the object; one monad does not see into another; but they are all in a harmony pre-established by the monad of monads—God.

The consequences of Descartes' subjectivism are, after all, apparent in Leibnitz's system, and they are even more apparent in later systems. Berkeley knew of no other way out, so he eliminated matter—body, and left only purely passive spirit; only the highest spirit can produce effects, and it causes images to arise in individual spirits, and individual images at that, for there are no universal images. A queer system—but do you not see how in it, side by side with Plato, Descartes manifests himself?

The difference between Leibnitz and Locke is shown forth in the difference between Kant and Hume. Through Kant Leibnitz speaks, and hence even Descartes and Plato; Hume, again, sticks to Locke and to the old empiricists and sensualists.

We see, then, whence Kant got his uncompromising noetic dualism. He speaks no differently from Plato and the Middle Ages about the difference between the senses and the reason. *De facto* such a difference does not exist, there is no such sharp dualism. Here is Kant's first great error. Between sense knowledge and rational knowledge there is not that absolute difference of values which in accordance with his pattern (Plato) Kant makes. To speak of the lowness of sense-perceptions and to place them in opposition to the loftiness of the rational processes as Kant does, is not justified and has no sense. That is Kant's second mistake.

Whence, then (and this is not a paradox) comes the uncritical aspect of Kant's *Critique?* He believed so firmly, in accord with the old school, in inborn apriori knowledge and in his whole deductive system that he is quite amazing. Just as a faithful Christian or Mohammedan takes for granted that revelation exists and that that revelation must regulate all his knowledge and "natural" conduct, so Kant believes in the deductive power of the human spirit.

With this fixed idea, for it cannot be called otherwise, with this presumption, he would fain refute Hume who, just because he saw all the weaknesses of rationalistic philosophy so well, took sides with empiricism so obstinately, but not so blindly as Kant would believe. Hume, having mathematics in view, does not reject all rational knowledge. Here is the way out of Hume's scepticism, but of course only for one who can be just as sceptical about scepticism as about non-scepticism. If Kant had just once asked himself what he really meant by apriority, if he had required of himself a clear definition of that idea—his *Critique* would have turned out differently and better.

After all, Kant's philosophy is not less sceptical than Hume's, and perhaps it is even more so.

When dealing with the question of the relation between subject and object Hume did not express himself so decidedly for the subjectivism of the senses as Kant did for the subjectivism of the reason. In itself the subjectivism of the reason is no less subjectivism than the subjectivism of the senses. Why particularly should apriori subjective knowledge be more certain than non-apriori, but still subjective, sense knowledge? Why should I trust in apriori knowledge? That is the point. I know that Kant holds it necessary and universal, but that does not suffice, as can already be seen from the fact that, ultimately, the most important apriori knowledge, the foundation of all knowledge, ideas, are only "illusions" even though "necessary" ones. Kant with all his reason, pure and impure, could not get out of himself; the whole world as we imagine it is a purely subjective world, it is our world, the world of our reason—how, then, does it differ from the webs woven by the brain? How from this standpoint may I, can I, draw a distinction between knowledge and opinion?

Hume denies that we have a causal concept: if we have not, we do not know and we cannot say that our actions are originated by the influence of the outside world; that which we call effect and cause is nothing more than succession in time. Very well.

Kant refutes Hume with the teaching that we have a causal concept, but he admits that it does not proceed from experience, but that it is deductive. But apriori categories according to Kant have but a subjective validity in the sphere of phenomena (*Erscheinung*)—whence do I know and how can I say that the external world (the essential thing) affects me? Whence and how do I know at all that any object really exists outside my consciousness? In truth even the category of causality, like all the rest, has only a subjective validity; it is not valid for external things, for things in themselves; it dares to say nothing about them. How, then, can I dare to say that the senses furnish me with material? If I assert that I admit that the external world acts upon the senses, I know something then, and something very important about things in themselves, though, as Kant would have it, I cannot know anything about them precisely because the apriori concept of causality is, as he says, valid only in the subjective sphere.

These disparities in Kant's aprioristic subjectivism were well grasped by G. E. Schulz so early as 1792 in his work: *Aenesidemus*; in which at the same time he defines well and correctly Kant's relation to Hume.

The development of German post-Kantian philosophy is the best comment on Kant's fatal subjectivism. The absolute idealism of Fichte and Hegel was the natural consequence of his doctrine. Fichte's "ego standpoint" scared Kant, but then again Fichte was right in calling Kant's head a "three-quarters" head. Descartes with his unfortunate *cogito, ergo sum* quite turned the heads of us modern philosophers—thinking Kant has come to lose himself by dint of thought.

And thus Kant with his aprioristic subjectivism did a great deal to strengthen scepticism. One very strong sceptical element in the *Critique* is the doctrine that our consciousness, too, is purely a phenomenon, not a thing in itself at all—Kant obviously carried his utopian doctrine of *Ding an sich* to extremes. If consciousness is not certain, if objective things in themselves are out of reach —what else is certain?

Hume was more objective, Kant more subjective. Hume

Religion is Morality

based his philosophy on the senses, not trusting the reason except in mathematics; Kant trusted the reason above all, but he wanted to trust the senses too. Hume was an empiricist, Kant a rationalist, but Kant also accepted empiricism. Only, he made both the senses and the reason too subjective.

After all, Kant did nothing more to Hume than to extend his doctrine about mathematical knowledge to all knowledge. The mind itself creates pure knowledge, not only in mathematics, but also in natural science and in metaphysics, and this knowledge is universal and necessary. Just as in mathematics I arrive at eternal truths, so with the same creative power of my pure reason. I arrive at eternal truths in natural science, metaphysics and theology.

What man is, both from a theoretical and a practical point of view, chiefly interested to know is the answer to each of the three old, immemorial questions: (1) What can I know? (2) What should I do? (3) What may I dare to expect? In the *Critique of Pure Reason* Kant gives the old, the immemorial answer: "The theological ideal," God, exists, there is an indestructible soul, and that soul has an absolutely free will.

It is true—and this is a novelty in that old answer—pure reason created these ideas, and because it created them critically they are not mere fictions, they are real ideas, regulative ideas. Criticism is to old metaphysics and theology what the new chemistry is to alchemy, what astronomy is to astrology. Criticism is just criticism. The old naïve faith is gone—if we must believe then let us believe critically. But Kant thinks that by his very criticism he has conquered knowledge and made room for faith.

The *Critique* defies theology, but itself ends with theology. Of course—as in everything—Kant makes fine verbal differences; he explains to us here too that theoretically he is a deist, but practically a theist; the proofs of the existence of God offered up to the present time do not suffice for him, hence he is a deist, i.e. a critical philosopher who attains by means of the pure reason to the knowledge that there is some kind of cause of the world: but that is not enough so he is a theist, that is, he admits the existence of a Creator of the world, and he pictures Him according to the nature of his own soul. The *Critique*, then, ends with theology, but natural, intellectual theology, and not one based on revelation.

Kant called his century a century of beautiful trifles and frivolities, but at the same time a century of "sublime chimeras." What is his *Critique* but critical illusionism?

Kant did not escape from Hume's charmed circle in noetics or in ethics; he follows, too, in his traces in his doctrine concerning religion.

He carries his strictly dualistic point of view over into ethics. He requires that our behaviour should be governed by reason, pure reason, and not at all by sensuousness. Our moral consciousness is infallible, and in its infallibility it dictates quite categorically to the senses and to the ego: You must—you can because you must! Man, man as a reasoning being, as *Ding an sich*, is absolutely sovereign, is a sovereign—of himself—that is, a sovereign of man, considered as a being without understanding, sensuous, egoistic. Then, you must—that is your sacred duty.

Here, too, in ethics, Kant with his categorical imperative commits fatal errors. And it is just here that he could have learned more from Hume. He comprehended well Hume's attempts at ethics and his attempts to escape scepticism at least in ethics, and in that he agrees with Hume. He therefore puts the main emphasis on practical reason. But in this way he comes to strange conclusions. The absoluteness of the moral consciousness gives rise, for him, to three postulates (postulates of pure, practical reason): freedom of the will—immortal soul—God.

Is it not a strange dualism—that division of pure reason into theoretical reason and practical reason? In the *Critique of Pure Theoretical Reason* we are to prove that the idea of God is purely an "illusion" (a "necessary" one), valid only in our (of course subjective) conception, while in the *Critique of Pure Practical Reason* we are to prove that that idea of God is objectively justified, that God really is, exists.

In Kant's method here there is fatal duality, uncertainty and incompleteness. Theoretically, critically, he proves that all proofs of the existence of God are insufficient, and that the idea of God, like the other two ideas (of the soul, of the world), is only a "regulative," not a "constitutive" principle at all, or, simply, reason cannot prove the existence of God, but rather it proves that the idea has no objective validity whatsoever, being at most a methodological idea helping to theoretically unify our knowledge. That, then, is valid, but at the same time the assertion that God exists is valid practically, and He has an objective validity as an ideal, external to myself and above me, whose commandments I must fulfil.

Does that not remind you of that good-hearted minister who threatened his sheep with the flames of hell and eternal suffering, but who, when his flock, moved by his words, began to cry and became afraid, comforted them thus: "Well, don't worry about it, it's not so bad as all that, and who knows whether it is the truth? . . ." Just imagine the position: I "practically" believe that there is an infinitely ideal God who created the whole world and guides it to certain ends, but I must not make use of that knowledge when I study this world of His "theoretically." Is such a method admissible at all?

This noetic dualism hinders Kant in his ethics too. As that absolute difference between the senses and the reason does not exist on the intellectual side, neither does it exist on the practical and the ethical side. It is not only the reason and the senses that are in question; man possesses also emotions and desires: where is it written that no emotions are justified, where is it written that all sensuous emotion is unjustified? Kant completely forgot the emotional side of spiritual life, despite the fact that he himself, and rightly so, subscribed to the (then) new doctrine according to which emotion as well as will and reason was considered to be an individual and independent force. Hume in ethics clings to emotion and *de facto* by means of it he overcomes the scepticism of his own reason. Kant could have kindled a great, warm flame from this spark, but by grafting old dogmatism on to rationalism he did not do so. Kant, discriminating between the senses and the reason, divided also emotion from reason—there is no reason without emotion, and no emotion without reason.

Kant turned Hume's fur coat inside out. Hume had a winter coat of strong material, made to encounter the bad weather of the period of the enlightenment; the material was strong and thick, but that was only the outside, underneath he had a fur coat, which kept him warm, not sufficiently, but still it kept him from the cold. Kant put on Hume's fur coat—he was cold in it. He turned it inside out and wore it as our Slovaks wear a fur coat in summer. But they do that in summer only. . . .

Religion is, for Kant, deistic religion "in so far as mere (no longer pure) reason permits." Morality is for him religion—genuine piety consists in the recognition of our moral obligations as the commandments of God. The categorical imperative becomes an imperative of God.

In the rest of his doctrine about religion, and especially in his judgment concerning dogmatic religion, Kant on the whole agrees with Hume. He sees in dogmatic religion up to his time an attempt at real religion; but he condemns "statutory" religion, ceremonialism and all kinds of clericalism, not less decidedly and consequently than Hume.

While dealing with theism I must call attention to one other aspect of Kant's doctrine, and the more so that it is generally rather overlooked. Kant, as we know, in his *Critique of Pure Reason* shows how inevitably we come to ideas about the soul, about the world, about God. These ideas are for our reason and knowledge only ideas,

95

not at all actual. We have already heard about that. But the new and interesting thing about it is that Kant is well aware that we anthropomorphize our ideas, for he goes on to say that ideas are first realized by man, then hypostasized, then finally personified—in these three stages he carries through psychologically the process of anthropomorphization. The question then comes up: Is that permissible? Is that not contrary to the laws of criticism?

I do not know whether or not the reader expects a negative answer to the question—I at least would expect it. But Kant permits anthropomorphism. In the part of the *Critique* where he gives us "a criticism of all theology, based on the speculative principles of reason," Kant sums up his doctrine in seven points, and there we read that we may anthropomorphize our idea of God without fear and without shame; by this, he says, that idea acquires a precise unity, and it is precisely this unity that we are seeking for our knowledge. Of course, despite this "more subtle anthropomorphism" an idea must remain an idea; but, says Kant, without anthropomorphism we should not be able to imagine anything about that idea, which we, after all, do imagine as the cause of the world.

Mephisto, if he should read the *Critique of Pure Reason*, would surely call Kant's attention to the fact that Hume's savage anthropomorphizes too—why, then, all this ado? . . .

Having compared Kant with Hume and judged here and there the virtues and the shortcomings of their philosophies, I do not find it easy to decide between them.

Religion is Morality

The best thing is not to accept either of them—but to learn something from both. And we can learn much from both Hume and Kant.

There is no doubt that the more consistent, the more consequential, the clearer one is the Scot. The German (also of Scottish blood on the paternal side) is more inconsistent, more uncertain, and more obscure. True, Hume does not construe so much as Kant, and, therefore, it is easier for him to remain clearer. Kant is interested in synthesis and, naturally, his obscurity and disunity are more evident, just because he craves for unity. It seems to me, however, that he is more inchoate than he need have been. Hume, again, kept convincing and convincing, but he did not convince; he is, in many respects, rather weak and incomplete. To be sure this half-and-halfness is a characteristic of the new age, and just in that Kant is a modern man, in the sense in which the term is generally used today, he is a philosopher who is much in request at the present time by people from various camps—the empiricists, the rationalists, the idealists, the materialist-optimists, the pessimists, the theists, the atheists, the theologians and the anti-theologians, the precise thinkers and the fantasts, all and any of them refer to Kant. Perhaps there is some kind of power in his philosophy—I myself lack sufficient understanding to apprehend it After all, Kant was not the only one who left things half-finished; Comte did the same, not to speak of the fashionable philosophers.

Out of Kant's subjectivism, German idealism naturally developed. What could be out-philosophized, German philosophy out-philosophized. It philosophized to the

limits of philosophy. Hence very soon the more critical
spirits sought a corrective in more solid psychology (for
example Beneke) and in a more solid method; this was
helped along by English empiricism and by specialized
education (e.g. Lotze).

That idealistic subjectivism ended in pantheism is
natural. Older influences led to pantheism (Spinoza),
but more recent thought in general has been inclined toward it; the older abstract, theoretical theism obviously
does not answer to the needs of the people—I see and
feel that, in the prevalence of a pantheistic view of the
world, there is a desire for a more living God; simultaneously, pantheism answers to the more materialistic mood
of the times and it answers to the ever strengthening
individualism. And so just from the ethical point of view,
Stirner, quite in the spirit of German idealism, declared
the ego to be God. After Stirner came Nietzsche, after
Nietzsche Panizza and his followers—even for absolute
illusionism Panizza can, without difficulty, find the proper
ingredients in Kant. From Kant's doctrine of the
autonomy of the will and from his categorical Prussian
imperative, anarchism draws reinforcements—wrongly,
but then what has anarchism, what has Titanism to do
with right?

But it is time to conclude, though I have not even
touched upon many of the views of Kant. To do that, I
should have to begin anew, and I should have to show
mainly how psychologically he constructed his apriorism.
I should have to show, for example, what importance
fancy has for Kant; it is a matter of course that not

only rational judgment but also fancy has its part in that synthesis of his. We should hear about sensuous fancy and non-sensuous, pure fancy—in short, there would be plenty of psychological problems. I am thankful to Kant just because he showed me how it is that our thinking is a concrete thing, and yet not a mere thing, but a complicated piece of work and of really fine work. I do not agree with him, but I respect his synthesism; I have already confessed that, and I repeat it. The reader must not think that I do not value, or that I simply reject, that with which I do not agree. No—I just simply do not agree. And so I do not agree either with Kant's synthesis. I do not agree with it even though it has taught me many things. When, here and there, I make use of stronger expressions they do not apply to the person with whom I disagree, but to the thing disagreed with and—to my weakness. Even in a modern wood when people walk alone at night they whistle, and when they trip over a stump or branch they curse—we know that. . . .

In that synthesis of Kant's (I cannot get away from it) I differentiate two elements. In the first place constructive work (synthesis in opposition to analysis) and then the effort to excel all previous philosophy—Titanism. The *Critique* is a philosophical *Faust*. Both in it and in *Faust* man's relation to God is in question. Kant was creating a god. It is true that already Cicero and even still more ancient writers knew that everybody created his gods in his own image—but that is a truism. Kant's creation of a god is something different and something more. In this respect Kant and Goethe similarly represent this century, the century of a great revolution which aimed to place humanity on an altogether new foundation and upon the throne of the Highest.

In this, in Goethe, as well as in Kant, there is that strong rationalism, that belief in the absolute power and omnipotence of the reason—Kant even went so far as to believe in pure reason. That reason was an intellectual extract, an intellectual elixir—lifeless. That is why the revolution also ended in a fiasco, and Titanic rationalism ended in a fiasco. The categorical imperative did not save it.

Rationalism forgot too much about the heart, about emotion. The rationalists could not even say as much about themselves as F. H. Jacobi, Kant's adversary, said of himself, that they are heathen by reason, Christian by feeling. Even a diligent study of Rousseau did not shake Kant in his rationalism. Hume was more careful.

But this rationalism of Kant's has a good side to it: his ethical rigourism was a good school for those days of Voltairian frivolity, and it was, no less, an antidote against the increasing sentimentalism into which, with Rousseau, those who were giving feeling precedence of reason were falling. Even at a later period the categorical imperative proved to be a welcome antidote against romantic mysticism.

Therefore, finally, it is comprehensible that so many theologians have likewise found support in Kant. (In our era the school of Ritschl and the so-called Neo-Kantians.) They are attracted by the sincerity with which Kant derives the validity of morality from religion, they are allured by his acknowledgment that he is clearing away knowledge in order to make room for faith, and they are allured by his critical attitude towards the mysticism into which the romanticists were sinking. It is true that the atheists could also appeal to Kant, at least those who understood the *Critique* as did Heine (*"Hort ihr das Glockchen klingeln? Kniet nieder—Man bringt die Sakramente einem sterbenden Gotte"*). The worst of it is that Kant, by reason of his half-and-halfness, and by reason of his faulty method, had a bad influence, and despite his critical faculty he opened the door wide to fantasticalness. Proof of that was given by Schopenhauer and his followers; proof of that is being given by many and various modern "geniuses." Am I to learn from that, that we cannot get along without fancy? Fancy, creative fancy we must, indeed, have—but fantasticalness?

Chapter *IV*

Modern Positivism: Religion is Superstition—
Auguste Comte

THE exposition of Kant's criticism and Hume's scepticism cannot, as I pointed out just now, be easy; but then, he who has worked through the problem of the *Critique of Pure Reason* will comparatively easily penetrate the further development of philosophical thought and its relation to religion. And at once, on the spot, the reader will be convinced of that by the analysis of Comte's positivism.

Like Kant, Comte begins with Hume, but, of course, in an altogether different manner. Comte accepts Hume's theory that it is impossible to get to know the causal connection, but that does not upset him: we do not know— we do not need to know! That is in a few words the whole of positivism.

Positivism renounces the knowledge of causes of any kind, be they called first, last or final—it is enough to observe appearances, phenomena; the observation of phenomena leads naturally to perceiving certain regularities, so-called laws, only two in all, namely the laws of resemblance and of succession. Phenomena are connected, then, by no means causally, but by these more or less universal laws—knowledge of these laws is the real subject of science and philosophy. As from facts we advance to laws, so from less general laws we advance to more general ones; the progress of thought consists in the gradual diminution of the number of laws until perhaps in one law, the most general, we shall comprehend the entire fulness of life and of the world.

Comte accepts also Hume's definition of religion as anthropomorphism. This definition he needs in order to explain why it is that the positivistic view of the world has gained and is gaining strength only in the most recent times, for it is evident that previously science and philosophy were seeking for causes. How could it be explained, then, that only in recent times have people adhered to positivism, disregarding continuity and the causal explanation of the world?

Comte had a historical explanation of this fact; he showed that only as time passed and quite naturally positivism developed out of anthropomorphism. Already Hume had shown that monotheism developed out of polytheism; Comte accepted Hume's idea and extended it into the so-called law of three stages, according to which the human mind passed through theological and then the metaphysical stages before it came finally to the positivistic, modern stage.

According to Comte every idea, every science, and the human mind were in the beginning theological. Man in this first stage of his historical development believed in causes of things and phenomena, and these causes he anthropomorphized—primitive man believed in gods and in God. Hence the theological stage. This stage lasted for a long time and therefore falls into sub-stages: originally man was a fetishist, then a polytheist, and finally a monotheist.

Fetishism is a spontaneous inclination of primitive man

to consider all bodies in the external world, both natural and artificial, as animated; the life atrributed to them is conceived of as analogous to our life.

With the development and the sttengthening of the reason (by observation, knowing, and abstraction) man began to generalize, the explanation of the world became simpler—from fetishism polytheism developed, finally from polytheism by further development of the reason there came monotheism. Similarly there has further developed the metaphysical outlook, which is in fact only a nuance of the theological and a transition to the definite, positivistic view of the world.

According to Comte fetishism is the purest type of theological thought, but polytheism is nevertheless the stage of the strongest and most really religious spirit; it is a naive and direct faith, undisturbed by metaphysical and positivistic views, it is in complete accord with fancy and emotion, the great number of gods satisfying perfectly both reason and emotion. A monotheist is not capable of being so naively pious; monotheism, it is true, leads to fanaticism because it is exclusive, but this does not render it theologically stronger; on the contrary it is theologically weaker, being disturbed by metaphysical and even by positivistic views.

It will not be difficult for the reader to come to understand these ideas if he bears in mind the manner in which Corite divides history up into individual stages. Fetishism existed and exists among altogether primitive peoples; polytheism we see among the classical nations, the Egyptians, the Greeks, the Romans. Monotheism is in substance the Catholicism of the Middle Ages under the guidance of the Papacy; Comte brings it up to the twelfth century, and with the thirteenth century, under the spiritual rule of scholasticism, the metaphysical stage begins. This metaphysical stage ripens in the sixteenth century and lasts until the Revolution. After the Revolution the last period, the positivistic period commences. Comte very much dislikes the metaphysical stage, even though it was necessary to carry mankind from monotheism into positivism; that is why he places the Catholic Middle Ages above metaphysical Protestantism (the sixteenth to the middle of the seventeenth centuries) and metaphysical deism, which ruled from the middle of the seventeenth century to the Revolution, and the last phase of which is formed by the Revolution. Positivism is called upon to reorganize post-Revolutionary society and to clear away definitely the intellectual and moral anarchy which prevailed during the transition stages of abstract metaphysics, of Protestantism, of deism, and of the Revolution.

Those are the main features of Comte's positivism. As our study continues we shall add one thing and another, but anyone can see that we have not here such difficulties as we met with in Kant and in Hume. As a matter of fact, you will read the six volumes of positivist philosophy in less time and more easily than one volume of the *Critique* or than the little volumes of *Hume's Essays*. With Comte it is all plain sailing—of course, he only gives us the philosophy of his history and no noetics whatsoever; not even in the parts where he gives us expositions of the special sciences with which he is concerned; there are no unusual difficulties in his hierarchy of sciences. Nor is his theory concerning these sciences hard to understand. Positivism begins in mathematics and is carried on to a greater or less degree through the rest of the principal and fundamental sciences (mathematics, astronomy, physics, chemistry, biology, sociology), so that, for example, in studying mathematics, people already thought positively, while as yet, in studying astronomy and the other sciences, they thought metaphysically, nay, even theologically. Thus, viewed historically, his hierarchy of the sciences helps Comte to complete and to present and to fill in the details of his law of three stages.

All that sounds very fine and at first sight one likes it. But Hume and Kant did not philosophize in vain, and so we must look into positivism—critically—and then positivism begins to waver.

I do not believe in Hume's dog, and that is the important point. Hume tried to prove that we have not the idea of causality, Comte accepts it as proved despite the opposition that was raised against him in philosophical circles. He did not revise the whole course of philosophy, so to say, but simply stated that modern man of the nineteenth century is a positivist who cares nothing about knowledge of causes—and that's that. But that modern man cares just as much about knowledge as his non-modern predecessors, and will be concerned about it for ever and ever. It is impossible to forbid man to crave to know about causes; but that is what Comte did. Comte's system of philosophy is a very fine one except for its foundation which is false—it has no noetics, it is uncritical.

Religion is Superstition

Comte is as regards noetics really quite simple-minded. Just read for yourselves and see how uncertainly and inexactly he speaks of the knowledge of causes, note the terminology, and you will see how Comte in the most fundamental matters makes words serve his turn.

Generally speaking, his formula sounds like this; positivism should make constant efforts to avoid any searching for causes, be they first or final causes, in the real sense of the word, because such searching is necessarily fruitless; instead, it limits itself to the study of the constant relations between things, which constitute the effective laws governing all observable events (*évènements*) which in this manner may be "rationally" foreseen one after another.[1]

As has already been stated, positivism can avoid whatever it pleases, and so perhaps even the study of causes, but the question is whether it has a right to avoid a given question or not. And who says that the desire for a knowledge of causes is fruitless? Comte himself values (and rightly so) the pre-positivistic period—did it not prepare the ground for positivism? And if we do not come to know all causes, the main causes—can we not come to know the lesser causes? Besides it is not true that our knowledge of those main causes is not improving—the point is that though we do not know them face to face, still we are continually coming to know them better and better. Comte himself is quite sensible of that, and that is why he speaks of causes "in the right sense" of the word, about "first" and "final" causes; in another place[2] he

[1] *Cours de philosophie positive*, 4th edition, VI, 599.
[2] Ibid., I, 9.

renounces the possibility of knowing the causes of "intimate" phenomena and "searching for the origin and the future of the universe" which is not correct either, for we can learn about these things by looking into any, even a positivistic astronomy or geology.

And finally, how many of these "first," "final" causes really exist? Concerning this Hume and Kant had no doubt that there is in fact a question of only one—of God, and that in reality the question is: theism or non-theism (not atheism), and then, what follows from that, the question of religion.

It will not surprise us to find Comte expressing himself so uncritically about his relation to Kant, and, implicitly, to Hume.[3]

Positivism, he states, exchanges absolute for relative ideas; for absolute ideas arise only when people look for a "cause" in the proper sense of the word, for the fundamental way in which various phenomena came about. The "famous" Kant is for him the greatest of modern metaphysicians (metaphysicians in his sense of the word) who nobly deserved eternal admiration for being the first to attempt to get clear of the philosophic absolute.

I need not call the reader's attention to the fact that Kant did not get clear of the philosophic absolute and was not even attempting to do so; on the contrary, he avoided the sceptical relative: the categorical imperative, the threefold postulate and theoretical apriori spontaneity are after all thoroughly absolute. Comte strangely depreciates the *Critique of Pure Reason* when he states that Kant's cele-

[3] *Cours de philosophie positive,* VI, 618, etc.

brated idea consisted of his grasp of the fact that all concepts are dependent upon, hence relative to, the influence of external circumstances, and upon their intrinsic nature which determines their individual results. But Comte thinks that after all Kant did not understand the full meaning of this relativity; he did not grasp, so he says, that it holds for all organic life and even for social evolution. Only now it is clear (he continues) to positivistic philosophy and sociology that all concepts develop in conformity with the whole evolution of the "collective intelligence of mankind," for all concepts were at first theological, then metaphysical, and only now are they positivistic—*ergo* they have always been relative not only from the static point of view, but even from the dynamic (historical).

Here Comte wrongs Kant greatly. In dealing with these questions Kant was not, to speak plainly, as superficial as Comte. According to Comte the whole content of the *Critique* would shrink to the eternal truth that all our knowledge is "relative on the one hand in respect to our surroundings (*milieu*) in so far as these are capable of influencing us, and on the other hand in respect to the organism, in so far as it feels this influence." Comte adds that this mutuality is immediately interrupted if the environment produces no effect or if the organism does not feel, and he cites as an example a blind man.

He goes on to explain that this relativity of our ideas should not be exaggerated, that all beings know the "real world" equally, the difference being concerned with secondary things only, and we must not, even from a historical point of view, he says, undervalue the past centuries in order to exaggerate the superiority of modern reason.

One can see without much trouble wherein lies Comte's noetical error, his uncriticalness. He judges the noetical problem from a biological and historical point of view alone, hence purely objectively; he does not seek certainty or trustworthiness in their subjective form, and then he does not even analyse psychologically the process of knowing. That, of course, is in accordance with his incorrect opinion that psychology is not an independent and precise science. (For Comte psychology is only a part of biology, but it is not right.) Hence the statement that every organism is dependent upon its environment and that all organic manifestations depend on the nature of the organism (again dependent on the environment), and the resulting uncritical view that by the recognition of this, Kant's work which is worthy of "eternal admiration" is expanded and corrected. On the contrary, after all, it must be clear that Kant's *Critique*, though it does not deal with historical development, is justified and necessary even from Comte's standpoint provided it admits, and it does admit, that the positivistic view of things always did exist even in the very beginning of development, though only indistinctly; and even for that weak, that weakest, intellect at the stage of fetishism, the question about the certainty of knowledge, its limit and its extent was also put, as it is, and will be put at the metaphysical stage, at the positivistic and at every future one.

It is clear that Comte does not refute Hume's scepticism—he simply sets it aside and passes on to history and politics. History, the philosophy of history, teaches him that the "collective intellect of mankind" developed until it reached the positivistic stage, and therefore the task to be accomplished is the restoration of Europe by means of positivistic philosophy. Knowledge is mainly anticipation, and thus Comte judges from the past of historical development what the task of the future will be.

"The noble *élite* of our kind will divide the work; France will have the guidance of politics and philosophy, England will bring her sense of reality and utility, Germany will be the teacher of systematic generalization, Italy will see to the aesthetic element, and finally from Spain it will take a deep feeling of respect for the individual and for universal brotherhood. By a 'final intimate combination' (*intime-combinaison ulterieure*) of these five cultural elements of western Europe mankind will reach its universal régime and by means of this the most perfect consolidation, the fullest mutual harmony, and the freest common achievement."[4]

The development of positivism after Comte shows us its fundamental shortcomings, just as the development of German philosophy after Kant shows us the shortcomings of the *Critique*.

The stronger intellects perceived in the first place an insufficiency of noetics. Mill (is he not after all an expressed adherent of Comte?) reduces positivism to a strange kind of phenomenalism—the world is for him, after all, nothing more than possibilities; Taine from

[4] *Cours de philosophie positive*, VI, 764 and 765.

positivism reached materialism. Littre, after Comte the recognized representative of positivism, actually defended Comte in secondary things only, and himself ended with orthodox Catholicism; the later positivists, and especially their leader Laffite, are only now beginning a critical study of noetic fundamentals. The majority of the positivists ended with dilettantism in Renan's style and eclecticism—with a "combination" of various cultural elements, even a cosmopolitan combination, as Bourget describes it.

A consequent positivism is theoretically and practically impossible. The requirement that in science we should observe properly, not give way to fancy, and so forth, is good, but has been observed in science since Copernicus, Descartes and Galileo, and it will keep on being observed even better and better. But to prohibit the search for causes and research concerning the destiny of the world and the like, is naive. As long as the world has existed people have tried to know all about it. Perhaps in the end they have said to themselves that it is impossible to know, but even the knowledge that it is impossible to know is not positivistic but critical. Thus Socrates himself began and thus Kant continued, and, as it has been said, the knowledge that our reason is weak, and that knowledge is positive, is a positive enrichment of our reason and philosophy, and is not so much a matter of course as it appears to be in Comte.

The thing cannot be done by a "combination" of "cultural elements." Such a "combination" does not satisfy any thirsting modern soul, with such a "combination" spiritual hunger cannot be appeased. It is not enough to appropriate to oneself the various elements of knowledge, ideas and desires, worked out and lived through by other people and nations, and to "combine" them somehow or other. I must work that which I receive together with my own into a whole (and woe to me if I have nothing of my own); the "combination" of various cultural elements is just dilettantism and eclecticism, but it is not a living, nourishing whole, Again and again the question will pursue us: how are we to combine and what?

Mohammedans pick up every piece of paper with writing on it because it might be a piece out of the Koran —why then should we not find in Comte too some good teaching? We do find it and plenty!

I have stated that the way in which Comte avoids noetical discussion is very uncritical and naive; but it is precisely from this that I take a lesson.

As is already known, the Scots refuted Hume with so-called common sense, and Comte's positivism has in it something similar. Common sense, is, of course, a strange thing; sometimes it is very unsound and it is certainly no absolute authority—but it is always good when we hear its voice; especially when it is the common sense of the English. The word "common," too, connotes socialness, collectivity; Comte, as the reader will remember, places the collective reason of all mankind in opposition to the individual reason, and therefore, I say, positivism reminds me of anti-Hume Scottish philosophy.

After all, let us leave Scottish philosophy alone—it is enough for us to be aware that Comte opposed the philosophy of history and of social outlook to Hume's scepticism, historicalism, collectivism, and politics.

Comte—and here we come to a thing which is very important for philosophy—lived through and felt through the post-Revolutionary hardships. Comte recognized, with the conservative and reactionary opponents of the Revolution, that the Revolution originated in the philosophy of enlightenment of the preceding age. He saw in it, even, the last phase of the metaphysical development of deism (Hume also was a deist!), and just because of this he opposed his positivistic philosophy and politics to the political and philosophical revolution. Even though Comte realized very well what Hume had done for positivism, still, by his own positivism, he amended Hume's scepticism.

Inasmuch as scepticism springs from over-emphasized subjectivism, Comte opposes historical and social objectivism to subjectivism.

And that is the important lesson which we can draw from Comte's philosophy. Comte stresses sociology and history; he holds that philosophy should be mainly sociological, and thus he more or less consciously aims a blow at Hume who recognized no philosophy.

Carlyle gave the advice to escape scepticism by means of work; Dostoyevski likewise tells the nihilist in *Devils* to win God by work—you can find this thought in Comte's historicalism and sociologicalism. After all, did not Hume defend himself from his own scepticism with his ethics?

I know quite well that Comte exaggerated his historicalism and politicism, but, nevertheless, his system does not cease to be a problem, and a great problem. Cômte is the very type of new-age, post-Revolutionary historicalism and politicism.

Comte's historicalism is devoid of deeper noetic criticism, and it is in this that his mistake and the mistake of all over-exaggerated historicalism and politicism lies. It is not enough simply to oppose to Hume and subjectivism the collective reason of mankind—for that collective reason also must be criticized, its limits must be fixed and its authority must be proven. In short, Comte did not present us with a *Critique of Collective Reason*—that was what was wanted after Kant's *Critique*.

I know very well that in Comte a part of that *Critique* is in a way implicitly given; I do not say that Comte's work was completely uncritical, for I know that he stressed the regularity of historical development, and that he established and recognized historical laws. By this he showed that he did not look upon collective historical reason as accidental, that in it he saw a certain order and guidance for the future, but despite that, his positivism and his positivistic foundations of history and sociology are inadequate. Comte's error is the greater because Vico was much further advanced in these things than he; in general the state of philosophy at the close of the past century and at the beginning of the new one required much deeper historical and sociological criticism than Comte has afforded with his positivism. As has already been stated I know that Comte saw many things very well; thus, for example, I value highly his correctitude in not recognizing the pretensions of the contemporary national economists, who wanted to base post-Revolutionary society upon their one-sided theory alone (and here Comte apprehended quite well one of the shortcomings of so-called historical materialism). I certainly value Comte, but I cannot agree with him, and it is just because of him that I realize the tasks of sociological and historical criticism.

The eighteenth century, even though it carried through a violent radical revolution, was not so unhistorical and anti-historical as it is often said to be; it is not altogether right to deny the rationalism of the enlightenment period all sense of historical development.

I have just mentioned Vico, whose *Scienza Nuova* is a remarkable piece of work. But even other thinkers of the eighteenth century, and even the rationalists themselves, were preparing the way for the modern philosophy of history and sociology; I mention only Montesquieu, Voltaire, Rousseau, Lessing, and Herder. Nay, I may even mention Hume and Kant. Rationalism is not opposed to the historical attitude; it requires, of course, a critical attitude, fearing, and rightly so, historical empiricism.

Hume, as has been pointed out, tried his hand too at scientific sociology and politics, and wrote a very clever historical book. Kant, with all his criticalness (or just because of it), in his well-known criticism of Herder's ideas and also in some shorter articles made a very serious contribution to scientific and critical history. It was from Rousseau, as he himself confesses, that he learned to understand the "rabble"—the people. And so it is just by way of Kant and Hume that we are led to complete the picture of the past age by mentioning Rousseau and Herder.

If we speak of Rousseau, we shall really be speaking of the great Revolution. Not that the whole Revolution was the result of Rousseau's philosophy; that claim, even though it is still repeated, is clearly unjustified—but Rousseau gives strong expression to the prevailing temper, and that temper he, of course, considerably accentuated.

It would be worth while to work out the philosophy of the French Revolution in the course of this work. In doing so we must necessarily become aware of the fact that the political revolution was preceded by a strong literary and philosophical revolution; but this philosophical revolution is in itself already part of the political revolution. Before the outbreak of the violent revolution the literary, philosophical and political views of England had a strong influence and Montesquieu, Voltaire and Rousseau (consider his relation to Hume!) kept on strengthening the revolutionary movement in France. Soon the influences of the American Revolution joined in. But those influences were not only literary, they were also religious—Protestantism acted upon Catholic France. And this Protestant influence was twofold: revolutionary and reformative. The fact that the French Revolution is a continuation of the revolution which grew out of Protestantism has appeared clearly enough already, Comte himself apprehended the connection very well. But Comte saw only the negative side of the influence of Protestantism. Freedom of conscience, Protestant individualism and subjectivism had been affecting Europe for ages already, and it was just in Catholic countries that they had a revolutionary effect. This constant influence of Protestant ideas and institutions is but little thought about. But it existed and exists. (*Nota bene* its effect in Catholic countries.) I ascribe the radicality of the French movement to a great extent to the result of the tension between Catholic absolutism and Protestant teaching and feeling concerning individual freedom.

And so strong was the influence of Protestantism on France, which had suppressed the Reformation by force, that it had not only negative, but also positive results, namely that the new French constitution and the proclaimation of the rights of man of the citizen were taken from the American constitution, derived from Protestant Puritanism. The motto "Liberty—equality—fraternity" was nothing but the political and economic result of the doctrines proclaimed since the Reformation.

The French Revolution was characterized by the fact that it extended revolution and reform into the political and economic field. But in no other spirit did Adam Smith and others work. The difference lies only in the radicalness.

By the Revolution political absolutism was overthrown and together with the king and the nobility, official religion was also overthrown, and the people—the towns —came to power and leadership. When the throne was rejected, the altar was also rejected; at least it was pushed aside and covered.

Reason and nature were to rule, natural rights and natural religion were preached—Robespierre was founding his church and papacy. Society and the State were becoming democratic, in practice equality and fraternity led to the rule of the majority, that is, after all, of the minority.

Religion is Superstition

But the new minority was after all greater, and it was new. Reason enlightened people's heads, but it also set fire to things, and the houses of the people were burned above their heads—up to the present time they have not got complete new ones, but they are being built, and a great deal of thought is being given to the manner in which they should be built. Meanwhile even the builders sometimes seek shelter in the old houses and palaces. . . .

One of such builders was Rousseau—a citizen of the Calvinist-republican Rome. Kant tells us that it was by him that he was taught to understand the life of the "rabble," that is, of the people—that tells us a great deal about Rousseau, everything, in fact. Kant was honest enough thus to point out the narrow-mindedness and triviality of the old régime, which is so evident in the pedantry and philistinism of contemporary philosophy, and especially of German philosophy.

Hume roused Kant out of his absolutist philistinism, and after being shaken by Hume he was shaken by Rousseau. Rousseau's *Emile* interested him so much that the orderly master and professor failed to take his afternoon walk. Hume and Rousseau revolutionized Kant, and Kant allowed them to—he entered into the revolution academically, but thoroughly.

The period was well on its way when, as well as Voltaire of the salons, proletarian Rousseau became an author of European fame, nay, even a prophet. Rousseau was zealous in defence of the oppressed and humiliated—the peasant was for him the nation; the will of the people as a whole was to be the deciding factor; he placed in opposition to the individual "I" the collective "I" (*moi commun*).

119

Modern Positivism:

The proletarian agreed with Voltaire about reason, but disagreed with him as regarded his over-estimation of culture; reason and culture were not, for the proletarian, synonymous. To culture he opposed a state of nature. He agreed with the doctrine of natural religion—but he really believed in religion and wanted to believe in it, and he summoned emotion too for its defence. In this he was in accord with Hume, but what Hume acclaimed intellectually, Rousseau defended emotionally, passionately. That is why Rousseau swayed the people. He was a fanatic—he ordained capital punishment for those who denied deistic religion.

He wanted morals to improve so he preached the return to nature. He did so the more absolutely because he felt upon himself the unnaturalness of the old régime. He wanted to inspire his contemporaries with faith and strength—he felt the decadence of the higher classes and of the towns; Christianity itself seemed to him to rear weaklings and slaves. . . .

A revolutionist is not capable of being a consequent reformer. The Revolution brought many reforms and valuable reforms, but it also strengthened old and bad institutions. A reaction set in: through this the Revolution and radicalism were stereotyped—declared permanent. That is the fate of France and with her of all Catholic lands.

Comte comprehended how incomplete and superficial were the Restoration and the reaction of Napoleon and the monarchy, and therefore he was for a far-reaching reform. He revolted against Rousseau also, he opposed his turning away from culture, blaming him for sophistry—

and still he himself was not so far removed from that sophistry as he thought he was. A positivist could not with impunity flirt with de Maistre.

The French Revolution was not only for France and in France, it was in all thinking and suffering Europe, only that it appeared differently in other places. In Protestant Germany it showed itself, as is comprehensible, less radically; southern Germany and Austria slept an anti-reformation sleep. There was little interest taken in politics in Germany at that time—people did not even understand Frederick of Prussia yet. Thus it was no wonder that Herder formulated more calmly than Rousseau the problems which Rousseau concerned himself about; but the main thing is that he did deal with them, and very seriously too.

Herder, like Kant, was whirled, was dragged by Rousseau into political philosophy—gradually, having come to know France for himself, he quieted down; he found a corrective in Hume. As early as in 1767 he tells Kant that Hume is *"im eigentlichsten Verstande ein Philosoph menschlicher Gesellschaft."* Rousseau lived more for the present day. Herder philosophized about history. He is for the Germans what Vico is for the Italians. In Herder we see, in the first place, an enthusiastic herald of the humanistic idea. That idea was generally accepted in the eighteenth century. It developed with the Reformation and Renaissance, and derived its main content from classicism (humanism) and the deistic conception of Christianity (humanity). Herder gave this idea classical expression. Humanity was for him the goal of the historical develop-

ment of mankind. To become humane was for him the
ideal of the individual, of the nation, of all mankind.
Humanity was for Herder religion, it was his ideal of pure
Christianity—nay, it was for him almost God. Thus he
forgot all about himself in contemplating the far past and
the far future. In history he saw the plans and the love of
Providence. Herder attained to humanity through
education and enlightenment; he was also a rationalist,
but he avoided the "paper culture" of the enlighteners.

In history Herder saw a continual advancement, and
progress towards perfection, mankind in history forming
one coherent whole; he believed that "the first thought
in the first human mind is connected with the last thought
in the last human mind." He believed that philosophy
should be guided by history and history animated by
philosophy. Humanity as a whole is composed of individual nations; nation after nation in a given period most
fully expresses humanity, the nation is an organ of
humanity. His belief that the day of a Slavonic nation
(Russia) will come and is coming made Herder so
sympathetic to the Slavs. He has become a teacher for us,
too. Herder places the nation above the State—seeing in
the State an artificial, mechanical structure; he had no
scruples (of course in theory) in breaking up into smaller
units his own Prussian fatherland—obviously it was from
Rousseau that he learned the value of small States.

But Herder did not lose himself in humanity, he found
himself in his own nation, even though entirely unsel-
fishly, and without prejudice he recognized the qualities
of foreign nations and other periods. He, a Protestant,
defended the Middle Ages against those who saw in them

only barbarism. ("*So wird an ihm zum ersten Male offenbar, wie die starkste Innigkeit nationaler Empfindung allein aus dem Gefunle fur die Menschheit hervorgehen kann.*" —Kuhnemann, Herder's *Leben*.)

Herder was seeking the spirit, the soul of his own nation and of foreign nations. Folk-song revealed that soul to him—but he found it also in real poets—Shakespeare, Goethe, were for him national. National was, for him, the Bible—he was capable of feeling the poetry of national-religious desires.

Poetry, philosophy, and history, this "sacred triangle" reveals to Herder the spirit of nations and by it of mankind. As Vico was able from law to deduce the spirit of the Romans, and as in the development of law he saw the evolution of the spirit of all humanity, so Herder saw nations and mankind in poetry. "Poetry is the mother tongue of mankind"—he could say with his friend Hamman. With the poetry he studied the language of a nation and by its development he appraised, in general, historical evolution.

In the views of Herder there is, no doubt, considerable vagueness, and it is no wonder that they did not suffice for Kant. Kant in politics was—Robespierre, as Heine said; he looked upon mankind and upon its evolution soberly and critically—critically in the sense of his *Critique*. . . . Though he did not extend his *Critique* to include the study of history and social life, yet in his criticism of Herder's main works and elsewhere he said much that was just. He, too, sees in history plan and progress, humanity and everlasting peace are his ideals too; he sees humanity in a manly upholding of the

123

personal dignity of himself and of others—man must not permit himself to be trodden upon, that is a commandment of humanity. What the nation was for Herder the State was for Kant—the categorical imperative demanded that the organization of society should be more righteous; he believed that all mankind was one family, hence by no means nations and individuals will reach the goal, but humanity as a whole. For Kant, man, and in this respect he differs from Rousseau and Herder, is by nature bad, radically bad; evolution towards moral freedom is, then, the principal problem. From this standpoint the continuity and the steadiness of progress is not so easily possible as Herder thought it to be.

Despite these and other differences Kant has a good deal in common with Herder in sociology; at any rate we see how the political and historical problem of the eighteenth century even before the revolution began to disquiet philosophers. Finally, after the revolution, and with the failure of the revolution, philosophy turned to the historical past; politics, sociology, the philosophy of history and history become the great object of European thought. In France, Comte, in Germany, Hegel, are the most obviously characteristic of this strong, peculiar historic trend of the first half of the post-revolutionary century. But I repeat once more: that very modern historicalism had its first heralds in the century before, and Herder, Rousseau and Vico did not stand alone; we must at least mention Lessing and his beautiful exposition of the gradual education of mankind, we must refer briefly to Condorcet—Comte's and Hegel's historicalism had its roots in Hume's century. The far-sighted reader has

Religion is Superstition

already comprehend what I am aiming at: our modernity smells more than we wish to say of the old régime.

Historicalism, leading so often to reactionary thought, became fatal, even to Comte.

Comte having finished his great work on positive philosophy, published a yet more extensive work on positive politics and founded his—religion.[5]

There is nothing strange in his publishing more precise propositions for the betterment of Europe; what is strange, of course, is that he was founding a religion. But, after all, even that can be quite easily understood from the standpoint of positivist philosophy.

For Comte as for Faust, his own theory became too grey; man not only thinks but he also feels, and for a feeling individual the dryness of science does not suffice, he needs also religion. Man as a being not only thinking, but also loving and acting, finds in religion his complete satisfaction; religion satisfies not only the reason but also the feelings and the imagination. In accordance with that pronouncement, religion is equally scientific, aesthetic, and practical, uniting "radically" philosophy, poetry and politics; by a "universal synthesis" of religion, the study of truth is systematized, the instinct of beauty is idealized,

[5] *Cours de philosophie positive*, in six volumes, was published from 1830 to 1842; *Système de Politique positive, ou Traité de Sociologie, institueat la Religion de l'Humanité*, in four volumes, from 1851 to 1854; finally, *Synthèse subjective, ou Système universel des conceptions de progrès à l'état normal de l'Humanité. Tome premier contenant le Systéme de Logique positive, ou Traité de Philosophie Mathematique*, 1856. A briefer survey of Comte's religious speculations is in his catechism: *Catechisme Positiviste, ou Sommaire Exposition de la Religion universel en XI. Entretiens Systematiques entre une Femme et un Prêtre de l'Humanité*, 1857.

and finally good is done. In religion all reality (*existence réelle*) is "condensed." Dogma is the rational objective part of religion, the emotional part, the subjective part is in the cult and in the organization of life; the cult is purely subjective, the organization of life moral and political, it is also objective (subjectively objective).

The subject of positivistic and dogmatic faith and cult is mankind—*Grand Etre.* This Great Being, however, is not mankind as we are to comprehend it according to positive sociology, but it is *de facto* a being, it should be for us what for a Christian and for a theist God is.

Positive religion has, in the end, its fetish and not only one fetish, but many.

I do not use the word "fetish" in ridicule, neither has it a purely figurative meaning, but it has the original meaning established by Comte; Comte by means of his religion completely rehabilitates fetishism; fetishism, which is according to him "the only source of mental unity"; fetishism, which is that subjective synthesis in which the whole man finds satisfaction.

Positivist philosophy leads, then, we may say, to positivist fetishism. This positivist fetishism does not differ from the original kind in any way, unless in that it does not anthropomorphize so universally; on the emotional and moral sides it differs even less, scarcely at all except that its adoration is no longer directed towards the natural material but towards the products.

What Comte wants is quite clear: ideas born of emotion and fancy must replace noetical fictions, out of the "realm of proofs" arises the "realm of fancy," and therefore not only does mankind live (which after all it does even without fetishism), but even the earth on which mankind lives becomes the Earth, and the space in which the history of mankind takes place becomes: Space.

The external world, then, is anthropomorphized. Comte has a proof of that: To prove that external things, for example, the earth, have not feelings and will is impossible; only so much is clear that we cannot ascribe intellect to them—but they had it before, now they only feel what is going on with them, and they want that which they cause; before, while they still had reason, they strove for that which they now desire, that is, what they cause blindly—but precisely by doing this they spent their intellect, and have only an active, not a theoretical life.

Hence, according to Comte, mankind at the highest stage of cultural development is returning whence it came—to fetishism. But there is a difference between the fetishism of the future and the fetishism of the past. Fetishism in the beginning was not capable of organizing society; theocracy went further in that direction, for it already comprehended all our needs. Greek polytheism developed the reason, Roman polytheism fixed practice, and Catholicism ("which might well be called the polytheism of the Middle Ages")[6] developed our moral sense. (Comte is chiefly concerned with the separation of spiritual from worldly powers.) But not even theocracy was able to definitely arrange society, because in each of its stages it based itself one-sidedly upon one of its constituent elements. Other causes of its insufficiency were its absolutism and egotism. In positivism and positivistic fetishism, sociocracy takes the place of theocracy. This

[6] *Système de Politique positive*, II, 134.

religion has all the qualities necessary to ensure that at last and permanently a "western republic" may be established.

Sociocracy constitutes in the first place a universal synthesis: it accepts all the former programmes and combines them suitably; and by means of this it becomes conservative, but at the same time regenerative; furthermore, it constitutes a relative synthesis; no longer are causes sought, only laws, and it is also altruistic; finally, sociocracy constitutes a subjective synthesis—that is, as above mentioned, a complete rehabilitation of fetishism; fetishism becomes a subjective method and thus "the only source of mental unity."

An objective synthesis—that is the main result of Comte's philosophy of history—is impossible; it was just this that previous ages attempted to arrive at. There is, however, nothing left for humanity except a purely subjective synthesis, and that is just fetishism. Fetishistic positivism, the religion of mankind, is the right and the perfect religion: it satisfies reason best, as well as the emotions and the will, for man must think, love and act; it satisfies the individual and society, it can set in order, but it can also assemble; it cherishes love, but it gives faith its due—in a word, in positivistic fetishism the whole of true reality is "condensed"; it is as scientific as it is aesthetic and practical, it fuses "radically" philosophy, poetry, and politics—it is a perfect universal synthesis.

Among the details of Comte's philosophy are many strange things, for example his symbolism of sacred numbers; or when we read that we are to place all geometrical figures (that is, in order to anthropomorphize them as much as possible) in the *Grand Milieu,* and when we are given advice we are to imagine it as green upon white—are not those queer things? They are—but Wilde's green pinks are also strange, and still he finds admirers. Were I a decadent I would call your attention to Galton—you can learn much from his psychology about what colours people associate with abstract ideas (especially numbers).

Mill and others see decline in the later speculations of Comte on religion. Perhaps, but I have a somewhat different opinion of such declines. Tolstoy also "declined" because he entered into religious philosophy, and the same was said of Dostoyevski, of Gogol, and of others. I do not altogether believe in that "decline" so long as critics do not prove to me that those men had not already declined before their decline began, or, in a word, I do not believe in sudden declines, and I am thinking more particularly of Comte, whose decline had already begun in his positive philosophy and just in that very part of it which was liked by so many and even by Mill.

I am not defending Comte at all, but I should like to show here how, in questions of religion, people perceive the weaknesses of others, but do not see their own weaknesses. The fantasticalness and, if you wish, the absurdity of Comte's views is not the worst thing—we shall frequently see this in the course of our study.

That Comte after positive philosophy approached the problem of religion is altogether natural, even though it is not altogether a positivistic problem. In positivistic philosophy he taught of course that religion was a pre-positivistic stage; but he obviously found that religion, like all the other cultural forces such as science, art, and so forth, had been developing from the very beginning, and that thus it was not possible to break history up into religious and non-religious periods, that it was not possible to make a division between religion and science, which Hume did, Comte at first accepting it. (It can be shown after all from Comte's work that he was not clear about this matter in his positivistic philosophy.)

Comte was not immune from views which were quite common in his time—it is just the extreme to which he pushed them and the form in which he presented them which startle us.

In the first place he proclaimed the religion of humanity —there is but little that is strange in that. Herder, Kant, and many others promulgated the same religion, meaning thereby the organization of all mankind—the only peculiar thing is that Comte made a fetish of humanity. However, even here to a certain extent, the word more than the thing startles us. Kant also allowed anthropomorphism. Not even Spencer completely rejects it, and in general the problem concerning anthropomorphism is not yet solved. And as has been said, he who does not permit himself to be put off the track by a word, will find anthropomorphism in Schopenhauer, in Hartman, and in many others.

In all that Comte could be excused somehow, at the worst by the argument *ad homines*—Schopenhauer's Will, Hartman's *Unbewusstes*, Spencer's Final Cause, and so on, are no better than Comte's Great Being. But Comte cannot be forgiven for conceiving religion so super-

ficially as to see in it only anthropomorphism and—
politics. Really only politics—for Comte the Church
absorbed religion. In attempting to reorganize society he,
in the end, believed as the liberals do still, that society
can be maintained and can be saved by politics. The
Revolution and the anarchy springing from it had so
impressed him that he wanted to have order at all costs,
and that is why he wanted to have a new religion and a
new Church. Obviously, after all, he did not trust purely
State policy. And thus he ended with politics which
upheld—de Maistre, and *nota bene* he came to this while
still a positivistic philosopher. Once at that point, seeing
the foremost place occupied by Catholicism in the world
of theocracy, he reduces Christianity to terms of policy
and ceremony. From this standpoint it is altogether consequent that for him Ignatius Loyola was greater than Jesus
—Dostoyevski's grand inquisitor would be completely
comprehensible to Comte. Even Jesuitism itself is, after
all, positivistic. It is Renan's dilettantism which would
fain construct aesthetically, but if needs be violently, the
whole social system and all morality. Father Gruber, a
member of the Society of Jesus, was well aware of this
side of Comte's positivism and made use of it.[7]

Comte's decline, in a word, begins in his positivism.

Comte succumbed to the influences of his period, and
succumbed to them completely. In other words, Comte
was a much weaker philosopher than we admit, and
weaker in that in which he thought he was strong.

[7] *August Comte, der Begrunder des Positivismus : Sein Leben und
Seine Lehre,* 1889.

Modern Positivism:

In his positivistic philosophy he made an attempt at an objective synthesis, purely scientific and even historical; the new age was to be a direct continuation of previous evolution, the philosophy of history was to show by what principles that development should be conducted. All of a sudden, however, Comte dropped that objective synthesis and took refuge in subjective synthesis— romanticism in the worst sense of the word flowed with the current into his positivistic policy. Emotion, forcibly excluded from positivistic philosophy, sat on the throne; positivistic logic became the logic of the heart and fancy. And like all mankind he sought the whole salvation of his over-sensitive heart in religion. Even severe Kant succumbed in this too. He who would study Comte's system more deeply will be bound to compare with some care his "subjective synthesis" with Kant's *Critique*. Comte, like Kant, placed the greatest emphasis upon the unity and uniformity of our knowledge: Comte would fain gain this "mental" unity by subjectivism, and hence he finds satisfaction in the notorious fetishistic myth. Kant finds unity in the transcendental ideal, which ideal, however, moved by practical motives he "postulates" (assumes without proof), then objectifies, and in the end also anthropomorphizes. Comte and Kant both attempt to make a place for faith, as Kant says. Comte expresses himself more strongly, he would have a "logic of the heart," not only of the intellect. In both fancy plays an important part—they differ, of course, in their concepts of religion and its moral code: for Kant religion is rigorous morality, for Comte, a romantic pill inducing quiet sleep and a carefree life.

Comte, like his contemporaries Chateaubriand and

Religion is Superstition

Musset, accepts romantic psychology and noetics—emotion and will have primacy over the intellect (Comte speaks of will like Maine de Biran and like Schopenhauer in his *Positivistic Policy*) fancy becomes a world-creative principle; the man of genius, the great man, is the rightful leader of mankind—Comte did not hesitate to proclaim himself the high-priest of his religion.

How contemporary were the views of Comte I see most strikingly proved in his agreement with Novalis. Novalis' "magic idealism" is Comte's subjective synthesis —in general a morbid subjectivism; Novalis finds in his heart an "organ of religion" and, like Comte himself, a Protestant, seeks to quiet his religious delirium by means of Catholicism. He condemns the Reformation as a "violent insurrection" and in quite the same way as Comte praises—the Jesuits. There is further peculiar conformity between them—Novalis like Comte was enthusiastic about mathematics.

Hence we shall not wonder at the rehabilitation of fetishism—romantic Rousseauism, though of a heavier calibre. Comte's modern man would like to become a savage—*voilà tout*.

Litchenberg, who had one of the clearest heads that ever troubled about modern problems, once said: "I think that the most certain way to forward man's progress would be to refine by means of philosophy the blind, natural urges (*Naturgriffe*) of the barbarian (who stands between the savage and civilized man) making use for this purpose of the refined intellect of civilized man. If there were no longer any savages or barbarians in the world, it would be the end of us."

Modern Positivism:

In like manner Rousseau judged, nor did Kant oppose it, and Comte believes it also. And people still believe it. Why, then, do the Slavophils and Tolstoy in their traces flee from philosophy to the moujik? Why does the German anthropologist Ratzel expect a renovation of European blood by Negro blood? What is Nietzsche's blond beast? What is the meaning of all that calling upon the younger generation for will, strength and barbarism which are to overcome over-civilization? One of the youngest of the younger generation, Wiegand, like Lichtenberg, wrote: "Every culture must close with Byzantinism. It is an awful thought that the world time after time needs barbarians." Why are so many afraid of "modern Huns and Vandals"? Why does France which is the most advanced seek out Russia which is the least? Are not the English so "healthy" because they live mostly among savages? . . .[8]

In a word, look upon this modern society of ours of the nineteenth century with open eyes and you will see strange things. You will see that Lichtenberg's "savage" theory was long ago put into practice—who was Napoleon? Did there not fall on their knees before the Corsican conqueror, who did not know how to write correctly, not only legitimate rulers of Europe (who did not know how to write correctly either), but even the very founders of ultra-scientific positivism, and dictators of modern thought like Byron and Nietzsche, who see in him the "synthesis of not-man and superman," "the aristocratic ideal incarnate?" Tolstoy has a word to say about this aristocratic ideal of Nietzsche's. For him it is nothing more

[8] Wiegand: *Essays*, 1894.

than a historical label for a mass movement. What, then, is the significance of this tremendous historical mass movement?

Post-revolutionary reaction is obviously not satisfied with a return to tradition and to pre-revolutionary administration, it returns to barbarism—that is, really, over-reaction, and it has a deeper and wider significance than that given it by the modern revolution in thought.

But to finish the chapter with Comte: The founder of positivism is a strange proof of the restlessness and incompleteness of our century.

Chapter V

Modern Historicalism: Ignorance is Religion— Herbert Spencer

AFTER the Revolution many people turned back to the past and compared it with the present, seeking in it, at the same time, consolation; others fled into the future— turning away likewise from the present. Utopianism turned towards the past, utopianism turned towards the future. The historical sense became in every way stronger, the new age in general is renowned for its historicalism, if so we wish to designate that historical sense and (romantic) delight in the past. Philosophy became mainly the philosophy of history. In general, every department and branch of history was fostered.

This historical sense, manifesting itself in political meditation upon social problems, manifests itself theoretically, too, in history, in sociology, and in the philosophy of history, and is carried over into nature and into everything in the whole world. From the history of mankind it progresses to the history of the universe, of everything living and dead. The so-called philosophy of nature, the continuation and renovation of which is modern evolutionism, is originated. Darwin derived the idea for his studies from Malthus' work on the sociological problems of population.

Evolutionism and historicalism blend into one another, but evolutionism is more than historicalism. The idea of evolution contains a new, unusual element; present

136

things and beings developed from previous things and beings by means of gradual and constant change (transformationism)—the progress in which the philosophy of history and history have taught us to believe becomes development, and that development into all forms of existence—forms continually more complex and more perfect.

The doctrine of evolution presented itself as a revolutionary doctrine, more particularly directed against religion. Strauss, for instance, was enthusiastic about Darwin because by his treachings, so he thought, he escaped the concept of a creator. The popular idea of the new teaching was limited to the content of the phrase, "man is descended from the monkey"; it was a provocative slogan, and positive religion was attacked, and not only its theory, but also, and perhaps even more so, its ethical views. Evolutionism promised an altogether new world view and, of course, an altogether new social system. The law of the struggle for existence seemed to be an altogether new and different law from the age-old law of love, and enthusiastic believers in the new doctrine pictured to us not only a new past, but a quite new future. The old utopianism was economically strengthened by the utopianism of natural philosophy—people already began to see a superman. . . . It is certainly characteristic of the moral and intellectual atmosphere of the time that evolutionism became the faith of the great masses but more especially of social democracy. Materialism, with which the philosophy of Hegel's left wing was incorporated, changed its discredited name and became evolutionism. Today evolutionism too is becoming old-fashioned: *Die Todten reiten schnell.*

Modern Historicalism:

Herbert Spencer is the leading evolutionistic philosopher. He attempted to construct a complete evolutionistic view of the world. Spencer's life-work is impressive in every respect, and it impresses me just because he carries the evolutionistic idea through everything with great consistency. As he presents us with a complete view of the world, Spencer naturally concluded his works with an ethical system. From the very beginning of his scientific journey he solves all the urgent problems of the age by means of his philosophy, but especially he solves the question of religion. And of course he attempts to solve those problems which Hume formulated and which Kant and Comte had solved before him. Spencer's philosophy is a conscious continuation of the line of thought worked out by these philosophers.

And Spencer, too, is, like them, above all things concerned with the problem of causality. Herbert Spencer studies the problem evolutionistically; he shows how the simple philosophy of primitive man gradually ripens into the convictions of the modern man, who thinks scientifically. Primitive man formulates the problem of causality anthropomorphically, he transfers the source of energy which he feels within himself, and which explains to him the changes which he himself causes, to all changes outside himself but more particularly to changes not caused by man. By degrees there matures within him the idea of a force unconnected with the human spirit, but connected with spirits outside and above mankind. As the many and lesser spirits lose themselves in one all-embracing origin, the idea of an objective force becomes disconnected from the forces of which we are consciously aware. In a man who thinks scientifically this dissociation reaches its height. Man explains to himself scientifically all kinds of physical changes as the effect of force; however, he imagines this force in the image of that inner energy which he is aware of in himself, in the form of muscular energy; we are forced to symbolize objective force in terms of objective force, because we have no other symbol. In the last phase of our evolution we have attained to the knowledge that the force which exists beyond consciousness cannot be similar to that which we know as the force within consciousness, and that as one can create the other both must be different modes of one and the same force. "Hence the final result of primitive man's speculations is that the power which reveals itself throughout the universe under different forms is the same power which manifests itself in us under the form of consciousness."[1]

Spencer, like Hume and Comte (in his positive philosophy), places anthropomorphism and scientific thought in opposition to one another, the one excluding the other; historical evolution consists in this: that in the course of time man keeps on becoming less anthropomorphic, contenting himself with a precise scientific explanation which is based upon the ideal that all changes are explained by the concept of force, a single uniform force. Hence historical development on the philosophical and scientific side consists of the surcease of original anthropomorphism, or in Fisk's words, a process of deanthropomorphization: science carries out this deanthro-

[1] See Spencer's *Ecclesiastical Institutions*, published as Part VI of *The Principles of Sociology*, para. 659.

pomorphization by substituting for anthropomorphisms even the finest, ever more general laws which deal, in the last resort, with that one and uniform force.

Spencer's exposition reads very nicely. We see at once how primitive, let us say savage, man becomes a modern philosopher: in the beginning he anthropomorphizes very crudely, but, having been taught by experience, he anthropomorphizes ever less and less, until finally he finds in an evolutionistic formula the answer to his original problem. The problem, of course, is always the same—the savage has to explain the same world as the philosopher—the answer of the savage is incorrect, but still it contains a seed of truth, for according to the evolutionistic theory it cannot lack it.

The points of agreement with Hume's theory are evident, but so are the divergences, and they are considerable and of such a nature as to leave a sceptic unsatisfied. How could it be otherwise? Hume would show Spencer that he is not sufficiently explicit as to whether a philosopher may anthropomorphize and if so to what extent. We read that a scientific man rids himself of anthropomorphic elements, but at the same time we read that he cannot get along without "symbolism," and that so he "symbolizes" an objective force by the concept of a subjective force. What does "to symbolize" mean? Does it mean to anthropomorphize or does it not? Evidently the philosopher, like the savage, has a respect for words.

Hume would, however, find still further cause for dissatisfaction. He would be dissatisfied more particularly with the theory that the objective Force (we will speak of the capital F later) is identical with the force within ourselves, existing under the form of "consciousness": where is the proof of that statement? "One can create the other": is that so? Is our consciousness created by an objective Force? Critical biologists and psychologists do not suppose even for a moment that consciousness can be thus easily explained. Spencer, of course, knows this too, and therefore he defends himself by proclaiming that the objective and the subjective force are "modes" of one and the same force: and what does a "mode" mean?

But Hume would in the end forgive Spencer for all that, for the question is not how the savage, how the evolutionist, formulates to himself the problem of causality—but it is whether we have a clear, precise idea of causal connection, whether we see that connection as clearly as we see that $5 + 7 = 12$. Hume does not deny that we have a conception of causation; nor does he deny that we get on well enough with that conception in theory and even in practice; but he asserts that that conception is null and void, that it is a blind conception, no more than a habit, and is not a sensible rational conception. It is valid, then, for things experienced (i.e. in the past) but not a step further.

Opposed to this scepticism Spencer's formula is weak.

From his solution (which is really not a solution) of Hume's question Spencer's further views and his attitude towards the religious problem follow naturally.

The great mistake which Hume and even Comte committed, namely, that they took original anthropomorphism for religion and the strongest form of religion, Spencer no longer commits.

He analyses better what that primitive anthropomorphism is and how it develops. Like Tylor, he points out in the first instance that primitive man believes in spirits and he tries to explain how this belief arises. Dreams and what he sees in them inspire the savage to think that he has his double, which leaves him in his dreams; he believes that what he sees in his dreams is reality. Peculiar and pathological states like faintness, epilepsy and the like support him in this animism (Tylor's expression), and also many natural phenomena such as, for example, echo, shadows, strengthen this belief. That *alter ego* of man is originally as material as his own ego; but with time it becomes more and more immaterial, it also becomes indestructible, immortal (in the beginning it is destructible), more spiritual. This spirit is taken as the cause of all that happens to living persons: for example, during sleep it leaves the living person and then again it can step into it, and thus are explained such strange pathological states as epilepsy, insanity, possession by evil spirits, and finally even death. Driving out spirits, exorcizing and overcoming them result—conjurers and sorcerers become important personages and sacred individuals. From these customs (overcoming or placating evil spirits) a cult develops; awe of the spirit makes the burial-ground a consecrated place, the grave in time becomes a place of worship, and so on and so on—all belief in the various gods originated from veneration for forefathers (the spirit of a forefather is, of course, the most esteemed) and all religious worship is in germ a funeral ceremony. (From the food allotted to the dead arose alms, the killing of slaves became sacrifice, abstaining from food for the benefit of the spirit became fasting, eulogies and pleas to the spirits of the dead developed into prayers, and so forth.)

Thus, according to Spencer, from the worship of fore-fathers all idolatry and polytheism can be derived. The concepts of spirit and good are identical for the primitive man. Just as the more he respects the stronger man (physically-spiritually) the more he fears him, hence the more he respects the stronger spirits—the gods—the more he fears them. The hierarchy of spirits and the entire mythological system arise; the head of the family is at first, in the family and primitive community, the earthly authority (the chief), and the spiritual authority (the priest); in time these two functions are separated, and as the communities are differentiated there arise various cults, polytheistic priests, and finally, the mono-theistic ecclesiastical organization, for monotheism naturally developed out of polytheism.

Thus Spencer very cleverly modernizes ancient Euhemeros, who already three hundred years before Christ in a strange work proved that gods and heroes are nothing but people who were worshipped after death. Just as Euhemeros pointed to the grave of Dionysius in Crete, so Spencer brings forward many, many proofs from recent literature in support of his theory, and there is no doubt that he is right to a certain extent—to what extent, is the question. But we are not concerned with that now, I only wanted to show how Spencer explains the origin of religion and how he compares philosophy with religion and opposes the one to the other.[2]

Spencer, just because he is an evolutionist, sees quite correctly that up to the present time, not only science but also religion has been developing, and therefore he thinks that even in the future the evolution of both will go on; nay, he even believes that the chronic antagonism which has existed and still exists today between them will disappear in the course of the further development and perfecting of both. Evolutionistic philosophy has even the task of reconciling religion and science.

Science does not destroy religious ideas and feelings; for what it takes away of mystery from "the old explanation" it adds to "the new one." Scientific development on the one hand is a gradual transfiguration of nature: where ordinary observation sees complete simplicity, science reveals complexity; where there seemed to be absolute immobility, science perceives activity; where there seemed to be emptiness we recognize a wonderful play of various forces. Every generation of natural scientists discovers in so-called "dead matter" forces which our elders never dreamed of, thus step by step by means of science we reach not the view that the universe is dead matter, but that it is everywhere alive, alive "if

[2] Not fetishism but animism is thus, according to Spencer, the original form of religion; out of animism fetishism first developed as an external result of faith in spirits, i.e. when a man believed in spirits and in many spirits, he looked for them also in objects similar to man, and finally in common objects.

not in the narrower still in the wider, more general, sense of the word."

The results obtained by natural science are reinforced by the results of psychological speculation. Introspective analysis forces us to admit that our scientific explanations of phenomena if adequate are the expression of our sensations and ideas, that is, they belong to consciousness and they are but symbols of something which lies beyond consciousness. "Although analysis later reinstates our primitive faith to the extent that behind every class of phenomenal manifestations there is always a nexus which is reality, remaining constant amid changeable appearances, still we know that this nexus of reality is always inaccessible to our consciousness." Into the activities constituting the consciousness there cannot enter activities lying beyond consciousness. These, then, would seem to be unconscious; however, the fact that the former are caused by the latter leads to the conclusion that they are of the same substance. And as in that case we are forced to represent external energy in forms of internal energy, the picture of the universe becomes rather spiritualistic than materialistic—even though further considerations force upon us the truth that the conception of this final energy which we derive from subjective activity cannot ever show us what that final energy is.[3]

Scientific analysis, then, does not destroy the main object of religion, it only changes it; in its concrete forms science broadens the field of religious emotion. From the very beginning of science the opportunity for

[3] *Ecclesiastical Institutions,* para. 660.

wonderment keeps growing—a savage is often indifferent. For example, what miracles do biology and other sciences too reveal in the most ordinary things—that "the heavens proclaim the glory of God" holds good for science also. And the progress of science and knowledge strengthens still more this religious feeling; for not even the strongest and most educated mind has either the knowledge or the ability "to symbolize in thought the fulness of things." We are all as yet limited to the study of a small part of nature, we know no other fields, and if we know them we are not capable of comprehending them as a whole; in the future the more developed minds will come to know, perhaps vaguely, all the individual parts in their fulness and by this means their emotion also will be raised above our present emotion in the same way as the civilized mind of today is emotionally raised above that of the savage.

Science will, however, force us into agnosticism, but at the same time it will continually prompt man to imagine some kind of solution of the great enigma which he of course knows cannot be solved. He will continually come to know better that the main concepts— origin, cause, and effect—are relative concepts belonging only to human thought, which probably cannot be used about this Final Reality, transcending human thought. But even though he suspects that explanation is a word without meaning, if it is used in reference to this Final Reality, still he feels forced to think that an explanation of some kind must exist.

There is one truth which must always become clearer to us—the truth that there exists an Unattainable

Ignorance is Religion

Existence manifesting itself everywhere, which we cannot find nor can we either think of its beginning or end. Amidst the secrets which thus become more mysterious the more we think about them, there will remain "only one absolute certainty: that we are continually face to face with an Infinite and Eternal Energy from which all things come."

Spencer, as we have heard, expects a reconciliation between science and religion, and expects that reconciliation, in so far as philosophy is concerned, from evolutionism, or, more precisely, from evolutionistic monism. For it is with monism that we are here concerned, in so far as Spencer's views are consequent and precise.

But there is this to be reckoned with—Spencer's agnosticism is in itself lacking in clearness and certainty. Spencer presents the cultural process to us as a continual deanthropomorphization, but he has already said that anthropomorphism (and with it religion also) is a positive force, whereas deanthropomorphizing science is to a great extent, or entirely, negative. And Spencer deceives himself very much when he things that religion will have great respect for his negative monism, and that it will reconcile itself with it.

Spencer himself speaks as if there were an absolute difference between anthropomorphism and scientific explanation. In the passage quoted above it is stated that the scientific concept of energy is free from anthropomorphic admixtures. We read elsewhere, too, that man is progressively ridding himself of anthropomorphic views, is coming to see that even theism is not adequate; for example, the doctrine of the existence of hell, that God could punish eternally, the doctrine that the whole race could be punished for Adam's trifling sin vexes him; he sees how the qualities attributed to God contradict one another, and so on—man rejects first the "lower" and finally the "higher anthropomorphic characteristics attributed to the First Cause," arriving at "consciousness surpassing the forms of determined thought."[4]

And is it possible to have consciousness, or, more precisely, to have ideas, without definite "forms"? Spencer has divagated strangely from Kant's *Critique*. Kant tried in the sweat of his brow to give his *Critique*, where it dealt with the main metaphysical questions, the most positive possible content. Spencer is satisfied with a mere negation, not even considering that he is requiring an impossibility—"consciousness surpassing the forms of definite thought." But Spencer himself knows best that such negative thoughts are not even possible. In his *First Principles*, where he presents to us the basic philosophical ideas of his evolutionism, he speaks in one instance thus of the problem: "We are forced to form a positive, even though vague, consciousness of that which goes beyond definite consciousness."[5]

Spencer, then, comes to know something about this Unknowable of his, here and there, as we have already heard, for he declares that there is a similarity between objective and subjective force. On the whole, however,

---

[4] See *Ecclesiastical Institutions*, para. 658.

[5] See F. Howard Collins: *An Epitome of the Synthetic Philosophy*, 2nd edition, 1890.

it can be seen that he does not like to speak of those things, he does not like to express himself precisely. Thus, especially at the end of his *First Principles,* he points out that his evolutionism supports neither the materialistic nor the spiritualistic view concerning "the final essence of things"; but in the same breath we hear him say that concepts of matter and spirit are only signs, symbols of "an unknown reality which is the foundation of both"—whence do I know that that unknown reality is the basis of my ideas of matter and spirit and what does that mean? The First Cause exists, it is an Infinite and Eternal Energy from which all things come— are these not positive characteristics?

This is a risky indefiniteness. Spencer can be sure that theologians will not be frightened by the capital letter with which he writes his "Unknowable" X, and they will not be in favour of reconciliation with such a philosophy. It is dangerous dilettantism. From agnosticism will finally result gnostic—ignorance, or in plain English: we shall return through agnosticism to superstition. I for my part will not raise my hat to a great "Unknowable," "Eternal Energy," "Great Enigma," etc.[6]

Comte was more precise in this matter for he declared himself definitely for fetishism. Spencer's agnosticism is nothing different from fetishism.

---

[6] In the original capital letters are used: Unknowable, First Cause, Power, Universe, Nature, Eternal Enigma, Ultimate Reality, Inscrutable Existence, Infinite and Eternal Energy, and perhaps even more. (Perhaps to the Englishman it does not matter so much since he always writes his "I" with a capital letter.)

Modern Historicalism:

Spencer's agnostic religion is a great nuisance. A certain vagueness and indefiniteness results from the fact that eventually he does not differentiate carefully enough between religion and anthropomorphism. He is not guilty of such a crude identification of them as Hume and Comte were, but it is enough that he opposes science to religion, where actually the contrast is between scientific (non-anthropomorphic) and anthropomorphic views.

We see this obscurity and indefiniteness in the fact that to "the religious consciousness" he assigns the realm of that which is beyond the senses and above them, whereas "the common consciousness" concerns itself with the sphere of the senses.[7] That is why he differentiates between religious and scientific ideas (in *First Principles*). He very often speaks of religious ideas and feelings—here again we see the influence of German post-Kantian philosophy.

As has already been noted, Spencer sees the cause of the chronic struggle between religion and science in the fact that they both until now were and are imperfect. The struggle will end when they become more perfect.

Religion, he says, is right in so far as it holds to the truth that things are a manifestation of a power surpassing our knowledge—but it is mistaken in presenting us with definite and absolute (hence anthropomorphic) representations of that unknowable force. It is just in this respect that science has continually been purifying religion from "irreligious elements"—science advanced "more religious ideas" than religion itself. But the

[7] *Ecclesiastical Institutions*, para. 656.

shortcoming of science was that it was satisfied with a "superficial," "unscientific" solution.[8] By that religion and science were "incomplete," their disparity and conflict began and continued. Between perfect religion and perfect science, then, there will be no disparities, a reconciliation will come about. Spencer demands tolerance, not so much for religious conservatism, as for progressive scientific thinking.

He pictures the future development of religion somewhat like this: the spiritual power will separate itself from the secular power even more than it has up to the present time, State Churches will disappear and full autonomy of each religious community will come about. The office of the clergy will completely disappear, but "certain representatives" of it will not disappear. On the dogmatic side theism will give place to agnosticism, and therefore worship, tending towards reconciliation with God, will be discontinued, but it does not follow from this that all ceremony will disappear, for it is this which keeps up our consciousness of our relation to the Unknown Cause, and gives expression to the emotions accompanying this consciousness. The need will remain to moderate the too prosaic and material form of life which eventuates when people are wholly occupied with common everyday interests, and those will always have their place who are able to inspire their hearers with a proper sense of that mystery in which the origin and the meaning of the Universe are veiled. Spencer therefore expects that more particularly musical expression of the emotions accompanying this sense will perfect itself,

[8] *First Principles*, para. 2F, etc.

already new Protestant Church music, less personal than any other, serves well to express the emotions awakened by reflection upon the unstable life of the individual and of mankind—life which is a trifling product of that unlimited Power. The music of the future will give these emotions much better expression.

The clergy will, finally, have in the future a mainly ethical task, and it will especially be their business to instil, not rules already known, but new ones necessary for social life, which is becoming constantly more and more complicated. . . .

I repeat, such a religion is a miserable pretence. Dilettante historicalism misleads Spencer to unnecessary concessions. Heaven defend us against such, *sit venia verbo*, philosophic lemonades, that is all I have to say. If I am to have religion in its old form, let me have the real thing—or, and this is what I would say in Spencer's case: "I am finished for good with all that old stuff."

Spencer reduces religion in the main to morality, as did all his teachers. Hume did not wish to be a sceptic in practice; Kant made morality the basis of religion, and Comte founded the religion of mankind. Spencer does not dare to reduce all religion to morality, but almost all; therefore he speaks with such emphasis of his ethics, proclaims it his main work and the completion of his philosophy.[9] And Spencer's ethics have their source in native English utilitarianism.

Adam Smith had the unfortunate idea of cutting man with logical scissors into two halves, the egoistic and the altruistic; that would, after all, not have mattered much,

---

[9] *The Principles of Ethics*, two vols., 1892–3.

but then he forgot to put that man of his together again. So it happened that the national-economist followers of Smith satisfied themselves with one half; somehow or other they healed up the half-creature with their ointments, but he had difficulty in walking on one leg, seeing with one eye. The worst thing about it was that the heart was in the half which no one bothered about. It was not until the good utilitarians bethought themselves of it and wanted to act the Samaritan that they found they were not able to join the unfortunate divided creature into a living whole, but they dressed him up in a tight-fitting suit of the finest English cloth, and thus the poor creature somehow managed to make his way through the world. Plato had not the least idea that his poetic thought would be so strangely dealt with by modern economists. Plato dreamed of a divine Eros—he was still very simple; the economists and that sewed-up Englishman of ours do not need Eros, they already have his progeny—their homunculus! . . .

It is said that man seeks happiness, and that happiness is secured for him, and especially for his descendants in the far future, by means of natural development: egoism and altruism, the individual and society will get into evolutionistic equilibrium. . . . I confess that utilitarianism in all its forms gets on my nerves.

Only narrow-mindedness and ignorance of man and real life could have hit upon the convenient formula that man craves for pleasure, bliss, and happiness for himself and then pleasure, bliss, and happiness for others (of course "and then"). I am not so bold as to include in one formula all the effort of life, but this I know for certain that man does not crave for happiness, etc., not even that merchant there, not even that banker there (*he* certainly does not), not even that *bon vivant* there. That many accept the hedonistic formula there is no doubt; it is so convenient and it explains the world and life so terribly simply—all our craving and striving, "that Eternal Enigma," for which even Spencer has such respect, is so simply solved—we want happiness and that's all! Let us, then, after all, take Bentham's list of pleasures and woes, and add to it his scale and tariff and we have life explained. . . . All those great prophets, saints, mystics and thinkers, inventors, politicians and military leaders, all those poets and artists, all those who were racking their brains and risking their lives—they were all seeking happiness, they were all buying happiness from society, so to speak, 1 kilogram, 5 grams, 7 decigrams, 3 centigrams, 9 milligrams of pleasure. Only now can we understand how unpractical were all those prophets, saints, and so forth; how unpractical, for example, Jesus was, He who did not give happiness and pleasure the least thought!

The late Professor Huxley once wrote (he had a scathing pen!) about the religion of the positivist: he said that he would rather worship a group of wild monkeys than their rationalized idea of mankind. Huxley when he wrote that never even thought that he would soon dispose in a similarly summary manner of evolutionistic ethics. I forgot to show in more detail that ethical evolutionism attached itself to hedonism, but the reader can repair the omission himself; furthermore, it is but too obvious that the struggle for existence—the preservation of oneself and of the race—the survival of the fittest, and so on, after all mean nothing more than what the hedonist, I mean the egoistic hedonist, preached long ago.

Huxley, too, formerly looked upon as the head of English agnosticism (the term is Huxley's and if I am not mistaken he used it first about Spencer), gave a lecture at Oxford University in 1893, which not only in England but also on the Continent caused a great stir; it has been the object of attention ever since.[10] "Cosmic nature," he said, "is not a school of virtue, but a camp of the enemies of ethical nature," in nature there is only the struggle for existence, and hence the rule for the ethical conduct of life is: to do in every respect the exact opposite of that which leads to success in the natural struggle for existence: ethics, "instead of merciless self-assertion, demands self-limitation."

Is it incomprehensible that this sharp opposition between nature and morals surprises us—the modern agnostic, the evolutionist, proclaiming the theory of descent and determining man's place in the scale of animal life,[11] in the year 1893, does he speak no otherwise than Paul, contrasting with one another nature and grace?

Spencer himself after the lecture rose to call[12] attention to this weak side of the argument; at the same time, however, he expressed his agreement with Huxley's condemnation of "the fanatic individualism of our age."

[10] Huxley: *Evolution and Ethics*, 1893.
[11] Huxley: *Evidence as to Man's Place in Nature*, 1864.
[12] *Athenaeum*, London, August 5, 1893.

Modern Historicalism:

Already in his ethics Spencer placed himself very decidedly in opposition to "the wretched *laisser-faire*," demanding state limitation of free competition and contracts, for he knew very well that there are not only criminal murders, but also "business" ones.

Furthermore, like Huxley, Darwin himself, Wallace, Fiske, and other Darwinists, evolutionists, condemn egoism and violence in society and in human life. That is: revolutionary evolutionism in practice and in ethics becomes conservative. Huxley speaks not only against the teachings of Ravachola and company, but he also turns against social democracy and here Spencer adds his voice to his. To-day, in fact, only the followers of Nietzsche deduce from evolutionism an aristocratic ethical system of domination.[13]

And not only that. The Darwinists and the evolutionists not only preach the old Christian ethics, but also seek for reconciliation with religion. Darwin himself in this respect behaved, as is known, in a very conciliatory manner; Spencer, the chief philosopher of evolutionism, from the very beginning and continually preached the reconciliation of science and religion.[14] Therefore, it is no wonder that already even the once militant Haeckel in his evolutionistic monism seeks "the link between religion and science." Vetter, professor of the technical institute at Dresden and a translator of

[13] See Alexander Tille: *Von Darwin bis Nietzsche,* 1895. Tille speaks of Spencer as of a "juggling philosopher."

[14] *Der Monism als Band zwischen Religion und Wissenschaft. Glaubensbekenntniss eines Naturforschers,* 1893.

156

Spencer's works, who died recently, takes the same way.[15]

Kidd[16] went furthest in this direction. He understands Darwin's struggle for existence in the same way as Huxley does; from this standpoint he sees in religion not only a corrective of that merciless struggle, but he sees in it the main content of historical development. Hence Kidd's demand to subordinate reason to religion, which *eo ipso* cannot be and should not be rational, but directly irrational.

Thus the newest, the really new philosophy and, mark it well, a philosophy which has grown out of natural science, does not place itself in opposition to religion; on the contrary it either itself tends to become a new religion (at least the theology of one), or it seeks a compromise with existing religion. The leading philosopher of evolutionism is making an effort, by means of an objective historical synthesis, to reconcile modern thought with religion, with Christianity.

That objective synthesis was not a success for Spencer, but is none the less interesting and instructive for us. (My reader must have already seen that in my opinion the history of the search for truth is a Calvary of errors.) And you see Spencer, a man with such a wonderful mind, a man who was certainly progressive, by means of his objective synthesis coming to the place at which Comte arrived by means of his subjective synthesis. There is a

[15] Benj Vetter: *Die Maternes Weltanschsujeng und der Mensch,* 1896.
[16] *Social Evolutions,* 1894.

marked difference between positivistic fetishism and evolutionistic agnosticism, just such a difference as there is between Catholicism (Comte) and Protestantism (Spencer), but, finally, agnosticism has weakened also and is falling into mysticism, into the mysticism of agnosticism—which is like all modern mysticism. I have not the least doubt that this religion of darkness, or at least semi-darkness and dusk, in some way or another does answer the needs of many wearied souls—but not mine. Not even the nicest Church music ever helped me or will ever help me in my life's difficulties. . . .

But as I say—Spencer's agnosticism is instructive. Anybody who has thought that all English philosophy is empirical, clear, and practical must give up that prejudice of his if he comes to know Spencer's philosophy, this greatest and most certainly English system of modern thought. Even in England alongside of a philosophy which is mainly empirical there has always been a philosophy which is rationalistic and that in Kant's sense of the word, and Spencer himself despite all his empiricism is *de facto* a rationalist who has passed through the school of Kant.

Spencer himself thinks that by his agnosticism he has only completed what, before him, was taught by Hamilton, the well-known adversary of Mill and his pupil Mansel. But Mill showed Hamilton clearly whither his teaching that philosophical knowledge is relative leads—Spencer did not heed the warning voice aright. Whither Hamilton's agnosticism leads Spencer could see from Mansel. From the doctrine that philosophy cannot know the absolute, Mansel simply showed that there is nothing left for the reason but revelation. Even the theologian Maurice rose up against Mansel—but not even that opened Spencer's eyes.[17]

I never trust at all those theologians or even philosophers who lay stress upon the weakness of human knowledge. Not only is a very heavy theological burden laid upon that weak reason of ours, but a certain amount of indecision and often of insincerity is added. I do not like to see that in Kant and because of it I do not admire Spencer. From positivism as from agnosticism there arises an unpleasant dilettantism merging into mysticism. Spencer came unpleasantly near to being a theological dilettante. Of course dilettantism as easily developed out of evolutionism as it did out of historicalism and this can be seen in Spencer himself. Spencer arguing in support of evolutionism endeavoured to unite different ways of thinking and to put them together into one synthesis, but this was not successful. It is a great illusion to think that, for example, Kant's criticism can be evolutionistically modernized (Spencer explains apriorism—by inheritance). Spencer here and there appeals to postulates in the Kantian sense[18]—such attempts of this kind lead only to uncertainty. Evolutionism does not necessarily mean that all peoples of the

---

[17] Concerning these controversies see Hoffding: *Einleitung in die Englische Philosophie unserer Feit* (1889), and Otto-Pfleiderer: *Religious philosophie auf geschichtlicher Grundlage* (1878); 2nd edition (2 vols.), 1883–4; 3rd edition (1 vol.), 1896, entitled: *Geschichte der Religious philosophie von Spinoʒa his auf die Gegemwart. Die Entwicklung der protestantischen Theologie in Deutschland seit Kant und in Grossbritanien seit* 1825 (1892).

[18] For example: *First Principles*, paras. 26 and 43, and so forth.

present and the past must inevitably be merged into one—but the idea of evolutionism leads one astray directly into that line of thought, towards an absorption of all things into one. Spencer, too, yielded to the desire to develop everything out of a few elements, and so he came to work out his dilettante reconciliation of science and religion.

Chapter VI

Modern Humanity: Creative Love is Religion— Augustin Smetana

THE one dominant theme of our history, to which everything else was subordinated, was a theme of religious differences and religious conflict. In the second half of the sixteenth century during the reign of Charles IV a more deliberate movement towards reform began. Milic, Mathew of Janova, John of Stekna, Waldhauser, and others came into prominence. In the course of two and a half centuries, if we go by Bielogorsky's chronology, this movement ripened and then it merged into Hussitism, the Czech Fraternity movement and Protestantism. The next hundred and fifty years saw an absolutistic anti-reformation movement which prevailed —in a word, the religious question fills all our modern history from the end of the Middle Ages to the century of the great revolution.

But with the end of the absolutistic anti-reformation the problem of religion did not cease to be a Czech problem. What for more than four hundred years had been the motive force of Czech thought could not be extirpated by a mechanical civil and ecclesiastical absolutism; an absolutism which, scarcely completing the anti-reformation, weakened and fell into ruin, while the Czech spirit naturally kept on developing its line of reform. History, like nature, does not take great leaps.

The main ideas and tendencies of Czech enlightenment took the same direction as that towards which our reformation had tended. He who descries aright in history and in its leading persons the real live powers leading ideas and urgent desires will not permit himself to be confused by external forms and subsidiary matters.

Our enlighteners went on pursuing the ideals of our reformation, and especially the ideals of our Fraternity. Humanitarian and national ideas are reformative ideas. Nationality, it is now held, sprang from the Reformation; humanity is likewise a new idea and it also progressively developed through the Reformation and the Renaissance.

The idea of humanity was in the eighteenth century the leading idea everywhere, and it was the motive power of resistance to the old order of things, not only in France, but also in Austria which, led by persons antagonistic to reforms, kept most closely to the old order.

It was the tenacity of the anti-reform leaders which made it possible for the counter-reformation to be carried through. But anti-reform absolutism was warping, and it was warping because of continual Czech opposition— until Maria Theresa, seeing the continual and spreading resistance of the Czech peasantry, realized that anti-reform absolutism did not suffice, and even Emperor Joseph II gave in to the European tendency towards humanity and enlightenment. When in France the rights of man were proclaimed, in accordance with the example set by the American religious independents, among us, Czechs, the process of regeneration was begun with humanitarian ideas and ideas of enlightenment.

The ideal of humanity guides our work for reform; our greatest and best thinkers and workers preach humanity, they base the idea of nationality on humanity, they themselves conceive humanity religiously and specifically in the spirit of our reformation.

Kollar, a descendant of the Hussite and Czech Fraternity refugees in Slovakia, was the first who clearly formulated the humanitarian programme; after him came Palacky, Havliček, Smetana—then Amerling, and others. They all followed the beaten track of Kollar. For these thinkers the idea of humanity becomes the Czech idea also, from them it gets its specific national content—the humanitarian reformers represent to us our national modern way of thinking, just as the Polish Messianists were the leaders of Polish national thought, just as the Russian Slavophils guided Russian national thought.

The strongest thinker among our humanitarians is Augustin Smetana. All the virtues and the shortcomings of the Czech thought and endeavour of that day are most clearly reflected in him; he understood the problems and the perplexities of reform down to their very foundations; and more deeply than others. But we are interested here in his philosophy of religion.

And it was precisely the problem of religion which was Smetana's vital problem, vital mainly too in the sense that he lived his philosophy of thought, as well as proclaimed it. By their spiritual strength, thought-content and depth, Smetana's life and philosophy are a great witness that the basis and the root of really reformed Czech life can be religion alone

Like all "awakeners" of their people, Smetana draws from the study of the past information as to how to direct his steps towards the life of the future. All our "awakeners" turned their eyes to the past; history was for them a great reformative teacher. Smetana too tends toward historicalism—which is, furthermore, one of the fundamental traits of our century. Smetana agrees in this with Comte, with Spencer and, of course, with the German philosophers in whose steps he consciously treads.

Smetana gave the clearest expression to this historicalism in his declaration that he himself does not wish to promulgate a systematic philosophy, he is satisfied with writing the history of philosophy: all possible systems have found expression in the course of the evolution of philosophy up to the present day—there is nothing left but to know these systems and to take out from them the substance of truth. He says that criticism of the philosophical past suffices. For Smetana believes that the human spirit has most fully manifested itself in philosophy, and therefore a history of philosophy, of course a critically and philosophically written history of philosophy, is the best history of human thought and endeavour in general. Smetana gives us the philosophy of the history of philosophy.

There is, however, a difference between Smetana's historicalism and the historicalism of the rest of the "awakeners." They searched in the most remote and the most ancient history, Smetana draws more from the more modern and from the most modern history. History develops gradually and his researches are concerned with the latest stages of its development. And thus his philosophy of the history of philosophy becomes an analysis of the systems of modern philosophy. Smetana with his criticism of the past comes upon a general law of development; from the past he determines the aims and the needs of the present. Uncritical historicalism does not satisfy him, only information derived from experience, such as is presented by history with its thousands of details,[1] suffices.

From history he would fain derive the meaning of life, he wants progress to be consciously continuous with the progress recorded in history. With this idea he gives us his history of philosophy, coinciding intentionally or not in this with his famous predecessors Herder and Vico.

Smetana ends up with a philosophical system. Just as Kollar had to complete his philosophy of history with his philosophy of religion, just as Palacky was forced to formulate from the history of the first centuries, and, even more, of the reformation brought about by the events of the year 1848 and of the subsequent period, a programme for the present, so Smetana by his criticism of history arrived at a system of philosophy.[2]

---

[1] Compare the opinion about Herder in the book: *Die Katastrophe und der Ausgang der Geschichte der Philosophie.*

[2] Smetana's philosophy of history is contained in his first work: *Die Katastrophe und der Ausgang der Geschichte der Philosophie,* 1850; the system of philosophy is in the book: *Der Geist, sein Enstehen und Vergehen. Philosophische Encyclopaedie,* 1865. Smetana's philosophy of history is in two smaller works belonging to the year 1848: *Die Bedeutung des gegenwartigen Zeitalters* and *Die Bestimmung unseres Vaterlandes Bohmen vom allegemein Standpunkte aufgefasst.* Smetana's autobiography was published by Meissner: *Geschichte eines Exkommunizierten*—"Eine Selbstbiographie von Augustin Smetana. Aus dessen Nachlasse heraus gegeben. Mit einen Vorwort von Alfred Meissner, 1863."

Modern Humanity:

Smetana's philosophy is anchored in German idealism, Hegel and Schelling had a decided influence upon him. Smetana, like the greater number of modern philosophers, is a pantheist, and starting from this metaphysical point of view he evolves his philosophy of history: metaphysics—noetics—natural philosophy—historical philosophy—ethics—in Smetana unite into one whole, and a magnificently conceived whole. Smetana's philosophy reveals marked noetical creative power, as can be seen by his German style alone. What is surprising in Smetana is his consequentiality—there is hardly an evolutionist who describes so clearly the continuity of world development and the system of world development in its totality as does Smetana—there is of course no doubt that fancy often masters experience.

Like many others Smetana wishes to penetrate the very sanctuary of *Sais*—with a determined hand he removes the veil—he beholds the picture; but further he, too, cannot go.

For Smetana the basis of the development of the world and therefore also of history is in the progressive reconciliation of opposites, which from eternity and for ever pervades the universe in a manner incomprehensible to us: The Infinite is eternally connected with the finite, though the one is exactly the opposite of the other. This opposition is metaphysical (transcendental), but it is at the same time historical, it exists in every individual, it is so to express it also moral. Smetana uses various terms: the Finite and the Infinite—the Temporal and the Eternal—the Earthly and the Divine—Lower and Ideal—Animal and Human—Darkness and Light—

Creative Love is Religion

Egoism and Love—Slavery and Freedom—Individual and General.

The spirit becomes conscious of this opposition from the world—the spirit and the world are of course one and the same thing, for it is known that everything that is, is a fusion of the infinite and the finite. One All-Being, All-Spirit has two halves—the Finite and the Infinite. The human spirit, the human consciousness is a transition form of both opposites together—the whole world is a transition form, a stage in the evolution of these opposites, in the transition and development of our spirit, in which the infinite and the finite are fused into a natural unity.

I will not deal with the chief metaphysical doctrines of Smetana in detail, I will only note them. Smetana, as has been already said, is a pantheist (an idealistic pantheist) and, with his idea of continual and uninterrupted development, comes in between Herbart with his pluralism and Hegel with his absolute monism.

That pantheism is just simply impossible, Smetana's "counter-endeavour" metaphysics show. The development of the world, we hear, is a continual transition from the infinite to the finite; this takes place first of all in nature and then in history, of which nature is the basis, and at the same time the pre-image. The consciousness fuses within itself the finite and the infinite, man is the real bridge between finite and infinite nature, and history is the actual translation from one to the other. Man carries unconsciously in his consciousness a unity composed of the finite and the infinite; it is not until he becomes conscious of it that he gets to know it, and by

167

doing so he solves the world enigma. The process of becoming conscious is philosophy. Philosophy ripens to fulness in history—history is the reconciliation of eternal opposites. In man the temporal and the divine fight their decisive battles, in man the temporal yields to the divine and that struggle and transition is the content of history.

This struggle of the temporal with the divine goes on continually, never does one of them rule supreme: but in the fact that the divine subjugates the temporal lies the divine power, which is the principal law of the eternal All-Being: man is the realization, he is the image of the All-Being. Smetana calls this an ancient law, the law that the equality of the two powers eternally neutralizes both, that the divine is continually in process of being victorious over the terrestrial—neutralization is the ancient law of the eternal All-Being, and this law was given form by the eternal All-Being by means of a temporal being, man: it is man's destiny that in him the destinies of the temporal and the divine are decided, and that the divine power appears in process of overcoming the temporal. History is this conflict and this victory. . . . If we wish to designate Smetana's pantheistic monism in a phrase— it is a system of relative identity.

We will not go into Smetana's speculations about nature, even though they are very interesting, for in them we see the development from dark and, for us, impenetrable nature to living organisms, plants, animals, and man; in this there is much of fancy, fantasticalness— but are not all the more consequent theories of evolution to a certain extent fantastic? Is not Darwinism, for example, fantastic?

I do not doubt that the modern evolutionists themselves would find much in Smetana of modern and certainly of fertile thought, even though they would have to free it of its mystical wrappings. The manner in which Smetana carefully constructs the transition stages of development certainly deserves our attention. Let us just look at the great complete kingdoms, the vegetable kingdom, the animal kingdom, and mankind; between each of these realms Smetana places an intermediate kingdom and the line does not end with mankind, but the evolution goes on beyond man, a superman—a super-superman develops. So, as Smetana himself says, we have this order of things:

1. Actual vegetable—True pre-animal. 2. Actual animal—True pre-man. 3. Real life (man)—Superman. 4. Ideal man[3]—Super-ideal man. 5. Emotional being.

Perhaps this scheme will frighten the reader away from the study of Smetana—but it should not; in the most modern philosophy and even in evolutionary philosophies based on natural science there is just as much terminology as in Smetana. But before we are really interested in the evolution of mankind, history interests us, and, included in history, the history of philosophy, forming according to Smetana not only a red thread through, but a fundamental part of, historical development in general.

The motive power in the evolution of the world is, according to Smetana, the fateful conflict between the

---

[3] "Ideal" signifies "actuated by pure ideas or ideals."

temporal and the divine, and this conflict takes place just within the spirit of mankind. The world and the spirit stand in opposition to one another. The spirit, then, has two main functions: to know and by knowledge to become conscious of itself, and just by means of this knowledge to overcome the world's opposition—which is its own.

History is nothing more than the evolution of consciousness, and up to the present time there have been three periods in it. The first period took place in the East. The spirit emerging from nature came to know the world and being, generally, directly, uncritically; knowledge and being were not yet in conflict.

In the second stage consciousness divided and placed itself in opposition to the world, to being, the consciousness became critical, man became conscious of conflict. This second period is occupied by western thought, beginning with Greek philosophy and ending with German philosophy, from Thales to Herbart.

The third period begins in modern times, in our age. In this period the divine is already decidedly victorious over the temporal, and just because of this begins a new and really human age, for in the transition periods the temporal still held too much sway. These two past periods were according to Smetana like plant life and animal life—then came the life of the spirit truly human, all-embracing life as contrasted with the life of the past, which was absorbed in detail. The significance of our age (Smetana writes in 1848) is already evident when we see its vital fulness and activity—the divine is decidedly victorious over the temporal.

Creative Love is Religion

Eastern man lived in the spiritual tranquillity of a child—the world and consciousness, nature and man were not in conflict with one another, man lived happily in constant contemplation. Western man lived altogether differently. In his daring, he wanted to know the world, he fell away from his god and there set in a tormenting consciousness of conflict burdened with guilt. He began to long for salvation. Reason did not suffice him to gain it, all he could do was to struggle with evil. All the ethics of the West demand effective morality, moral will, whereas eastern man lived by his uncritical, poetical vision. Western man became practical—eastern man was satisfied with his contemplation.

The new age, which will therefore be neither oriental nor western, had the task of reconciling these opposites of eastern and western thinking, and at the same time of evolving something better—a higher, a unified, synthesis.

We must not of course imagine that the preceding periods were entirely and absolutely different. Not at all. In the first and second periods the same conflict, the same principles exist, only that in the first period the world is more the deciding factor, in the second the spirit is more the deciding factor; the oriental way of thinking is never entirely absent, just as the western way of thinking is not always victorious.

The first period is characterized by absolute submission of the spirit to nature; the spirit and the world were already in conflict, but there was not the consciousness of it. In the second stage conflict and knowledge began to make themselves evident.

Modern Humanity:

And in the second period religion began.

Smetana teaches the following concerning the content and development of religion and its relation to philosophy:

Accepting Schleiermacher's definition, Smetana sees in religion two principal elements. As soon as man noticed the conflict with the world and the disparity between the divine and the temporal, he presumed that the divine had deserted him; and he felt his weakness and his dependence upon the divine which he now imagined to be outside of and beyond himself. That was an illusion— for the divine was not beyond man; but by means of the temporal, of matter, nature caused a conflict within him and overpowered him just because he sought the divine in it. Primitive man, in a word, worshipped nature and this primitive religion attained its greatest beauty among the Greeks.

The Greek gods disappeared, the human spirit developed beyond them, but it did not satisfy its desire for the divine. Religion became even more important, and it was especially the Jewish people who, throughout their history, lived through that religious conflict the most painfully and the most fervently.

But the desire for salvation was satisfied—Jesus of Nazareth in His person combined the divine with the human. The Christians of the first ages again lived blissfully and happily, but this happiness soon came to an end, for Christ after all did not altogether reconcile the divine and the human—the Christians began again to yearn and to be sad. The Church became a kingdom of this world, the original sacred teachings degenerated into vain forms and the original helpful love into purely

172

external ceremonies. Catholicism did not appease the desire for salvation, and out of religion it made yet again the Old Testament struggle between the worldly and the divine.

And again the desire for reconciliation and salvation was strengthened and this desire grew in the same measure as the dominating religion became earthly. German mysticism of the thirteenth century gave expression to the desire for association and union with God. (Eckhart—Suso—Tauler—Frank—Weigel—Jakub Böhme.)

Catholicism was outdone, but by no means permanently, for not even mysticism is the right reconciliation of the conflict between the world and the moral law. Mysticism gave up all earthly things, it made a complete surrender to subjectivity. Mysticism was therefore a transition and an introduction to a new period of religious life—to the Protestant Reformation.

Luther finished what Wickliffe and Huss began. Huss was the morning star, Luther was the daylight. The content of Lutheranism can be expressed in one phrase: mysticism transferred from the emotions to the reason. That is the meaning of the new teaching about the faith by which man was to attain inward union with God. Religion for the first time became the concern of the reason. Reason, the spiritual element, becomes the motive power of progress, the motive power of the whole new era—the Reformation was the signal for a new period of development for the world and for history.

Luther himself and his orthodox Protestant successors were frightened by reason and its effects, but were no longer able to stay them. There was a renaissance of classical studies, and in a short time a new, free, liberating philosophy made its appearance. Protestant orthodoxy renewed the old conflict. It was the task of the new philosophy to put an end to the conflict in the course of which it conquered mysticism.

Spinozaism was the first to succeed in doing this. As far as scientific thinking was concerned, it put an end to the conflict between the human and the divine; after Spinoza, all European philosophers worked with this end in view, until Kant by making a religion out of morality struck off the shackles of revelation from religion, i.e. Protestant rationalism vanquished religious science.

This conquest was completed by Feuerbach. Feuerbach showed that the idea of deity and its attributes is the result of historical development. Man came to know error and conflict and thus he was led to theology. Man became a real man, religion became an interior interest of the heart; man no longer longed completely to dissolve himself in the divine—he simply learned then that the age-old conflict arose out of the fact that the deity had forsaken him, but not the deity of which religion taught. The divine had become human, man saw through the religious illusion—theology was conquered, and its results were handed over to human science, to science dealing with man, which covers both the human and the divine.

Smetana, we see, like Comte and other philosophers of the new age, takes religion for a myth and for a transitory phase of evolution, but whereas Comte, Spencer, and others place religion right at the beginning of evolution, Smetana places its origin in the second stage. Thus, religion becomes an even more transitory phase of the spirit. Comte, although he presumed the theological period to be transitional and preparatory, in the end returned to religion; there is something analogous in Smetana, yet he differs from Comte.

Smetana, in a word, regards religion as something inadequate, a weakness; he takes Schleiermacher's definition of religion literally. Religion is a stage of illusion: man was frightened by his duality and in his fright he falsely imagined that the divine in him was for ever lost—meanwhile the temporal, worldly, low elements gained the upper hand for a while only. Man came to himself.

This process was initiated by philosophy. Religion is, according to Smetana, an ante-room, a step towards philosophy. The task of philosophy is to determine the real basis of man's conflict with the world and with himself, and then to make that conflict cease.

Philosophy, then, arose from religion. Or was it from theology? To this Smetana does not give a correct answer, for, for him theology and religion merge into one another. In this matter he is neither clear nor consequent. In Protestantism, then, he sees half religion, half philosophy, and the new philosophy is nothing but a continuation of Protestantism, and then at the same time the conqueror of religion.

In the seventeenth century, according to Smetana, the historical disintegrating process had already gathered considerable force. This period was the real transition period to modern times. In it there began a definite reconciliation of eastern with western thought—hence, too, individual philosophical systems, in unequal measure of course, contain eastern and western cultural elements.

German and Italian philosophy have a stronger oriental element, as appears in the various systems of pantheistic mysticism. In opposition to this, rationalistic philosophy represents the tendency of western thought and that in all its forms: in the aprioristic system inaugurated by Descartes, in the empirical systems beginning with Bacon, and finally in scepticism.

German idealistic philosophy: Kant—Fichte—Schelling —Hegel—Herbart—completed philosophical development, and prepared the way for the final reconciliation of the conflicting elements in human consciousness.

In German idealism all the principal original rationalistic elements were resumed: Kant and Fichte continued in the rationalism of Descartes, in Schelling and Hegel Spinoza was renewed, Herbart was in a way a new Leibnitz. German idealism has in it also elements of scepticism. Thus in German idealism both eastern and western tendencies are represented. Eastern thought we see most clearly in Hegel, the most extreme Westerner is Herbart.

German idealism thus completed the task begun by Protestantism and previous rationalism. Oriental thought found excellent expression through Hegel—all that that thought has of good and right in it is presented in Hegel's system. In Herbart western thought reached its height. But just because of this Hegel and Herbart are one-sided—in Hegel the infinite swallowed up the finite, philosophy became purely knowledge, contemplation; Herbart, again, like Kant before him, placed a one-sided emphasis upon the agent, upon will, upon morality, but thus they both lost the unity of the divine life. What was to be done, then, to reconcile those opposites, represented in ancient times by Hindu and Christian philosophy, and in German idealism by the opposing philosophies of Hegel and Herbart?

That reconciliation, however, could not be carried out by philosophy. Philosophy, the daughter of religion (theology), would die with her mother. Just as religion is a transitory period of the spirit, so also philosophy has a transitory mission to inform man of the conflict between the earthly and the divine, between eastern and western thought. Philosophy is that information—it stops of itself as soon as man has been informed. German idealism is the peak point of this informing process, hence a catastrophe follows, a catastrophe in the sense of artistic drama: the various philosophical systems were not mere accidental episodes in the history of the human spirit. The history of philosophy, the history of the spirit in general is a great drama gravitating towards its destined end, towards catastrophe: philosophy is a transition to a new, a third period of history, and German idealistic philosophy more particularly is the last word, the final act—philosophy consumes itself and it consumes religion.

The preparations for the new age are, Smetana believed, completed, but even now it is in the future. But it is beginning, though only in minds which comprehend the tasks of the new philosophy. Comte likewise rejoiced in the thought that the new age started as soon as it began in the mind of even one—in himself alone. According to Smetana "the rabble" and its blind leaders will still remain for a long time in darkness.

But there are many who, though they are as yet unable to live in the spirit of those few chosen ones, nevertheless do not trust the blind leaders—and this mass of people has fallen into indifference. Indifference is for Smetana the chief characteristic of the times—it is an ugly, an intolerable state of mind, but it is the ground into which the ripened fruit of the tree of knowledge must fall in order that it may grow into a sturdy vigorous tree of life.

And what will Smetana's tree of life, of truly spiritual life, be like?

Religion will turn into art—artistic creation is the basis of the future spiritual life.

History began with the conflict between the human and the divine. The human and the divine have equal rights, but in man a conflict arose between them and the rule of the human element began. The human element is the cause of the conflict. But finally reconciliation will take place, and by this reconciliation is meant the assumption by the divine of power over man and its victory over the human. As in the beginning there arose the illusion that the divine had for ever removed itself far from man, and as by reason of this illusion there arose that yearning which was incompletely appeased by religion, so now the opposite illusion will arise, an illusion more beautiful and more blissful: man will imagine that the human has been removed far from man in order that it may be improved and glorified in the world beyond by the divine. Of course, the human too will remain in man, but it will be entirely subordinated to the divine.

As we see, Smetana ends like Comte: with a myth. Just as Comte renews positivistic fetishism, so Smetana arrives at conscious illusion: by means of art a conscious illusion will be created, religion will change into art, man, humanity, will attain satisfaction in art, in artistic creation.

Smetana's idea that in the new age art will change places with religion has been often and variously expressed. The same idea is implicit in Comte's positivistic fetishism; art lays claim to the rank of a religion even in Spencer. The views of Strauss are known, though, of course, they would rather compromise Smetana's idea than support it. Smetana does not mean so-called passive artistic enjoyment (horrible word!), but he means activity, creative activity: just as man created gods in religion, so in the post-religious period he will create matter, the world. Man with that art of his will glorify the world, the glorification of nature will be the accomplishment of the highest, the universal work of art.

Smetana's predecessors in this way of thinking were Schelling, Friedrich, Schlegel, who glorified the creative power of genius. Perhaps Smetana knew Saint Simon. In the new age ideas of this kind were being expressed. To a certain extent also Herder was Smetana's predecessor, inasmuch as he connected religion with poetry, and especially with folk-poetry. Smetana certainly gave philosophical expression to our attempts at regeneration, which, on the spiritual side, most readily found expression in poetry, literature, and art.

Smetana's thought shows far horizons to psychology—in itself of course it is not clear. Smetana sometimes speaks about art in the general sense, at other times he speaks of religious poetical inspiration, at other times again he sees the seeds of this future art in primitive sorcery, and yet again he regards the new creative state of mind which he contemplates as art. That will be, he says, the higher art, and everyone will take part in it.

Art, Smetana goes on, has ennobled religion already in the past, and therefore that new state will be only a perfecting and a fuller development of the elements already existing. Religion will only lose itself gradually, people will, without knowing it, cease honouring the gods—the divine will be within them. Art has the same content as religion—namely, the correlation of the two opposing powers which form the one and only all-being. In religion the human subordinates itself to the divine, in art the human is glorified by the divine. In religion man as compared with the infinite is finite, in art as compared with the finite he becomes himself divine. The man of the past is pious, absorbed in the worship of the divine: the man of the future is artistic, he is enthusiastic in glorifying the things of the earth.

Perhaps we shall better understand these ideas of Smetana's if we survey his views on moral development which proceeds simultaneously with mental development, and which, of course, has its causes and reasons in the whole state of man, of mankind, of the All-Spirit or All-Being.

The primordial conflict caused in man not only a religious, but also even a moral and a social illusion, for people began to think that they were not only not one and the same being, but that they are many and set in hostile array against each other. A period of selfishness set in. Only when they subordinated themselves to the divine, which they had placed outside of themselves, did they agree that the earthly elements in man should have their own fixed sphere of action—then law came into existence and law as well as religion became a great force in the selfish life devoted to earthly things.

The Asiatic peoples lived under the greatest oppression from egoistical despotism; the Greeks by their love to their beautiful fatherland formed a free community. But it was the Romans who first formed a really free community. Roman freedom was developed from monarchical despotism more deliberately than in the case of the Greeks. That is why the Romans were the real representatives of law—they were for law what the Jews were for religion: but just as the Jewish religion was egoistic so Roman law was egoistic, it was recognized as applying only to the Roman people themselves. Roman Italy was free, but its freedom was based on the slavery of many—the Roman republic fell. Cunning Augustus stood up to defend the republic—his followers strengthened Roman despotism. Asiatic despotism was revived in Roman despotism.

This despotism disappeared for a time owing to the migration of the peoples, only to revive again. In the name of Christianity, Christian despots came forward, who based their egoistic government upon the grace of God. Feudal states from the fifth to the sixteenth century only modified the old slavery into subjection and bondage—therefore in the sixteenth century feudalism without difficulty changed into absolutism.

But from the fifteenth century onward, men striving for freedom arose. They were political mystics like Thomas More, Campanella, Harington: they called the enslaved people's attention to the natural state in which the divine and the earthly were not yet separated, and to family love. After these, the way of political freedom was prepared by the political philosophers Vico, Sidney, Montesquieu, Franklin, Adam Smith, but chiefly by Rousseau. The Encyclopaedists joined forces with them.

In the meantime religious emancipation ripened, and so at the end of the eighteenth century despotism was broken and removed by the French Revolution. Louis XVI had to answer for the sins of his predecessors: "Publicly as a criminal he was executed as an unforgettable warning that despotism is the greatest crime by which man can be branded."

But in 1793 freedom disappeared before the despotism renewed by Napoleon. So also the Reformation was only gradually victorious against spiritual oppression, and freedom had to constantly subdue despotic attacks upon it. Napoleon showed the nations what despotism is and how it originated. And the nations comprehended. After two attempts at restoration the Second Republic was finally proclaimed in France in the year 1848, "so that she should no more ever permit any dynasty to make its nest in her heart."

Smetana in his fiery enthusiasm for freedom believed that Italy would do what France had done, and that also "consequent Germany" would do politically what it had done in its literature, and that even the Slavs would still in this century overturn their own despotism. An age of liberty, equality, and fraternity had come; liberty: an acquisition from the past; fraternity: the hope of the future; equality: the symbol of the present.

Only the symbol, for Smetana did not believe in communism, as, in accordance with the watchword of equality, it was proclaimed in the year 1848. For him communism is in the social and political realm what indifferentism is in religion. Equality is certainly a rightful claim; but the communism of the period was a pure abstraction, never realizable, an abstraction derived from law and love, a purely theoretical transition from law to love.

People are not equal, they are more than equal— identical, but of course only when the divine has subjugated the human within them. And only when this takes place will the age-old egosim be broken—egoism will turn into love. The rough, awkward communistic theory will be a transition to the general and all-comprising love. And love, of course, is not and cannot be anything but a transformed egoism—namely, divine egoism.

Mankind will become one family: love will at first seize individual nations, it will change whole generations, and finally the whole of humanity will unite in divine

183

harmony. What was attained by individual associations in the past, such as, for example, the Pythagoreans, the Essenes, the early Christians, the Neoplatonists, and later on various brotherhoods, will become general.

Law and love have the same significance: they govern the relation of man to man. Law makes people stand comrade against comrade—love unites them. People, as looked upon by law, are finite beings and therefore, in their masses, they limit themselves by law in their relations to one another—in love they are the diivne itself. The man of the past was a stranger to his fellow-man, the man of the future will be to him a kind brother.

Smetana himself summarizes human development up to the present in this statement: "The whole history of mankind seems to be a great sanctuary built upon a million graves. In the middle of this sanctuary the present rises like a sacred sacrificial altar upon which science, the ordained high priest of humanity, sacrifices religion and law, that is, the animal-human element in our race, and changes it into the human-ideal. This sacred uplifting is the content of history and at the same time the meaning of the present age. All the rest is to the world-spirit deafening noise-making, meaningless play, and blind chance."

Our age, a period of real humanity, is not the last period. We have already shown how Smetana conducts natural and organic development through five main forms; to this plan history corresponds.

The whole course of historical evolution according to Smetana must be represented thus:

Creative Love is Religion

In the first stage, lasting thousands of years, man vegetated in spiritual rest; it was a somewhat plant-like life, undeveloped, but happy. But, man awakened out of this rest; mortal conflict and by means of it the historical process was inaugurated. The first stage had no history, was prehistorical. In his second stage man was overpowered by earthly things, he lived a rather animal-like life, instinctive, sensuous, without real consciousness—a life governed by religion and law.

Man awakened out of this life too—with the new age; with the Reformation in religion and the Revolution in politics consciousness began, man in truth became man in that he came to himself, in that he began a spiritual life. In this third stage, for the first time, man will begin to develop new spiritual and social forces—out of religion he will make creative artistic enthusiasm, he will change law into universal love.

After a period of general pure humanity an ideal life will come. Man by his creative love will change and glorify all nature; and, finally, in the last period, for thousands and thousands of years, he will lead a happy and again a quiet life. By "quiet" is meant that the fifth period is again without history, above history; man returns again as it were to the vegetative life, but of course to vegetation in the highest sense of the word—humanity will live in the most ideal happiness.

How we are really to imagine this further and final development is not clear. In the work, *The Significance of the Present Age*, Smetana speaks of the future in the earth, he even fixes the places where the fourth period (in America) and the fifth (in Polynesia) will end, but in his encyclopaedia he contemplates the development of superman as a biological process too; out of man there will develop by degrees a being of ideas and emotions.

But I will not criticize Smetana's philosophy of history in detail. Not because I should have to reproach him for fantasticality, for the vagueness of his thought, and so forth—in these respects Smetana succumbs to all the shortcomings of similar philosophies. But as the reader sees, Smetana wrote during the period of the French social utopians (Fourierism), during the stirring years of the forties. Smetana is a Czech, a Slavonic utopian.

The humanitarian period and the humanitarian order of society will, he declares, be established by the Slavonic race.

Although mankind forms one whole, its historical evolution is limited to places and to persons. For Smetana Europe is a limited ("charmed") sphere of the terrestrial region, forming the geographical basis of our era. Nations and races, too, have a marked influence on their own development. Races are, according to Smetana, the work of nature, in the sense that nature itself has attempted to reconcile the earthly and the divine, and that that attempt manifests itself in the evolution of races. Thus we see that Smetana everywhere and consequently places his pantheistic metaphysics in the foreground. It cannot be denied that by this method he comes to original and often nice analogies, but they are nothing but analogies and not explanations; we get symbolism, not analysis.

Creative Love is Religion

Smetana accepts the old division into five races. The Ethiopians (the blacks) represent plant life, vegetative life, they are the lowest; the Mongolians are a sensual race, corresponding to animals; and finally the Caucasian race represents man; there are still the Americans and the Australians left—they are the failures of nature, they are imperfect, degenerate types.

Like the races the individual nations have had and have their special cultural missions. Of existing nations, the French have already fulfilled their task, having broken political tyranny for good; the English bring culture to the distant parts of the earth, they have, like the French, mainly a practical task. The task of the Germans is theoretical—by science and philosophy they are to make the life of the few the life of the many, and in this way to complete what the French and English have done, they having subordinated the particular to the general in practice.

The symbolism here is obvious, but the philosophy of history would need a more real explanation of what individual races and nations contributed to evolution in general. Of course for Smetana racial differences have necessarily a subordinate significance—the evolution of the spirit and the consciousness is a purely spiritual and metaphysical process. Smetana knows this and therefore tells us that the course of history does not depend on nations and peoples, but on "various physical and moral combinations"—to speak as a critic, Smetana deduced his history of philosophy from a preconceived idea rather than based it on experience. This can be well seen in his essays on the Slavs and their cultural tasks.

Modern Humanity:

Smetana derives from Herder and from Kollar the view that the Slavs are good, quiet, and peace-loving, and are thus fitted to lead culturally the third period of development, a purely human period. The Slavs by nature have all the necessary qualifications for this; they are a robust strong race, they have an ingrained tendency to socialism, they are distinguished by depth of artistic feeling, and finally, by their racial and national awareness, they show that they are in every way very active. Hence the Slavs will accept all western culture and they will create from it a new element of culture, and that will develop into creative love.

The Slavs will more particularly assimilate Germanic culture as a whole. The Teutons, especially the Germans, will live on in the Slavs as the Greeks and the Romans lived on in the Teutons.

Smetana had no more precise ideas than these about the Slavs and their historical task. We hear, however, that the northern Slavs will be the first to take up the new cultural work, and that the Slavs in southern Russia will complete their task, but even that does not give us a clearer picture. Clearly it is Herder's idea as symbolized by Smetana in his own mind: the Slavs in southern Russia will come into contact with Greece, the cradle of European civilization, and thus the cultural and geographical circle will be as it were completed. We know already that such a return to beginnings is often to be found in Smetana. It is an old idea often transferred to the new era —Rousseau, Kant, Comte, Spencer gave expression to it —and in any event it means nothing more than that

188

man's historical evolution has at bottom not changed him radically, and that there lurks within it that romantic yearning for savagery. Smetana, not less than Comte and the others, paid his debt to romanticism.

Smetana in his philosophy of the Slavs is much more indefinite than his contemporary Russian Slavophils and the Polish Messianists. It is just because he is more of a metaphysician than they—the Russians gave a more detailed historical and social exposition. The Poles were more political. Nevertheless the similarity of the Czech humanitarians especially to the Russian Slavophils is great. Certainly the conformity of thought is marked.

With all his metaphysical vagueness Smetana did not forget to designate the special task of us Czechs: in view of our geographical position and our connection with the Germans we are destined to become the mediator between the East and the West.

We Czechs must absorb the entire content of German culture up to the present day, and especially the philosophy, for it is just in philosophy that the human spirit, hence the German spirit, has expressed itself most fully. And because German philosophy is the deepest philosophy, there is nothing left but to master it by means of exhaustive critical study of its content. This task falls to us Czechs—to collect, to explain, to put into practice, to criticize, to co-ordinate, and then to expand all the ideas worked out by German philosophy; in general, then we are to undertake the completion of German culture. The eastern Slavs will then take up the results of our cultural work, and then they themselves will hand it over to the farther east. . . .

Modern Humanity:

On the moral side this transition from western, Germanic-Roman culture is to mean a conflict, not a physical but a spiritual one—the Czechs are (with the eastern Slavs) to give an example how two nations have been able to comprehend the laws of historical evolution and to subordinate themselves to them.

Smetana did not hesitate to oppose Havlíček in order to defend German philosophy against unfounded attacks.

The reader will excuse me if I add to my outline of Smetana's religious philosophy a few things which have less connection with the matter—but Smetana is not known to us, is almost foreign, and therefore I take this opportunity of calling attention to him.

Smetana is in our philosophy what Dobrovsky is for our knowledge of things Slavonic and for our history—a Czech writing in German, but feeling Czech—a Czech much more Czech than dozens of writers writing in Czech. And as Dobrovsky contributed to our awakening with his Latin and German writings, even so will Smetana, I hope, perform his task. A revival will not come about by the Czech word, but by the Czech spirit.

Smetana's Czech nature shows itself in his leading ideas and in his spiritual character.

As regards the latter, Smetana, in a purely Czech manner, unites within himself mysticism and criticism. At least in my judgment, that is a characteristic of our Czech spirit. That characteristic showed itself in a great measure during our reformation. In the period of revolution it manifested itself again. And not only in Smetana. That same characteristic can be observed in Čupr, in

Creative Love is Religion

Klácel, it can also be remarked in Havliček, though in him it is less evident.

Smetana's moral character points to the same origin. Meissner understood this well when he was writing his biography. I think he compares him aptly to Havliček: "Smetana war durch Gehurt wie durch charakter ein Czech. Er hat in seinem charakter wie in seinein Lebenslaufe und seinem Lebensende eine Ainlichkeit mit Carl Havliček, jenem edlen Uberzeugstreuen und unerschrockenen Kämpfen der böhmischen Presse, der unter dem Bach'schen Régime, von Weib und Kind getrennt, im ultramontanen Buiten 'interniert' wurde, und die Heimat nur Widersah, um in ihr zu sterben. Er hatte wie dieser denharten Kapf, die Mischung von Schwarmerei und schonungsloser Logik und den unbeugsamen Charakter."—Meissner, *Geschichte eines Exkommunizierten*, p. xi.

Smetana's Czech nature shows itself in his religious philosophy. The same spirit that guided the pen of Chelcicky speaks to us from his pages. The conformity is striking. Like Chelcicky, Smetana does not tolerate dogma in religion, limiting it completely to the moral sphere. Smetana expresses this Czech idea thus: "Religion should cease to exist and should transform itself into creative love." This does not mean anything more than that Smetana sees the substance of religion in love. Smetana so emphatically insists upon the moral side of things that he sacrifices philosophy too—theoretical philosophy and science will give place to more practical activity, they will also give place to artistic creation, which is not only to be manifest in art, but is to dominate in practice the whole of nature.

Religion will become a universal brotherhood, through creative love—the Czech ideal of brotherhood becomes in Smetana an ideal for humanity.

Smetana means, of course, humanity according to the requirements of his time: humanity must be social and political.

For this reason he rejects the State as Chelcicky does: law must give place to helpful love, and when this has taken place there is no longer any room for the State. He rejects militarism. Smetana is an enthusiastic defender of political and spiritual freedom in general—he welcomes enthusiastically the freedom of the year 1848, as contrasted with the "stupefying" absolutism of old Austria. He has even a kind word for liberalistic religious indifferentism.

Smetana comprehends religion socially. He awaits social reform from the Slavs. Smetana is zealous against the caste system and nobility, reason is his highest authority. He hopes that the real noblemen among the nobility will understand the great struggle between the poor and the aristocracy, that they will unite with the citizens and will prevent a hostile encounter between the two classes. If love is to abide with us, to be our quest, we must sacrifice our selfishness. "To want to be happy is almost a crime, if we understand what our time is— sacrifices are more needful now than ever before."

World evolution, revealing itself as the spirit coming to a knowledge of itself and victorious over matter, in our period particularly leads to far-reaching moral reform. Out of the old man the new man is to arise, out of the man of the past the man of the future—superman.

The idea of superman for Smetana follows consequently from his whole evolutionary system.[4]

But the Czech superman is different from Nietzsche's. Nietzsche arrived at the idea biologically, Smetana morally. Rousseau's German longs for blond beasts, the Czech for the peace of plant life. In a word, the Czech superman is peculiar and individual: the Czech man becomes a superman by victory over the senses and through true love towards his fellow-man: the sensuous man is not capable of sacrificing himself for the common good, which is precisely what would elevate him; only he who is able to sacrifice all is able to progress: the Czech superman does not live for the sake of power, but "for the sake of sacrificing"[5]; he feels the collective guilt, taking the bad actions of others as his own. Evil is for him the common enemy; the Czech is in no way an aristocrat, he does not claim to be a saviour, but for him the whole modern era is the saviour; the Czech superman loves the oppressed, even though their crudeness displeases him; the oppressors he hates even though they tempt him with their culture; for the Czech superman love and friendship are the highest virtues, unfriendliness is for him the ugliest

[4] Smetana does not use the word "superman"; he speaks, however, of super-senses, super-plants, and uses the expression "the kingdom which shall come after man" (*Nachmenschenreich*), from which an ideal state of existence will develop. In Smetana's sense the expression "after-man" might be used.

[5] Smetana says "Wille der Aufopferung" in *Der Geist, sein Entstehen und Vergehen*, p. 219.

thing in human life—Smetana therefore, like Dostoyevski, does not believe in hell, only in heaven.

Smetana's philosophy has also non-Czech elements. His whole system had its roots in German idealism. The Russian Slavophils had their roots in it too. Smetana himself knows this, for he declares that it is the Czechs who are to take all the good from German thinking, and complete it.

Like all idealistic systems, Smetana's system of relative identity has an elaborate structure, but is not based on experience.[6]

In Smetana there is much that is arbitrary and unproven. Why, for example, should we hold that German thought has already exhausted itself for good? It is not exhausted, as we see. But, of course, the Russian Slavophils also thought so; in this Smetana is in striking agreement with Kireyevski.

The root of its defects, in so far as religion is concerned, I see in pantheism. I know that pantheism is modern, and I can understand that. But it is impossible to explain the world by pantheism, all experience speaks against it. I repeat I can understand why people in our times are delighted with pantheism. People want order and unity

[6] Philosophical thinking is very much dependent upon language; a great deal of German teaching simply cannot be conceived in Czech. A Czech would never, for example, have attained to the differentiation between Kant's *Vernunft* and *Verstand*. We simply have not those words. In Smetana there are many examples of this. For example, his *Bewusstsein der Bewusstsein*, designating a high stage of ideal evolution, in Czech must be said in another way, for "consciousness of consciousnesses" does not suffice.

Creative Love is Religion

in the midst of chaotic multifariousness, for modern people paper-theism does not suffice, they have artistic aspirations, and these can be satisfied by pantheism; all that I understand, but nevertheless I cannot accept pantheism. Smetana also was conscious of the weak side of pantheism, and did not surrender to it entirely (*relative* identity); at least he avoids its absolute subjectivism. Thus, at least, I explain his efforts towards noetical and moral collectivism. The final aim is the unification of the object with the subject, but Smetana pictures that differently from Hegel: the German consumed the world with his reason, his idea; the Czech conquers the world simply by his emotion, his love: the German is weak because of his strength, the Czech strong because of his weakness. . . .

Chapter VII

The Religious Question and Modern Philosophy

WE have made the acquaintance of a number of modern thinkers of several nations, and, among them, what are called the leading minds; we have nothing to do but to co-ordinate their doctrines and to come to understand the significance of their views for the religious question.

Well, then—in the first place from the survey of modern philosophy it is evident, as I asserted at the very beginning, that the religious question is an open question for philosophy, it is a permanent and the principal problem; those who say we have done with the religious question have not the least idea of the real state of things. . . .

Hume with his scepticism aims a blow at theism, and *in concreto*, socially and politically, at the Churches and the clergy. From the examples brought forth as a proof that popular religion is superstition it is evident that among the Christian Churches he thinks mainly of the Catholic Church.

Philosophy overcomes religion. He proves that the weakness of the reason excludes metaphysics, theology and religion from man's purview; which is the exact opposite of what theologians generally prove from the same weakness. The senses are in reality the reason, and God cannot be seen since no cause can be seen at all. The logic of the senses submits to the authority of habit; it is a blind logic, a dog's logic—but that can't be helped.

It is by a lucky chance that we have from nature a

bit of human feeling one for another—there is not much of it, but there is enough for life and society to exist; if we can help ourselves a little in addition by means of scientific politics we may be satisfied. True political science, like all sciences, is blind too, purely empirical, but we can't help it, "poor people cook with water." If you can busy yourself with philosophy and literature (Hume admired Cicero!) you will endure life somehow— and if you cannot endure it: *exitus patet*! Hume wrote an unusual essay in which he proves the permissibility of suicide—it is a paper as characteristic of Hume as it is of the new age. However, he did not publish the paper, in fact, he destroyed it after publication (but before distribution). That is also characteristic: he did not venture so far yet.

In so far as we can judge from his biography Hume's scepticism sufficed him. He had no family and did not care to have one; so-called high society in which he lived quietly and reasonably, taking care (by moderation and simplicity) to be independent, was sufficient for him. Scepticism did not disturb him, at any rate it was no poison to him.

That theologians saw devilry in Hume's scepticism is comprehensible. But philosophers were also indignant. The century which so ostentatiously delighted in reason suddenly hears: "habit, instinct, no reason at all!"

Kant, like many others, was disquieted. After twelve years of contemplation he published his *Critique of Pure Reason* in defence of reason. Experience is blind, but it is made possible by reason and its deductive faculties, reason gives it meaning. And, finally, the deductions of the reason are justified, especially those old ideas of God, immortality, and free will. But, of course, our reason is dependent upon the world. It is God who, when He thinks, creates the world. At the same time, in Him between thought and object there is no difference; we do not create things, only ideas, the objective world obtrudes itself upon our eyes and calls forth thoughts—but, after all, we are not entirely passive, we are active through our reason; our senses give us the raw material, our reason works it up with its own forms of perception, with categories and ideas. We are not gods, but still we create our world for ourselves. We form even sense-experience.

But what right have I to trust these forms (if they exist) and formations of mine, and to trust them more than the senses? Is that world of ideas more truthful than that world of facts, and is it more genuine?

Kant exchanged the logic of the senses for the logic of reason, of practical, pure reason. Hume would have greatly rejoiced seeing that for Kant, after all, *practical* reason, the vital needs, are the deciding factors: *sic volo sic jubeo.* Of course we can immediately complete the verse: *stet pro ratione voluntas.* ("So I wish and so I command, let my will stand for a reason.") Reasonable? What is left of the critic? That is the question. Schopenhauer thinks that he completes Kant when he teaches that the will is blind—Hume may again exult.

Comte came. He accepted the logic of the senses; he added to it the logic of reason, not of pure but of historical reason. Reason has developed. It has reached a mature age—that which our fathers and predecessors thought and did, youths and children used to think and do. And now we are men. We are positivists. We will arrange society according to our own matured views and it will be good for us all. True, man ages, but cannot forget his beautiful youth and childhood. Hume is right though, that that youth of our humanity was superstition, but it was warm and pleasing, and therefore—let us return to superstition! Let us blindly believe our positive views, let modern science be our religion, our superstition. After all, the whole thing in life is that emotion, not reason, should be satisfied, reason must serve emotion. To this end we will build up a great universal Church just as our fathers did. Let all humanity, the past, the present, and the future be our god—politics will build up that Church for us, and I, announces Comte—will be your Pope, the high priest of mankind.

No, says Spencer, in opposition to Comte; you are right in many respects, I accept almost everything; but Hume and Kant after all gave superstition a great blow—there is nothing to be done but to arrange society more critically, according to its historical development, of course.

But its development must be conceived in an evolutionary manner. Now, don't be afraid—evolution is not so bad! That which was, is and will be is really one and the same—don't you see that evolution is actually conservative? A Pope, a high priest you need not be, for you are *de facto* more, you are a part of God, developed by evolution; by evolution from a pre-monad. We are a part, we are a manifestation of the universal All-power. History is a part of cosmology, study history and you will know where in the world process we stand today. Calendars with historical and individual prophecies science has not given us yet—but listen to your emotions and instincts, look for pleasure and avoid pain. Spencer concludes the rationalistic credo quite in accordance with the ancient hedonistic rule. . . .

And so we see: the meaning of all the philosophizing from Hume to Spencer can be briefly stated: We want to, nay, we must believe—but in whom and in what?

Scepticism or belief? —that, then, is the question to be solved.

From Hume to Spencer we can observe the decrease of scepticism. That is: of a thought-out scepticism, a scepticism full of conviction. Philosophy after Hume would fain believe. After all, Hume himself believed in the senses, at least he did not distrust them entirely—and he believed in reason, at least in mathematics, too. He knew, of course, that consequent scepticism is impossible. That already Descartes knew, Augustinus knew it, the old sceptics knew it. Scepticism is only relative.

Kant rejected scepticism and fought especially against Hume's scepticism. He allows Hume to be dogmatic, to be empirical, but he criticizes his scepticism. He examines the sources of knowledge themselves, not only the knowledge obtained so far, and thus he escapes scepticism. He trusts in reason and the faculties, he believes, too, in the senses guided by reason. He believes not only in mathematics, but also in natural science and metaphysics. In the end he comes to a belief in God.

The fundamental idea of Kant's *Critique* is law; without the critical faculty man cannot get along. But Kant, concentrating on his own ego, did not tell us why, really, we ought to believe and to believe like the old dogmatists. Modern man needs besides criticism, a criticism of criticism. We need it so much the more because Kant fought against scepticism but, just because of that subjectivism of his, did not conquer it.

Comte greatly simplified the problem for himself. He believed in Hume, but also, uncritically, in the senses. His method is fairly good, but that's all! Even Comte's disciples take us no further. Spencer is more careful—he knows Kant and modern criticism better; here and there he even comes close to pure reason. Comte believed most in mathematics—Spencer in history. Kant completed Hume's logic of the senses with the logic of reason, Comte with the logic of the heart, and Spencer with the logic of history.

Hume did not care about religion—philosophy sufficed for him, it is for him religion. Kant did not reject religion so easily, but for him the morality derived from it was enough. Religion (the old one) did not suffice for Comte —he rehabilitated fetishism. Spencer was willing to compromise with religion as it is.

Hume is altogether indifferent as regards theism—he has no objection to it if it is philosophically conceived *à la* Locke. Kant is for theism. Of anthropomorphism, which Hume so disliked, he is not afraid, at least he admits a more subtle anthropomorphism. Comte becomes absolutely a fetishist, and takes pleasure in polytheism. Spencer, as has been said, makes a compromise, inclined towards pantheism.

Upon ethics, as we see, they all lay stress—Hume,

The Religious Question and Modern Philosophy

Kant, Comte, Spencer. Hume is in haste by ethics to escape his own scepticism. Kant holds on to the categorical imperative, which gives him common sense; Comte even becomes the founder of a Church and proclaims social and political rules in a very detailed manner; Spencer sees in his just-finished ethics the fulfilment of his life's task.

Hume does not care about the Church, neither does Kant; on the other hand, Comte sees in the Church and its management the principal thing, while Spencer in agreement with Kant subordinates it to the postulates of ethics and the development of reason.

Hume and Kant are rationalists. But Hume patched his rationalism with emotionalism, if we wish to designate by this term the view that emotion and will are above reason. Kant is the hardest of all—at the command of pure reason every emotion must humble itself. Reason is a despot. Comte almost dissolves in emotion. Spencer moderates himself as befits a utilitarian gentleman. Comte, of course, lived through the last period of the Revolution. All the French became softened by it. Hume and Kant represent the eighteenth century, Comte and Spencer the nineteenth. Modern man is softer—but it is not always the emotion which he gives as the reason of his softness that makes him so, very often it is only an imitation of emotion, emotionalism. But the fact is, he is like that— the rationalists of the past century with that reason of theirs were different. . . . It is certain that Hume and Kant do not care about religious ceremonies; Comte cares about them, and nothing else; Spencer does not oppose them.

The Religious Question and Modern Philosophy

Our Czech philosopher concerned himself with the religious question no less than his German teachers. It was for him a vital question in the most real sense of the word—Smetana was himself at first by conviction a Catholic priest; through his life's experience and philosophy he gradually lost the faith of childhood, until finally he gave up his priestly office. He himself tells us of those struggles and afflictions.

Mankind, he believes, is continually reaching for higher and higher goals. Progress and development is the lot of man, therefore he cannot satisfy himself with faith— scepticism was always nobler than faith. Smetana sees scepticism as a phase of knowledge, salvation is only in knowledge and awareness. Smetana esteems Hume highly.

Smetana, just as he does not seek absolute spiritual peace in life, does not seek even for absolute bliss in it. "A very faint touch of suffering always remains in the infinite." In Smetana himself, this touch of suffering tinged his thought and emotion: Hume with his little essay on suicide was only teasing—Smetana gave real expression to the modern suicidal weariness by teaching that to depart from life for moral motives is the best proof of immortality, and that such a death alone is worthy of man. . . .

The real essence of man is in emotion, never in reason only, hence also mankind is hastening towards the new age of social love and artistic creation by men of genius; philosophy, having risen out of religion and law, will lose itself in love and artistic creation.

Smetana, like all his great predecessors, believes in an

ideal of humanity. Hume conceived humanity purely individualistically, humanity is for him sympathy; according to Kant the individual as an individual must respect mankind. Comte, like Herder and Rousseau before him, conceives humanity collectively; humanity is for him identical with mankind, mankind is for him god. Spencer similarly conceives history and the mankind of the present as an organic whole. Smetana, finally, connects with the idea of humanity the idea of nationality as did Herder, Hegel and others before him.

Modern man—we see that clearly—is tired and irritated, irritated and tired because of doubting. In his weakness he demands the right to take his life. . . . "Man *can* die by his own will, that is the proof of his freedom, that thought makes him a god, by means of it he is independent of everything; after all, human affliction deserves this divine gift." No otherwise than Pliny at the time of the Roman decadence, the modern philosophers praise voluntary death. And our modern Czech philosophers praise it too. Modern man is a sceptic. He does not trust, he criticizes, he rejects. But at the same time, and just because of this, again and again, he concerns himself with the question of the certainty of his knowing, and so doing, he does not believe, but he would like to believe; he criticizes, but he seeks; he denies, but he really wants to construct. He looks for foundations for himself, and wants to have them deeper and stronger. That is why he inspects them.

Certainty! What is certain? Upon what can I stand firmly and sleep peacefully? What is truth?

The Religious Question and Modern Philosophy

What is truth?

Do we get certainty from the outside world or from the world within us? Or do we derive it from both these sources? What, then, do we derive from the outside, what from ourselves?

Is it to be objectivism or subjectivism? Is there, after all, a difference between object and subject?

The object forces itself upon us, it prescribes the progress of our thoughts, it presents definite objects to our desire; by means of fantasy and reason we can unite and disunite in all kinds of ways those given and determined elements. We can analyse and synthesize in our laboratories the materials given us by nature, but—to create, and to create out of nothing we are unable.

Do we not create anything at all of our own power? For in relation to the present world we are not only passive, but also active, and very active—and can that activity of ours be really nothing but passivity? What is that continual and eternal searching and delving of ours? Are we not, after all, if not gods, at least little gods, demigods—and was not the serpent in paradise right after all? Is Hume right? In nature we find, or at least we anticipate, order, a firm, age-old order—whence comes it?

And do we not perceive just as firm an order of our thoughts, our emotions and our desires? All our ideas, all our knowledge, all our action tend towards unity; we have not a chance mixture of individual thoughts, wishes, emotions and doings, but there is in it system and systematization—where did it come from? Is it also forced upon us from outside, or do we create it ourselves?

And if we do create this unified system of the inner

spiritual world ourselves, out of what do we create it and how? Does not the object contribute some elements and if so, which?

And how is it with the question of certainty? Is that certain which is given us from outside? Is that certain which we create ourselves? And if so, which is more certain? Still, I see that I err here by my senses, there by my reason. I begin to doubt, but that firm objective order confuses me in my doubts; that order of my mind, that peculiar unity of all knowledge, and that purposefulness of my desires and doings confuse me in those doubts. To doubt and only to doubt, to deny and only to deny, I cannot—I must acknowledge something, and I do acknowledge, I must believe and trust.

Again and again comes the question: subjectivism or objectivism?

The object for me is not only nature and perhaps the animal kingdom, but also my fellow-men. And they come first of all, for with them and among them I grow. What, then, have I from them? And again: I observe that social order exists, I observe that order in evolution exists—what criterion of knowledge is that order, and what standard of conduct is it and can it be? What, and who, am I, in relation to the whole and in relation to the social whole? Where is my place in historical evolution? Am I to trust in myself, in my reason, in my will alone, or also in others, in their reason, and in their will? Where is certainty here? In me, in the individual, or in the social and historical whole? In my intimate family circle, my circle of relations, friends, acquaintances, or also in those unknown to me, the community—the State, history, as a whole, the Church, Europe? Of what value is social and historical logic?

Again and yet again: subjectivism or objectivism?

The object for me is nature and society: am I not an object to myself—I myself? Am I not embodied nature? Am I not embodied society? Am I not bone of the bones of my fathers? And if bone of the bones—am I not spirit of their spirit? Of the spirit of my forefathers? And of the spirit too of nature? What then am I at all? What is that self of mine—that most essential ego? And is it not strange, very strange—I become for myself an object of observation and investigation! Is not that really a strange, the strangest enigma—I, I must in the end observe myself, as, at an observation station, they observe a suspicious person; I must study myself because I do not understand myself—I do not understand my own "I"!

To study that ego I must get out of myself, out of that ego of mine, that self of mine, I must continually compare myself with that "not-I," with my own body, with yours, with your spirit; with nature and, and . . . with what else? With what? And what then is that ego of mine at all, that "I"? Whence did I come, what am I doing here? I did not create myself, it was not by my will that I was created (otherwise I would have made everything different, oh, quite different). . . .

"Why, then, don't you make alterations, why don't you supplement? Why?"—And am I not criticizing it all, am I not condemning it? Am I not overturning it all, am I not putting it in order; am I not fighting against all those commands given by nature, society, history?

You are carrying on a fight—but master of it all you

are not, and without a master you see yourself that it cannot go on; you are fighting, but precisely through this fight of yours you recognize that master; you are a general defending, and perhaps only a private, nothing more. You are not God.

Who, then, who is that master?

And again and again—am I object or subject? After all, that means: how do I know about the object, I, the subject. Psychologically it means: senses or reason.

That is what is the concern of modern philosophy. The ego analyses itself psychologically, it analyses itself again and again—does nothing but analyse. But that is just the way to the real aim which is *synthesis*. That wholeness, that system, that unity always occupies our minds. That is why synthesis plays such a role already in Hume (the synthesis of the senses), in Kant (a synthesis of pure reason), in Comte (a subjective synthesis of the heart), finally in Spencer (an objective historical synthesis), Smetana finally admits of one synthesis only—synthesis of philosophical systems up to the present time.

A synthesis—what kind? An arbitrary one? It is out of the question, since I have only analysed, analysed—and not created. The synthesis may be a critical one, but only a critical one.

Since individual branches of science and social functions and obligations have specialized themselves and divided themselves into individual classes, we feel the need for philosophical unity. The problem which modern philosophy has placed before itself is: How can I live with full and complete self-realization? Can I accept the scientific, social, and world order given to me through experience?

What am I to accept: what must I not accept? Know everything and choose the best for yourself? It is just this matter of choosing which concerns us, here is the stumbling-block. What am I to choose, how much am I to choose, for I cannot take everything. Yet again: a critical *synthesis* is required.

A critical one: no mechanical but accidental combination, but synthesis; not eclecticism, but *criticism*. System in the midst of accident, wholeness though all is mingled, unity in complexity: a unified view of the world. Smetana asks point-blank for a creative synthesis of genius.

Man does more than think, he feels and he wants. This was really why modern psychological analysis posed the problem of the relation of the senses and the reason to the emotions and the will. Already Hume said: "I believe in my senses, but feeling guides me more surely." Kant said: "I believe in the reason, I do not trust the emotions; that which you, Hume, looked upon as the guidance of the emotions, is, after all, only the guidance of reason, of practical reason, of course pure, practical reason. The categorical imperative commands you what you must feel; the emotions are blind, the reason decides." To that, Comte answered: "I trust only the senses guided by the reason, but the fact that I know, see and think at all can be explained by the fact that the feelings and the will are matter."

Last of all came Spencer: "I trust in the senses, the emotions and the reason, but they developed from the same primitive spiritual embryo; reason, emotion, will, are only different sides of one and the same spiritual activity. Activity is, however, the basis of spiritual life." Smetana's ideal being is a purely emotional being.

We see that our age, in contradistinction to last century, appeals rather to emotion. Maine de Biran, Schopenhauer, with their teaching concerning the primacy of the will over the reason, have expressed the general mood. Schopenhauer especially is the herald of the new age and of the will. Romanticism is the opponent of rationalism. To the older dualism of the senses and the reason there accrues a further division of the soul into emotion (including will) and reason.

The old problems crop up even here. Is there such an abyss between feeling and reason? Is there an abyss between the senses and the reason?

And not only that. Again the object-subject question pursues us: are not the emotions more subjective than the reason? And if so: have we not by reason of this a threefold world: object (nature, history)—object-subject (reason)—subject (emotion)?

And, finally, which is dependable—which is the more dependable—reason or emotion? Why should I trust emotion, why should I trust in it more than in reason? Because it is more subjective? Is that "I" more in emotion than in reason, and am I, then, master there, in that most inward part, and only there? Is there, then, truth in emotion, is truth an emotional thing? Perhaps there are two truths, one emotional, the other reasonable? Perhaps there is a third truth, perceptive truth? Already today this is proclaimed and quite generally too—what, then, is truth?

The Religious Question and Modern Philosophy

It is not a matter of thought, of emotion, of individual thought and emotion, it is a matter of the whole man as a thinking, feeling, acting being. Thought—emotion—desire, are the products of our psychological analysis; but our aim is synthesis, critical synthesis. Our psychical and physical life is more than those individual tendencies, thoughts, feelings, desires, it is all of them put together. It is not a combination of these individual abstract elements, it is a whole—it is life. Life, physical and psychical.

Every philosophy is a manifestation of that life, but at the same time it has a real influence upon it. And it is with this that philosophy is concerned—though academic philosophers forget it. Modern literature has not forgotten it, hence its great influence just on that very philosophical education. Hence the modern attempts to make a literary genre out of philosophy. The modern novel is becoming more and more philosophical, metaphysical. So also are drama and lyricism. Is Goethe's *Faust* a drama—only a drama? Is Rousseau's *Héloïse* a novel—is it? Is Dostoyevski a poet? We call these men poet-thinkers, but what does that joining of the two ideas mean?

Yes—what we want here is synthesis. What we want is that critical, that creative synthesis, of which Kant and Smetana dreamed, and which is far from being accomplished. Modern philosophy must make an effort to complete and to perfect the synthesis of Kant, Comte, Spencer, and Smetana. Philosophy must become synthetic—synthetic in the modern sense of the word, it must stop being a lesson for school, it must be a lesson for life.

Scepticism, criticism, positivism, historicalism, humanism, are not merely systems of thought, they are the sources of moods, momentary and permanent, they are an expression of the whole soul, they are an expression of character and a school of character.

Modern man would have from philosophy an explanation of life, of real life, of the whole of life—he wants to know how to live. But people live life and merely talk about philosophy, hence that effort toward a new and living philosophy, that desire for a new word and—for a new life. Does philosophy long for new life? Is it itself an expression of that life? What then is the relation between philosophy and life? Are we the creators of our life, of the new life? And to what extent?

Or was Rousseau perchance right when he fled from philosophy and civilization? Do we need savagery and not philosophy? Or do we want a super-life—a super-man? Is the modern man, as Baron Münchhausen says, to pull himself up by his own tuft of hair—that, then, is the question? And where will he pull himself up to? Where?

And what about religion in view of all this? What is that religious belief, what its dogmas, and in what relation do they stand to philosophical belief? And ritual and morality, and Church administration—what does it all mean?

Part Three

Modern Titanism

Chapter I

Modern Man in His Literature

SO-CALLED Church statistics give us information as to the question of religion at a certain time and in a certain place. We learn thus how many churchmen attend church, how many go to confession and so forth; to Church statistics moral statistics are added. But this quantitative estimation must, if we are to judge rightly the condition among the inhabitants, be also qualified by observations and considerations which cannot be comprehended in statistical enumeration; we ought to have as far as possible an idea of all the thinking and doing of the people. It is not necessary to point out that thus to judge and to estimate the whole condition of religion and the Church is not very easy; is, for instance, only that person pious who goes to church so many times?

Difficulties grow if we want to form an opinion of the religious conditions not only of a single place and region, but of all modern society, the society of civilized nations in this century. A valid judgment can be formed of this only if we know the whole state of culture. I will not describe in detail how to undertake this study; we shall certainly make good progress if we know the state of thought and effort, first of all theological, then philosophical and literary. By a careful analysis of the theology, philosophy and literature of our period we shall come to know its religious condition and to grasp the religious question quite completely—in theology, philosophy and literature the fulness of the heart certainly overflows. Where else should the spirit show itself by which people really live? Where else should we find expressed and formulated what people attain, what they aspire to and long for, what they hope for?

If, then, we wish to find out the spiritual state of modern man, we shall have to listen to what that man tells us *in his literature*. Theology and philosophy are of no less value to us, but art, and especially literary art, speaks to us directly with just that fulness of life which is characteristic of art. The motto *L'art pour l'art* cannot hold us up. If that has a meaning, it is mostly this: that the artist—the real artist—takes the greatest care about artistic expression, but even with this care about form, art is an expression and an emanation of life. At the same time it is automatically understood that the artist does not create at the order of and for the advancement of, a tendency foreign to him; it is understood also that an artist creates, as the saying goes, unconsciously, spontaneously, simply. It must not, however, be forgotten that that creation does not exhaust itself in a single thought and concept—for man does not live by single thoughts, feelings and desires, but he lives by that vital effort, by that endeavour and searching, hoping and suffering out of which individual ideas, feelings and desires fly like sparks from flint. Art—poetry—is always social in the sense that it is connected with the endeavour of its own times, and that it is anchored in that endeavour. And, therefore, let us leave *L'art pour l'art* to literary bibliographers and hair-splitters, as also philosophy for philosophy's sake, science for science's sake—it is a wonder that nobody has said (and they have indeed said it) morality for morality's sake, piety for piety's sake!

That finally, in pursuit of our aims, we should go direct to the smiths and not to their apprentices, will probably be objected to by none. That is done everywhere. The psychology of the so-called masses (mobs) is in its infancy, and I take leave to remark that it will remain in that infancy, and, therefore, we have every right to turn to the literary giants. The lesser men will lose nothing by it, no jot or tittle, since these lesser men give expression to the same thing as the greater ones and many of them say it, too, after their manner. I think it was Berlioz who said that the only fault of every great composition is that it calls forth twelve bad ones—that is true of literature, philosophy and, in general, of everything. And it is not such a bad thing as Berlioz thinks—we all live in the same spiritual atmosphere.

If we choose, then, the leading representatives of the literature of individual nations, we shall get from them a fairly good picture of literature as a whole. At least, so I think: Musset, Byron, Goethe, Mickiewicz and Krasiński, Dostoyevski and Tolstoy have expressed the longings of modern man and even his religious endeavours quite fully; if we add a few more to them, and if we look upon the whole of them in a literary and historical light, the picture will perhaps fairly resemble modern man.

Chapter II

The Disease of the Century—
Alfred De Musset

FROM the title of these sketches ("Modern Titanism")
the reader probably expected that I should speak of Faust
first. Certainly Faust is the type of the modern iconoclast,
whether we take this word in the Russian or in the Czech
sense. Still, however, I will deal first with Musset's
Confession of a Child of Our Age (*La confession d'un
enfant du siècle*): Musset analyses more, Goethe constructs
more: and, therefore, Musset's *Confession* gives us more
directly the spirit of the times. Musset's *Confession* gives
us the colour for the first coat of the whole picture, that
colour shows through in all the figures and it shows them
up. Musset provides a psychological basis for all the rest
of the analyses. The reader will later gather from the
whole that we were right to begin with Musset.

In the *Confession* we have the whole Musset, the mature
and ripe Musset; I should say his *Faust*, if that comparison
were possible, but how can passion be compared with
reason and philosophy? Furthermore, the *Confession* is a
summary of experience and a life testament; but what a
difference between the old man of twenty-four and the
old one of eighty! . . .

The story in the *Confession* is simple, and similar in
manner to those in the author's previous pieces of work,
smaller and larger: an egoistic, passionate heart wounded
by the unfaithfulness of his beloved in vain seeks appease-

ment in ever new love-passion. Octave, a young man of nineteen and yet already a libertine, comes to know that his beloved is betraying him with his best friend; there follows a duel, in which Octave is wounded. His illness and renewed love-madness, his jealousy and love-hatred he drowns in wine, he stupefies himself with coarse sensual orgies until finally he finds a pure soul, Brigitte, who sacrifices herself for him, but in vain. Love no longer offers him tranquillity, on the contrary it forces him into a desperate rage, which vents itself finally in cruelty to his beloved; nay, even he is on the point of killing his beloved —but by a miraculous flash of the piety which has been preserved in his crippled heart from childhood, he is saved from murder. He loves Brigitte, but still he must part with her, and with the parting the novel ends.

For a French, for a Parisian novelist it is certainly a simple novel; but how much life there is in it—a whole heaven and hell of chaotically mixed feelings! The *Confession* is written (1834-6) after the parting with Sand, and is to a great extent the history of Musset's relations with her. The very fact that rarely were two such great writers united, makes one feel that the *Confession* is a deep study of that which is called love.

Within this frame Musset paints a picture with his own blood. All his emotion and thought express themselves in the idea of the fallen angel—the fall of the angel and the fall of Adam are united into one artistic and philosophical notion: a man having lost his sexual purity and innocence can no longer find happiness and hope.

". . . Ah! malheur à celui qui laisse la débauche

planter le premier clou dans sa mamelle gauche! Le cœur d'un homme vierge est un vase profond. Lorsque la première eau qu'on y vers est impure, la mer y passerait sans laver la souillure, car l'abime est immense, et la tache est au fond."

"The heart of a chaste man is a deep vessel; if the first water which you pour into it is unclean, a whole sea could flow into it and still it would not wash away the impurity: for the abyss is bottomless, and the stain in its very depths. . . ."

How does a chaste man-angel fall? Science giving birth to scepticism kills faith; a man having lost his faith falls under the tyranny of unclean love; and from that domination of matter and the senses there is no liberation, not even through the love of a pure woman. The obstinate logicalness of Kreutzer's *Sonata* has its roots deep in Musset's works.

In Musset we see the fatal division of love into physical love and spiritual love, into clean and unclean love; the age-old metaphysical and ethical dualism becomes in Musset a quite concrete dualism of sexual impurity and purity, and the problem is quite definitely stated: how, and by what, can the fall of the first man be undone, how can Adam be regenerated, how can he cleanse himself from sensuality?

In some passages faithful and pure love almost overcomes impurity (*Le Chandelier*); in the *Confession* Brigitte's pure love almost saved him from a deeper fall, but that fall is inevitable. Just read how pure and innocent Brigitte, in order to attract the unhappy man, adapts herself to his corrupted fantasy, imitating his former sweetheart in dress and in everything that might be agreeable to him—the angel of darkness has caught hold of the angel of light, and with him casts himself into a bottomless abyss. . . .

The love of a sceptic becomes the passion of a savage, seeking satisfaction in terrible and tormenting pleasures: Musset is continually complaining that it is just from that fundamental unbelief by which the soul is poisoned that corruption and coarse licentiousness result.

That type of love is simultaneously hatred. Kreutzer's *Sonata*, Dostoyevski's analysis of love, again have here their psychological predecessor. We see in the *Confession* how the corroding unbelief turns into a distrust in the faithfulness of a sweetheart, and how this distrust becomes cruel, even bloodthirsty; in the beginning the unhappy man tortures and torments Brigitte with his distrust in every possible way, in the end, however, in his increasing madness, he wants to kill her and is just lifting the dagger to pierce the faithful heart, when by a miraculous chance —a cross round his sweetheart's neck—he is turned away from the black thought.

Modern psychologists, dealing with sexual depravity and perversion, will find in Musset more than one instance of such close association of sensual love and cruelty, even bloodthirsty cruelty. Even in his first tales from Spain and Italy (Musset was only nineteen years old when he wrote them) we read of a passion leading to murder—with one hand the lover drags the corpse of a murdered man, with the other one the yielding wife of the man he has murdered. In *The Cup and the Lip* the thing is presented even more coarsely—there Musset forces the unfaithful woman to commit an act of unfaithfulness beside the coffin of her husband-lover; there is indeed in Musset's presentation of this kind of thing a kind of childishness. (He wants by means of coarse examples to show that there is no such thing as faithfulness, but it is enough that his fantasy is inclined to go that way.) In the *Confession*, too, the disease went deeper and further; a psychologist will find there many a type of sexual abnormality to add to an increasing collection.[1]

And so Octave's life hangs between two terrible abysses, between murder and self-murder. There is no other way out, but to destroy the object of his insatiable desire and finally to destroy himself. In the *Confession* we see many a time these two poles of death. The loss of faith leads by scepticism through cruelty to death. . .

How does the Voltairian sceptic end? By physical and moral suicide. Musset himself killed himself by drinking absinthe.

That, then, is in short the disease of the century, the disease of the child of our century.

Its historical origin and development Musset sets forth in his introductory chapter. It is a remarkable analysis, summarizing in a few pages the philosophy of modern French literature.

Our age—this is the kernel of Musset's philosophy of history—is a transitional period, and at that a transitional period between Voltaire's eighteenth century and the new era. "The whole disease of the present century

[1] For example: "le spectacle de la nature dans sa splendeur ayant toujours été pour moi le plus puissant des aphrodisiaques."

The Disease of the Century

proceeds from two causes: the people who lived through the years 1793 and 1814 have in their hearts two wounds. Everything that was, is no longer; everything that will be, is not yet. Do not look elsewhere for the secret of our evils." Voltaire destroyed faith in the old saints, Napoleon destroyed faith in the old kings—the old régime fell and the new one does not exist yet. Napoleon removed the kings but he himself fell, and the youth brought up for him and for his world-conquering plans was left suddenly without an aim.

With the Restoration the king was again installed, and a bit of the old order came back, but the old parchments could not give the new generation new life. The king and the priest, religion and the old political system were restored only *de facto*, but nobody believed in them any longer. The king fell and kings were falling, the younger generation was intoxicated with liberty, but it was not capable of acting freely or living freely. The rich became libertines, the middle class grasped offices, the poor got drunk with liberty, with a horrible, ineffective enthusiasm —big words caught France and drowned her in a horrible sea of aimless action.

A real life, an inner life there was not; hypocrisy and falsity spread and smothered everything in a monotonous, tedious lifelessness. It was not for nothing that a black dress suit was invented and worn in France for the first time—reason, dispersing all illusions, wore mourning.

There were hypocritical politics, there was hypocritical religion, love also became hypocritical. Egoism, terrible, cold, killing egoism held its orgies. Love became egoistical, the prostitute, the courtesan pushed back the dreaming, romantic, gentle, sweet grisette. Man separated himself from woman, for he had begun to disdain her, he threw himself upon wine, and leaving the cosy fireside of love, he killed himself in foul places. Love succumbed to the spirit of the times. As they did not believe in the old kings and the old religion, so love also became for them an old illusion. . . .

Musset does not forget the physiological causes of this social and moral change. At the time when husbands and brothers were on the field of battle in Germany, anxious mothers were bearing a fierce, pale, nervous generation. Born between two battles, educated in schools while the war drums beat, they fell into premature melancholy testing their flabby muscles in imitation of their fathers. From time to time their fathers appeared to them, red with blood, lifted them up on their chests which were decked with gold, but they immediately mounted their horses again.

The moral consequences of such an upbringing are, of course, as plain as daylight, and everyone, too, will comprehend the influence of the fact that France paid Napoleon yearly a blood-tax of three hundred thousand young men: in the ruins of the old régime moral and social anarchy took up its quarters. . . .

The child of the century lost its faith. "Neither as a child, nor at college, nor as a man did I attend church: my religion, if I had any, had neither ritual nor symbol, and I believed in nothing but a god without forms, without cult, without revelation! Poisoned from my youth up by all the writings of the past century [Musset's father

224

The Disease of the Century

published the works of Rousseau], I early sucked in the unnourishing milk of impiety. Human pride, that god of egoists, closed my mouth to prayer and my frightened soul fled through a void after hope."

We can imagine what the mind of this distracted being was like. As the century is formless, so the spirit of the individuals has less character; Musset compares his spirit to those temporary residences in which furniture from all ages and from all countries is accumulated and mixed together in discord, in disunity. His spirit is a cabinet full of various inharmonious curiosities . . . "I read much; among other things I learned to draw; I knew a great number of things by heart, but nothing in order, so that I had a head which was empty and at the same time swelled like a sponge. I fell in love with all the poets one after another; but I was by nature very receptive, and so the last one could make me dislike all the rest. I made of myself a great storehouse of ruins until at last, being no longer thirsty for the new and the unknown, I saw that I was myself a ruin."

Nevertheless, he was young, in fact he was still a child, but a child who had already been poisoned by the unfaithfulness of his sweetheart. And it was just at this point that he had no help. Voltairian philosophy did not help him; on the contrary with its scepticism it consumed even his love, pure in the beginning. He philosophized about every trifle which concerned him, but still he had no real philosophy; he had not a unified view of life, he had only the dust of thoughts, as has been said in the words of Bourget's *Disciple*.

The Disease of the Century

Musset analyses this "shameful moral disease" in detail. The disease consists of total scepticism and hopelessness—the youth of France believed in nothing. In this terrible condition people were not able to be enthusiastic even for evil, their enthusiasm was only for rejecting good. Hopelessness became insensibility. The fatal influence went from the head downward. Vital power was being destroyed by licentiousness, the spirit and the body were being killed—at the same time the spirit was destroying the body, the body the spirit. The rich said: "Nothing but wealth is truth, all the rest is illusion: let us enjoy ourselves and die." The moderately rich said: "Nothing but oblivion is truth, everything else is illusion: let us forget and die." And the poor said: "Nothing but unhappiness is truth, everything else is illusion, let us blaspheme and die."

Blasphemy—that was the result of the feeble efforts of the bloody and bleeding romanticism of Musset's times. "In blaspheming," says Musset, "the unfortunate, distracted being looks for and, sad to say, finds relief for his brimming heart: when an atheist pulls out his watch and gives God a quarter of an hour to kill him by lightning, that quarter of an hour, it is certain, is a time of anger and cruel delight." That was a paroxysm of hopelessness, that wordless invocation of all the heavenly powers; it was the protest of a poor, miserable being writhing under the foot that crushed it; it was a great cry of pain. And who knows? In the eyes of the One who sees all, it was perhaps a prayer. . . . "The distracted one finds thus a sort of occupation in imitating real despair—he laughs at fame, he laughs at religion, he laughs at love and finally he laughs at himself—he makes a fool of everything on earth. But then he does not know what to do more and finds consolation in empty blasphemy; and besides the sensation it is so pleasant to think oneself unhappy, when one is only empty and bored."

The sceptic consequently goes on towards enfeebling licentiousness and unnatural living—licentiousness is the very first effect of the fatal influence and it comes from the head—from philosophy *à la* Voltaire and Diderot, and from atheism itself; for every philosopher is, as it were, the cousin of an atheist.

Musset's Titan was, as he had to be, of the school of Goethe and Byron. Musset is well aware of that, and he himself determines for us his relation to both of them: Goethe and Byron for him are, after Napoleon, the greatest geniuses of the age, they are demigods—Musset's child of the century cannot but bow to them.

Musset derives not only from Goethe but also from Byron his extreme nervous depression and his strange inactivity. And in Faust—but still more in Werther—he sees the saddest human figure of all that ever represented evil and unhappiness; Byron, too, with his Manfred answered him only with a cry of pain, and, therefore, even though he worships them he simultaneously curses them.

From the gnostic Faust and the energetic Manfred was derived the feminine and depraved Rolla. Faust conquers the disease of the century with his philosophy, he does not give himself over entirely to pleasure, and at a great age he dies in full activity; Manfred also takes his life, but until he draws his last breath he remains an unreconciled rebel, who, even in his death, challenges heaven with his last denial. Rolla destroys the old world with foreign philosophy, Voltairian philosophy, but all he can do upon its ruins is to grow weaker through excess. It is suicide also, even though not physical and accomplished with one blow; it is moral, chronic, long-drawn-out, piecemeal suicide, it is more and many suicides.

In this weak passivity the spirit continually attaches itself to sensuous pleasures and with them it occupies itself. If it does not actually practise these pleasures at least it philosophizes about them. This progress of Rolla's scepticism Musset describes for us in all his works and in the *Confession*, too, he has explained it *in abstracto*.

Debasement and licentiousness either make a beast out of man entirely or, if he does not stop thinking, they develop in him a peculiar curiosity. Every man, sooner or later, through one kind of suffering or another, penetrates to the truth, to the "skeleton of the phantom"; that is what is called knowing the world, experience is paid for at this price. Before this trial some retreat frightened, others, weak and shaken, are like shadows after it, constantly wavering; some, and these are perhaps the best, die immediately, most forget—all stagger on to death. But there are people, and they are really unhappy, who do not retreat, who do not waver, do not die, or forget—as soon as ever they have come into contact with misfortune, otherwise called truth, they approach it bravely and resolutely, they even stretch out their hands to it. They are those who are drunk with the desire of knowing; *they* do not just look at things, they examine them through and

The Disease of the Century

through, they do nothing but doubt and examine, chasing through the world like the scouts of God. Their thoughts are as sharp as arrows, and a lynx gnaws their inward parts.

The licentious are seized with this rage more than others, for the simple reason that they, figuratively speaking, are accustomed to penetrate to the heart of things, and, if we may say so, by means of criminal contact. That is, also, why they are to the rest of the world of man like actors backstage. Thus the licentious man inevitably becomes either indifferently lazy or curious. Although he tries to see the worst in everything, he nevertheless sees that other people do not cease to believe in good. He takes no interest because he even covers his eyes, lest the voices of the rest of the world rouse him into disquietude.

Musset calls this strange state of mind "the curiosity of evil" ("*la curiosité du mal*"). It is an ugly disease, resulting from all kinds of unclean contacts. It is an instinct spying in the night after ghosts and in graves; it is an inexplicable torment by which God punishes those who have sinned—they would like to believe that everything may fall, but privately they would perhaps be unhappy if it should. They are feverishly active, they search, they analyse, they dispute, trying to see what they wish to see. They laugh to see evil done, they would swear that possible evil will come to pass, though they would fain see good in the background—a great formula that— Satan's first word perchance, when he saw Heaven's gates closing behind him!

Musset is a sincere man, for him God is no poetic

decoration, for him He is really the *ultimum refugium*. He gives me the impression of blaming God for caring so little about the order of this world when once He had created it—acting towards it like a nobleman towards his illegitimate son; Musset being in his place would arrange it differently, but, after all, so would all of us. Musset, anyhow, stands higher than Garborg's hero; Gram goes to a priest (not to a god!), Musset argues with God! Gram is only a "wearied" soul, Musset is a quite broken one, but proud, aristocratic.

Machar (in a recent letter) very correctly points out that Musset seeks God, and he remarks upon the difference between Musset's hero and Garborg's. It is indeed characteristic of Musset that he is not looking for a merely philosophical God, but for a religious one; speaking plainly, a revealed God. Musset is like Thomas: he also would like to touch his God, he does not trust in syllogisms and proofs. Between absolute faith and negation Musset recognizes no third state, or at most indifferentism. In the profound poem, *Espoir en Dieu*, he explains to us this theodicy of his: he goes through all the philosophical systems up to Kant, but he rejects them all, for even Kant is for him but an orator, and he ends up with a despairing cry to God to show Himself and thus frighten away scepticism. In truth He himself is guilty of that scepticism —why does He permit all that evil before which reason and virtue stand in fear? That is why scepticism has laid waste the land—and so it is not enough for man in his presumption to guess at God with his imagination. "God, reveal Thyself and evil and scepticism will be eradicated, they will be eradicated for ever and completely. . . ."

The Disease of the Century

Musset's scepticism is of a different type from Hume's. It is deeper—it has poisoned the very heart. Hume's scepticism is higher—it abides in the brain. Musset's is akin to Pascal's. The Pascals die of scepticism. Scepticism does not make the Humes uncomfortable.

In Rolla Musset has given us the pungent essence of his confession.

Rolla broke down all the bridges leading to the past—he lost his faith in antiquity, he lost his faith in Christianity and more particularly also in Christ.

> Les clous du Golgotha te soutiennent à peine;
> Sous ton divin tombeau le sol s'est derobé;
> Ta gloire est morte, o Christ! et sur nos croix d'ébène,
> Ton cadavre céleste en poussière est tombé! . . .

And just as he apostrophizes Christ, so the poet apostrophizes his seducer, Voltaire. Mr. Vrchlicky has expressed doubt as to whether Voltaire could have so much significance. He has, since Musset says so; Musset does not describe what he has not lived through, and have not other great poets since Musset lived through the same?

Rolla is God-fearing. He did not commit sacrilegious murders through philosophical reflection, but in excitement and agitation. Scarcely has he committed the act—and he commits it continually—he is sorry, he is anxious. He has insulted Christ on the altar, but he is frightened by the act, just as a believer is afraid of dishonouring a holy wafer. Having lost faith in the old world-order he wants to re-create the world and man, but only with his imagination, and thus in the end rationalistic pride throws him

231

into the embrace of his prostitute. He is passive in everything. Like Faust he buys love for gold, but he does not
seduce Marguerites, he only seduces himself. Faust becomes his own saviour, Rolla waits for his saviour and
waits for redemption—"which of us," he asks, "will now
become a god?"

Rolla fell because of the pride of his reason, but he
felt that fall deeply, more deeply and more sincerely than
Faust—therefore, Faust played more with the idea of
suicide, Rolla, in his delirium of pleasure alternated with
profanation and blasphemy, took his life. Faust at the
end of his life's journey is carried up into the heavens—
Rolla dies in despair, though wearing the mask of a
dandy.

Faust never felt sin, only restraint; Rolla feels sin, his
heart bleeds in the midst of his dissoluteness. Faust
philosophized his way out of the disease of the century—
Rolla does not speculate; he ends up with plain Rousseauism; he rejects civilization altogether. Longing for a
natural life, having given expression to a terrible satanic
formula, he would like not to think: it would be better to
do what the sheep do, which do not know where slaughter
awaits them and go to it chewing grass. That is better
than to be an *esprit fort*. Musset condemns his Titanism.
Like Schlegel, he wanted to vegetate like a plant and, like
our Smetana, he looked for a higher future in the vegetative life. . . .

Faust always remained more objective and did not
lose sight of the world—Rolla is submerged, is drowned
in his emotions, in passions, in love—and love is for him
"faith, the religion of earthly happiness." Rolla took more

The Disease of the Century

from Don Juan than from Faust, but he became a sentimental Don Juan. Rolla is continually and constantly subjective, the whole world is for him concentrated in emotion, in his own inner self. That is emotional egoism; Musset knows very well that in the depths of his heart he is as cold as marble towards the world, except that he feels the disease of the century. In the *Confession* in contradistinction to the egoistical Rolla he portrays quite deliberately the altruistic Smith. Faust in his objectivism becomes the ruler of a nation, Byron's Don Juan is capable of fighting for his own freedom and for that of a foreign nation—Rolla dies by the hand of Rolla. Musset also wrote, it is true, in a moment of transport, a national poem against the Germans, but his usual mood was non-political and unsocial.

He is disturbed by the anarchy of the times, but he does not take part in events in order to help society. The trend of the times (especially in 1830), did not make of him a fighter for freedom. The disorders of the times only roused him out of his emotional hysteria. He bemoans the ruin of faith in Christianity, but only because by faith in a future life all the poor and weak were able to endure, that is, to leave things alone. Freedom (that is the essence of Musset's social philosophy) made out of them enemies of Christ and they said to themselves "There is no future life." The poor said to the rich: You are only men; they said to the priests: You lie. Thus the masses called for equal rights for all, demanding for themselves the goods of not a future world, but of an earthly one: poverty and want uprooted faith among the masses, the poor believed already in themselves only and in their own hands. A

The Disease of the Century

social struggle took place and communism appeared as the only way out. That same want and poverty, Rolla is well aware, forces purity and innocence into prostitution. The tormented, enfeebled Voltairian sinks deliberately into vice and in it and by it ends his life. A strange finale for an aristocrat—or have we in Rolla, with his aristocratic Bohemianism, the first of the democratic Titans? Almost all the Titans think aristocratically, not democratically. But it was just the disease of the century which caused Rolla's death, as we read in the chapter of the *Confession* where he describes how he was waylaid in a saloon and his association with a harlot: "That was the disease of the century, in truth, that girl herself was it."

Musset's Titan did not conquer hostile Heaven, but the heavenly doors were hardly closed before him. . . .

Faust got himself into heaven with pomp but also only through mercy and by the help of metaphysical policy.

Musset is great because of his real sincerity: if we sin, let us sin—he does not conceal any of his thoughts or deeds, or his aims (in so far as he had any). Musset produces such a strong effect with that truthfulness of his because it is the truthfulness of the emotions. In this he is more modern than Goethe who is even more a man of the past, rationalistic century than of this one. Goethe too is truthful, but his truth is not so direct. This directness consists not only in sensitiveness, for even in emotion it is possible to be untruthful. We see this clearly in Victor Hugo, that Jesuit of passion and emotion.

Emotion of itself does not guarantee righteousness and truthfulness. Musset himself is a lesson for us how emo-

The Disease of the Century

tion tempts and leads astray. Read over in the *Confession* the scene where Rolla wants to stab Bridget. He is looking already on her chest for the place where her heart is—and there between her breasts he notices a small crucifix—the murderous hand weakens, repenting, he falls to the ground, and with a faltering voice cries: "My Lord, my God, my Lord, my God, You are here!"

I am not going to relate at length and in detail by what a strange chance Bridget received that miraculous cross from her dying aunt—that is neither the first nor the last accidental happening which guides Rolla's steps. And in this matter our Voltairian man is quite in accord with the ancients; chance is the master of the world and of life, and to this belief Rolla's whole religious mood corresponds—and this mood is best expressed by the term: *superstition.* A superstitious Titan!

By means of superstition that eternal wavering between belief and unbelief comes to equilibrium; thus Rolla's blasphemy is comprehensible—now for him Christ falls from the Cross into the dust, immediately afterwards the symbol of Christ saves him from the most fatal step in his life.

This is the romantic relapse into the Middle Ages, which neither Rolla nor any of his contemporaries could escape from, and in this he differs from Faust, though Faust also paid his toll to the Middle Ages. Musset in this is a Frenchman, a Catholic. Goethe's Faust is a rationalistic, a Protestant Titan.

The view of the world taken by present-day folk differs from the medieval view fundamentally in this, that it subjects the whole world and life to deterministic causality: it does not believe in miracles *ad hoc*, but it searches for the causes of phenomena, and in this knowing and foreseeing lies its power. The people of the Middle Ages were indeterminists, they believed in constant miracles, about the real cause of things they cared very little. The people of the Middle Ages were also more unconcerned, jollier. With the new age determinism, foresight, calculation, preciseness are coming into force; people are beginning to be more concerned about their future, they are more economical, they are more serious.

Catholicism holds (of course not entirely without any change) the medieval view, Protestantism passes on to the new view, which in its fulness has up to now been formulated only by science, and in the past also by philosophy. Hence the decided antagonism between science, philosophy and Catholicism. Protestantism stands in the middle, it wavers.

Protestantism is, in fact, closer to modern science and philosophy than Catholicism; modern philosophy is thoroughly Protestant. Even the modern social and political organization of life up to the present day, basing itself more and more upon science, is more advanced in Protestant countries. It is not mere chance that the national economic system which sways today the minds of all political and social thinkers, is English, Protestant, just as industry and commerce are mainly Protestant. Catholicism adopts a negative attitude towards science and philosophy: the believing Catholic refuses them and only unwillingly and inconsequently accepts their practical results; an unbelieving Catholic is a philosophical radical. But he is still so much a Catholic that in moral and social practice he constantly goes back to the Catholic cult. I am thinking of what I said about Comte's social philosophy and about his religion. Catholicism, with its firm thousand-year-old order, has such power and attraction that even Protestantism submits to it—of course Protestantism mutually has a strong influence upon Catholicism.

The influence of the Church and of the religion in which modern man was born, in which he was educated, is still very great and greater than people admit. If what Komenius and all educators tell us is at all true, namely that we become human only by education, then the power of the Church must be obvious: its educational influences act upon the most tender soul and direct our line of thought and action. They establish and strengthen habits in us; the influence of religion and the Church acts upon us in the most serious moments of our lives (birth, marriage, death), it acts upon us through the younger generation, through our children—in short, the influence of religion and the Churches is stronger upon everyone than most people are conscious of.

Even if people reject religion and the Church, and become declared atheists, they submit to its influence; nay, those who fight religion and the Church submit to them the most. The influence of the Church and religion does not lie, of course, only in accepting or rejecting single ideas, dogmas, but it shows itself, as has already been said, mainly in the direction which it gives to our life, it shows itself in the ideals which it instils into us and sets before our eyes.

237

The Disease of the Century

Many modern critics forget, when explaining personalities and works of art, the so-called milieu: philosophy and poetry betray to a much greater extent their origin in a Catholic, Protestant, or Orthodox milieu than, for example, their origin in such-and-such political or constitutional surroundings. Whence comes that fundamental difference between French and English poetry? We find real Titanism in English poetry. The Faustian idea is Protestant; Catholic and Orthodox poets changed the idea basically, submitting half-consciously to the influence of their Church.

Catholicism influences its believers and even its atheists not only through its doctrine and ritual, but also through its Church organization; Catholicism, just because of its organization, is a great and impressive social and political power. This is the reason since the Revolution of the ecclesiastical and political authority of Rome, not only in Catholic, but also in non-Catholic countries. With the Pope not only Napoleon, but even Gambetta's republic, agreed upon a concordat, although neither the soldierly Caesar nor the capitalistic democrat was a real Catholic. But the Popes no longer require so much as that.

Musset's Titan is a Catholic Titan.

Poetical Titanism is a pregnant expression of the age-old fight and of the emancipation of the human spirit, and at the same time an attempt at a new spiritual and social order. In it all the philosophical and religious problems are summed up, hence its close relation to the Churches and to positive religion.

Musset, like many French thinkers, ends his fight by accepting the external side of his Church. Not only does

238

he, like Augustine, give us his "confession"; despite all his resistance he does not go outside the external frame of the Church, its charmed circle. Musset's Titan prays, he does penance, he wants to have an absolute authority over him, and so forth—in everything you see a copy of a believing Catholic. Just as Satan is God's opponent, so the Catholic Titan is the priest's, the Pope's opponent. Blasphemy is, after all, his main revolutionary act, and that, as he himself says, is really a prayer. The Catholic Titan is too liberal not to have any fear before his Church and its spiritual and political power. But that fear does not lead to pure religion, but to superstition. That despairing fear is modern superstition *par excellence*. The superstitious Titan is the natural product of French Catholicizing policy and Catholicizing philosophy as we see them to the present day, as we see them more particularly in French Catholic romanticism taken as a whole.

Musset's Titan, like more or less all his French brothers, is a dandy. The French dandy is a strange type. He is a philosopher, but his tailor and his newspaper are for him considerable authorities, for the former mends his physical garments, the latter his spiritual. He is proud and conceited, and dreams continually of fame, but he has about him a bit of the classic theatrical hero. The French dandy is brave, he sacrifices his life for high ideals, but he cannot bear ridicule, and kills himself for a trifle and for a folly with equal ostentation. He is a knight without fear, but within him the worm of doubt gnaws, and, therefore, from resistance he falls into a compromise with the stronger, for his pride continually falls into despair.

The Disease of the Century

He carries on his Titanic revolution only in thought, theoretically, not morally and socially: the most violent radical in words and theories, he is a conservative and a reactionist in his actions; he is an enthusiastic revolutionist, but still he remains an old philistine.

Of course, it is no little thing to put off the old Adam. To overcome—to regenerate—what easy words, and what a terribly hard deed! Real victory over old views, to which we are attached, a genuine moral regeneration, what a great task! Revolution when compared with this reformation is child's play.

The French Titans penetrated no further than did the revolution. "A duel between man and God," as Lamartine called Titanism, ends, among the French, either in reconciliation or in despair, always in submission, even though sometimes Byronic obstinacy must mask retreat.

We see the romantic relapse as early as Rousseau—Rousseau even accepted Catholicism for a while; the severe determinist Calvinism in which he was brought up was too strong for him and did not accord with life. Chateaubriand's Atala ends in suicide, and René plays with it like Senancour's Oberman. Chateaubriand's Titan has a good deal of the external, the superficial, even the trifling; he despairs and doubts, but in the blood of the first martyrs (*Les Martyrs*), he only wades, he does not cleanse himself in it for a new life. Lamartine (*Job lu dans le desert—Chute d'un ange*) seeks purification in suffering for his fall, but he satisfies himself with poetical purification, in his fancy. His forte (and that holds for them all, for Constant's Adolphe too) is an analysis of suffering; he knows of no cure for it, and really does not want any. The strongest is perhaps Vigny. With his cold reason he concludes to reject God stoically, but he too has a few relapses and in *Elöe* he ends according to the traditional pattern: Satan was on the very point of raising himself by his love towards Elöe, but in the end chance conquers, bringing about his defeat. Victor Hugo raised himself no higher than great and prophetic-sounding words, Sand (*Sept cordes de lyre—Lilia*) gives us a Titanist mixture, composed of Faust, René and Byron. Leconte de Lisle flees back into antiquity, to the old gods, and contents himself in the end with some kind of purely imaginary mythology, nay, with a belief in foreign names.

The latest writers have resolved Titanism into its realistic and naturalistic elements, but they have not shown any more than the others evidence of its decline. Flaubert analyses brilliantly the romantic life of the modern bourgeois Eva; you recognize all the features of Musset's work in *Madame de Bovary* but without the romantic decoration and transferred from the aristocratic milieu into country provincialism. Madame de Bovary ends with suicide like Rolla, and she was similarly used to take refuge in religion and in God—a parallel striking even in its details, only that Flaubert describes the life of a woman.

A woman, and a courtesan at that, had been already portrayed by Hugo; after Flaubert we have the Goncourts' *Germini Lacerteux*, we have Dumas' *The Lady with the Camellias*, we have Zola's *Nana*, Daudet's *Sappho*, and others—naturalistic brutality spoils à la Marsyas the gentler illusions for that Titan, Don Juan.

The Disease of the Century

And we can imagine how, under the influence of philosophical positivism, the youngest Titans fight. Richepin, for example, parades with stupid, antiquated atheism (*The Bible of Atheism*) and with a none the less stupid materialism, seeing something magnificent in reducing his father and mother to spermatozoa. Bourget has more taste and more education, but not strength; the philosophical negation of the psychologist concludes with a prayer by the corpse of the Disciple, which Lermontov described so beautifully. Messrs. Huysmans, Coppé and others conclude with an express compromise with Catholicism.

The positivistic realists and naturalists in Zola's style proclaim their faith in science and its obstinate determinism, but Zola himself goes on a pilgrimage to Lourdes even though he does not believe yet, but with an obvious desire to be convinced and bring the struggle to an end. All the rest of the Parisian Titans are already content with symbolistic aristocratism, and the ritual of some kind of exotic neo-Buddhism, polytheism and so on and so forth.

In a word: the descendants of René and Rolla flee, the French Titans go from one defeat to another.

That my many clerical friends may not be needlessly aggravated, as they were about my study of Zola, and attack me in a swarm, I hereby declare that I did not derive all the referred-to and not-referred-to characteristics of French Titanism from Catholicism and only from Catholicism. As a matter of fact I was not writing about believing Catholics but about Titans. The Titans oppose Catholicism, they revolt against it. Of course, despite this and often just because of this, Catholicism has a marked influence upon them. What kind, how, and because of what, I have already stated and will state immediately more clearly.

It is to be further understood that in my literary-historical generalization I do not overlook the differences between persons. I know, for example, what the difference is between Vigny and Musset (I pointed it out), I know that in Bourget we find scientific and philosophical views which at the time of Musset did not exist, and so on.

There is a difference between Lamartine and Mickiewicz, between Musset and Byron. A Frenchman and a Pole, a Frenchman and an Englishman do not wear the same hats and clothes, and so also the blood in their veins flows at a different rate. But despite all these differences it is possible among the poet-Titans to empirically demonstrate such marked points of agreement that there can be no dispute about the decisive influence of Church and religion.

Therefore, for instance, Lenau's Faust may quite well be numbered among the French or the Polish Titans —from Goethe's Faust he differs just in so far as Catholicism differs from Protestantism. I will, therefore, save myself the trouble of analysing Italian Faustism and Titanism—its philosophical pessimism, its blasphemy, will be found in France, too. French poetry is the representative and leader of the poetry of Catholic nations taken as a whole. The poet of the *Ode on Satan* has also already and in the same manner reconciled himself with Rome. Satanism in all its forms is a weak and blasphemous phase of Catholic Titanism, as has been already perceived

The Disease of the Century

by Musset, and d'Annunzio could well be a French poet. And it is not only with him that French influence prevails; even our little Czech Titans are led by an inner impulse to the French School.

In my study of Zola I have already quoted the statement about "Catholic fancy": Saint-Beuve well perceived how Catholicism, with its sensuous ceremonial apparatus and with its Church organization, does not cease to have an effect even upon unbelievers and opponents. A Protestant feels this external influence of his religion in a much smaller measure, the Orthodox again more, yet less than the Catholic.

To Saint-Beuve's words about "Catholic fancy" I add here Flaubert's equally expert diagnosis of "Catholic melancholy" of which, he says, only ethereal souls are capable; Flaubert characterizes this melancholy in the statement that Madame de Bovary prayed to God in the same flattering words which she whispered to her lover.

We can explain a great deal in post-Revolutionary French poetry by means of "Catholic fancy" and "Catholic melancholy" which are, after all, only two aspects of the same spiritual and moral condition.

More particularly we shall comprehend what the French call love. Catholic teaching and the moral code of celibate chastity leave to weak people no ideal save a fantastic one—not corresponding to reality; but such is the influence of teaching and the influence of the moral code that the greatest libertine is disquieted by the teaching instilled into him already during his childhood. Reality hides and covers itself, and the exact opposite of purity dresses itself in the robe and brightness of purity;

there arises a peculiar insincerity, a peculiar hypocrisy, a peculiar lying to oneself.

Just because the attention of a child is soon turned to a thing, the influence of false purity is the more dangerous. Musset well analysed the strength and the significance of aroused curiosity about evil. *Curiosité du mal* leads naturally to *fleurs du mal.*

A man having sinned against the commandments and the rules of religion is disquieted, and that unusual spiritual and moral state which Flaubert called Catholic melancholy develops. It is a condition made up of many elements (sensuous fancy—different degrees of insincerity—self-deception and deception of others—analysis of our own condition—wavering between the extremes of purity and impurity—occasional penitence—fear of the authority of the Church, and so on). That state we can study not only in Musset, but in a whole series of French (Catholic) writers: Baudelaire, Barbey d'Aurevilly, Guy de Maupassant, Zola, Prévost and others.

A psychologist will comprehend, too, why in French literature the courtesan is so enticing. Dostoyevski too has his Sonecka, but with him the prostitute plays an altogether different role than with the Frenchman. Almost every French writer describes and worships a courtesan; Musset sees in her and in her influence the disease of the century, but already before him that modern French "woman" was portrayed by old Prévost and, after him, as we have already mentioned, by Hugo, the Goncourts, Murger, Dumas (son), Zola, Daudet, Bourget, and legions of lesser writers described her.

For the French—Stendhal has already said—there is

245

nothing in love but vanity and physical desire; and he is right in so far as modern love is concerned. It is not by accident that French literature, beginning with Stendhal, contains a series of psychological analyses of this kind of love; after Stendhal come Balzac, Michelet, Dumas (son), Bourget, Richet.

The poetry of Protestant peoples is purer than the poetry of Catholic peoples. *Ceteris paribus*, I attribute it to the Protestant conception of love, marriage, and family life.

The Catholic writers know that difference: Stendhal, Balzac, Zola, Bourget stated it. Przybyszewski stated it too, not so long ago. In outstanding English writers you do not find such provoking, analysing, sophisticated impurities as you do in French literature. Sexual problems are taken more simply, more naturally, without that sentimental illusiveness. That holds also for Byron, and for later writers, Garborg and others.

And what holds for men, holds also for women writers; George Sand, Eliot!

Between French literature and writers like Dickens, Thackeray, Eliot, Tennyson, E. Browning there yawns an abyss. These are two worlds. Taine, concluding his history of English literature, also notes this difference; he compares Tennyson and Musset and, of course, as a Frenchman and a materialistic positivist, sides with Musset and his Rolla, even though he recognizes the moral supremacy of Tennyson over Musset. It must be confessed that for Frenchmen (and for those who like their literature), Protestant literature and especially its conception of love seems monotonous, cold, insincere.

The Disease of the Century

French writers have themselves expressed this antipathy of theirs in various ways. *De facto* the difference here is one between two moral worlds.

It is impossible for me to enter here into the matter in more detail, though it would not be untimely or unsuitable in view of our literary and moral conditions; but more particularly the subject of the view taken of women and love in various literatures would require a special essay and much study. I would call your attention briefly to this only: that even in French literature there are differences due to period and to personality. *Manon Lescaut*, for example, is different from *The Lady with the Camellias*—I know all about it, but there is no time for that now. Here we are concerned only with characterization of French Titanism from this point of view also, in order that the difference between it and English, German and Russian Titanism may be understood. For example, Mephisto too laughs at Faust because he runs after every apron, and Dostoyevski analyses Karamazovism very carefully; but Taine, using a mild word, called Bohemianism, does not exist in non-Catholic non-French literature. (In Viennese literature it exists, of course, and in ours, though in different forms.)

We are not concerned here with the question as to who is most moral and where. We are not concerned here, either, with outbursts of licentiousness and lust; literary critics got the better of Schiller owing to an outburst of this kind, by threatening to publish his, as they called them, licentious poems. Musset himself was here and there very licentious; his *Deux nuits d'excès* was strong even for Heine, as Meissner relates in his diary (I, 231). But, as has been said, we are not concerned with such single events, but with that peculiar permanent moral condition showing itself in Musset's and Baudelaire's poetry and elsewhere, with that peculiar union of sexuality and religion—in a word, with that specifically French Catholic *sexual mysticism.*

That *Catholic* fancy and *Catholic* melancholy form a specific kind of *Catholic* mysticism, a sophisticated cult of instinct, a ceremonial apotheosis of matter and sensuousness under a religious, or even metaphysical and scientific veil. It is the Jesuitism of sexuality.

That Titanic revolution, in its character as a moral and social revolution, will always concern itself with sexual relations, the relation of man and wife, of family and children. If anyone wants to summarize it by misusing the word—then, with love.

Musset put his revolution most effectively into action through his philosophy of love. Woman became for him embodied pleasure and, at the same time, a punishment, woman is a sacred altar before which believers pray, and also curse:

> O femme! étrange objet de joie et de supplice!
> Mysterieux autel ou dans le sacrifice,
> On entend tour à tour blasphemer et prier!

And it is just Musset who explains how philosophical scepticism turned against love and how, then, libertinism became a cult, "the religion of earthly happiness." This strange union of mystical enthusiasm and sensuousness, that concentration of all thought and being on one object, we see first of all in Musset, with him and after him in

The Disease of the Century

Baudelaire, in the realists and the naturalists and finally in the dilettantes, in the symbolists, in Satanists and in all kinds of decadents. Decadence grows upon the ruin of the old régime, the Titanism of Musset and of the French in general is its cousin, nay, its stepbrother. With them, of course, Rolla had become old (he had got rejuvenated, some of the "young ones" would say); but just look at him for example in Prévost's *Demivierges*: here, too, the hero is a Voltairian sceptic and atheist, but he has modernized himself, he is a dilettante, he has passed through the naturalistic and the positivistic school, and therefore he has a somewhat different scepticism. He has not even a firm scepticism. And such was also his love, if it can still be called love. In very truth, the dilettante decadent already satisfies himself with airy emanations from hair and arms. . . .

The end, of course, is always and ever Rolla-like— a bullet in the head. So also ends Bourget's *Disciple*, the positivist—Huysmans satisfies himself with the recipe for moral suicide, and Zola on his old naturalistic knees begins to believe in miracles . . . the French Titan kept too much to the example of the Spanish Don Juan and thus forgot his own revolutionary aims. The Encyclopaedistic atheist, like a real libertine, likes to slip into church by stealth, and there in the dimness and the quiet of the Gothic arches he seeks new strength for his shattered nerves—even though only for new orgies—in the end only for orgies in his imagination, pictured 'mid the fragrance of the incense and to the melancholy tones of the organ. . . . Musset unsuccessfully rejected Christianity, he even unsuccessfully rejected antiquity. In Paris the

249

The Disease of the Century

Neo-Catholics rise from their romantic grave, the atheist, despite his "blasphemies," publishes the *Bible of Atheism* (Richepin) and becomes Tribulate Bonhomme, the dunce (Villiers de l'Isle Adam); then there are the Parnassians and all kinds of classicists, who celebrate their resurrection by inviting all the pagans in their organ (*nomen omen*), *Don Juan* (the organ of the League for the Extension of Paganism), to the celebration of bacchanalia and saturnalia. In the Oriental Museum a Buddhistic "mass" is heard, magicians are listened to—the French Titan has softened a great deal . . . Garborg's Gram if he saw all that would not wonder so much why a man becomes the more sentimental the more he defiles himself with revelling.

We can now reduce Musset's problem to the basic elements of philosophy and history.

The great Revolution undermined the pillars of the old political and ecclesiastical régime, but it was not able to build up a new régime; the Restoration could not do it, nor could the new republics. France is living in a century of transition. In this transition period the evils of the day are making themselves felt, and especially by the poets. Leibnitz philosophized metaphysically about evil; the poets and the thinkers of this century feel that evil within themselves. It is in the heart, says Musset, and Lamartine complained of the same thing, while de Vigny stoically stated the fact.

Evil, then, is in the heart—how did it get there? This old question Musset answers thus: Science and philosophy by scepticism killed Catholicism upon which the entire old régime rests. Voltaire tore Christ down from the Cross and threw Him into the dust; but though he made new demands on his believers, he did not give them anything to live on—so that to Voltaire we could apply Merimée's statement just now applied to Musset. Evil comes from unbelief, despairs Musset, proclaiming this no otherwise than did the reactionary opponents of the Revolution and of the rationalism of the eighteenth century; the difference, of course, between the poet and the believing Catholics is this, that they believe while he does not and cannot believe.

But he as an unbeliever, knows no other moral or metaphysical powers than the believer. This constitutes for him negation, and it is the negation of a weakling.

To the sceptic every share in the management of State and Church is denied, there is nothing left for him but his own "ego" and a private life. There is nothing left for him but love. But scepticism has undermined not only faith in the State and in the Church, it gnaws love to pieces too; scepticism, corrupting the whole of society, also poisons our emotions and our desires of the strongest and the most intimate kind, it destroys the child of the century in his very soul. Perturbation and conflict in the soul means conflict in love; sensual love, which is impure love, and pure love, which is spiritual in man, wage a fierce and constant war. We know beforehand which side will win; in this fight between the devil and God the Voltairian sides with the devil.

The old metaphysical and noetical dualism becomes in Musset this dualism between sensual love and pure love. Only that in him his god—pure love—must necessarily be at a disadvantage; if, as Musset believes, man is altogether weak and evil, if man and woman are fundamentally bad, whence and how can their union ripen into good? There arises not only the question of the origin of evil, but also the origin of good.

In this Musset and the French in general find a stumbling-block, and there is no way out until the old dogma about the impurity of matter and the flesh is returned to: there is no such thing as purely physical love; and the impurity does not lie in the body, It is a mistake to believe that the soul is elevated above the body; it is a sin, however, to proclaim that the body is above the soul. In this matter modern man is conditioned by the old period; chiefly by Catholicism.

Musset's Octave longs his whole life for love, and still he does not know how to love. In the *Confession* Musset shows us three kinds of human love, and we see not only the passionate Octave, but also the calculating Epicurean Desgenais, and finally there passes before the reader's eyes the person of self-sacrificing Smith. It is another proof of Musset's great honesty and sincerity that he did not conceal Smith from us—of course, Octave and Desgenais and Smith all in one are the child of the century. He analysed Octave and Desgenais in detail, he only outlined Smith. Smith's manner of love was not akin to Musset, for Smith could sacrifice for the sake of love; Smith also loved Bridget, quite differently from Octave, nay, only Smith really loved her. And Smith loved his sister and other persons, too—but for Octave love exhausts itself in sexual passion.

Octave knows very well and feels greatly that he does

252

The Disease of the Century

not love, that he is an egoist; scepticism has smothered love in him. The Voltairian pride in reason is the god of egoists. And, therefore, even his love is not love, but hatred. He hates those women he sacrifices to his passion, and he finally hates himself too. His love is death—it kills others and itself. This death has made its way into his head through sceptical philosophy, mainly through atheism; from the head it has penetrated into the entrails, into the whole body. Not even Bourget in his analysis of modern love knows of any other problem than the problem why love is at the same time and quite specifically hatred?

The atheist in the eighteenth century fashion succumbs to Satan—to sensuality, and in alliance with him carries on a war against the Highest—but in this war he gets no farther than blasphemy. The atheist *de facto* is not an atheist, by his anger he recognizes God, and by his weakness he subjects himself to Him. Musset's Titan only peeps at God, and just gossips philosophically about Him; his whole desire for knowledge has been converted into curiosity about evil. To deny the existence of the good entirely he has not strength.

Scepticism turns into emptiness and monotony, and all effort is devoted to filling up that emptiness; Octave, therefore, does not seek regeneration, new birth, it is enough for him to enjoy himself, and if the worst comes to the worst, to forget, to become insensible.

Octave is a sceptic, but at that an uncritical one. He sees the old world in ruins—instead of finding out what was imperfect in it, what had to fall, he laments over the ruins; nay, when his body has become enfeebled, he even returns to the ruins.

253

The Disease of the Century

In his longing for faith he becomes superstitious; he leaves life to chance, for a definite aim, an aim which governs and arranges individual deeds and ideas into a whole, he has not got. "*S'en aller chercher un hasard et rapporter une souffrance*"—to go out into the world blindly, carelessly and to return in woe, that is Octave's life work.

Work? No, no work at all, he feels, but he does not work—thus might Octave, with Oberman, have betrayed the secret of his unhappiness.

Musset's Octave and Rolla are of the order of those strong-weak Atalas, Renés, Obermans, Adolphs, who in the sombre habit of a monk, but with a belled cap on their heads, still chase the faun through France's vale of tears. "The only good that is left for me in this world is that many a time I have wept."

We see that in French post-Revolutionary literature the French soul has narrowed its purview down to its own ego—extreme subjectivism and individualism predominates in all poetry. Musset is a typical representative of that subjectivism, a subjectivism, we must add, which is purely emotional. Brunetière in one of his last works (*L'Evolution de la poésie lyrique en France au XIXᵉ siècle*) characterizes this lyricism quite correctly; he shows that Musset's dramas, Sand's novels, Michelet's history, Lamennais' political philosophy and Saint-Beuve's criticism are manifestations of that lyricism.

Morally and socially this subjectivism is egoism, just as philosophically it is scepticism in the various forms it took before arriving at modern dilettantism.

Gradually the French are turning from subjectivism to

objectivism—Gautier, George Sand signify that change. Literature is becoming more social. Saint-Beuve makes the lower classes the subject of his description, the Goncourts in the introduction to *Germini Lacerteux* promise us not a mere morbid dissertation on love, but a social analysis of morals, a history of the times in the spirit of the religion of humanity. Zola carries this farther.

But not even this objectivism suffices, as we see from the influence of the objectivism of the Russian novel. Poetic objectivism must be based upon the objectivism of the heart—upon *love*, and that love is of an altogether different kind and character from Musset's and that of all his melancholy followers. To the French even social poetry served only as a means for the mechanical emptying out of the emptiness of the soul. Hence their revolutions too were spasmodically violent, but they did not produce those reforms which the French always dreamed of and still dream of. The efforts of the impassibilists, positivists, naturalists, dilettantes, symbolists, decadents, and so forth are objectivistic attempts without depth and without sincerity, and thus the descendants of Octave and Rolla waver between superstition and belief, between sentimentality and emotion, between public opinion and truth, between sensuality and love, between Satan and God—the Titan has become an old, wanton dandy. And an old dandy, every one who knows the perversity of present-day literature will admit, is a terrible being, a terribly sad being.

Chapter III

Goethe's Faust: Superman

FAUST both formerly and today is looked upon as the typical representative of modern Titanism, and yet I began my sketches with Musset. I have given my reasons: in Octave's plain confession and in the person of simple Rolla—Faust's problem—the problem of us all—is analysed with so much mastery that we have a prototype with which to compare all the other types we meet with.[1]

Faust also is afflicted with the disease of the century, the complaint of Musset, the child of the century, but the disease is at a more advanced stage. The patient has, also, a different, a stronger constitution, therefore the symptoms form a different syndrome. At bottom, as has been said, the disease is the same: the division and the breaking up of the soul, the fight of the spirit with matter, the flight from the past into the unknown future, efforts towards or at least plans for a new life. Whereas Octave and Rolla live and die through emotion, Faust is a philosopher and a metaphysician, whose reason, even in the most violent fever, retains its power. The child of the century at once despairs and kills himself; Faust lives to an old age and quietly dies at useful work.

[1] For the purposes of this study the reader should recall to memory besides *Faust* the following works of Goethe: *Werther, Tasso, Wilhelm Meister, Prometheus* (a dramatic fragment), *Geheimnisse, Mahomet* (a dramatic fragment), *Der ewige Jude, Pandora*, also some of his poems such as: *Grenzen der Menscheit, Das Gottliche*, and others, in which the Titan and the Titanic mood and idea are renewed.

256

Superman

The French Titan carries on his fight vehemently, aggressively, blindly, the German Titan makes an attack on the basis of a great and thoroughly thought-out plan; Rolla falls while running at full speed, Faust stands unshaken, and his fellow-fighters cry: "Victory!" . . . Victory—over whom and how was Faust victorious in this fight for God and with God? . . .

> Zwei Seelen wohnen, ach! in meiner Brust,
> die eine will sich von der andern trennen;
> die eine hält in derber Liebeslust
> sich an die Welt mit klammernden Organen,
> die andre hebt gewaltsam sich vom Dust
> zu den Gefilden hoher Ahnen.

A conflict, then, as in Musset; the same fight between body and soul, sensual and ideal love, the world and the spirit; only that in Goethe the site of the conflict is rather the reason than the heart. Faust to a much greater extent and from the very beginning of his journey looked for all satisfaction and happiness in science and philosophy, but he did not find them; the more he knew the more strongly did he believe that he knew but little, after all, nothing. All philosophy leads in the end to weariness of life and to suicide. What Rolla came to by oversatiating the senses, Faust came to by overstuffing the brain.

Faust leaves philosophy and plunges into life—but by this way, too, he comes to the same end:

> O wär ich nie geboren!

he despairs in Marguerite's prison.

It is science and science only which brings us to the

conclusion that the serpent in Paradise lied when it said,
"Ye shall be as gods":

> Den Gottern gleich ich nicht! Zu tief ist es gefuhlt;
> Dem Wurme gleich ist—

This fiasco forces itself upon the Faust superman
soon, and with all the horrors of disappointed pride
and Titanic revolt.

> Welch erbärmlich Grauen
> fasst Ubermenschen dich!

cries the earth-spirit to daring Faust, the Titan before
he becomes conscious of his nothingness.

There is nothing left but poison. The recollection of
the faith, faith of his childhood, revived at the last moment
by the Easter bells, awakens in him the elementary instinct
for self-preservation; Faust yields to it, but the end is the
same—despair.

Pleasure and satisfaction are not, then, offered either
by philosophy or by love, either by reason or by the
senses. Musset's scepticism destroyed faith and by its
destruction, life. Faust loses faith because of his great
sceptical erudition and with it the love of life, but he also
loses that life by misusing it.

Faust's development is more complicated than Rolla's
and Octave's. In Faust we see three stages of development.
Faust, when he despaired of philosophy, plunged into
life and love, but from a life of love he flees to a life of
action. Rolla shot the Gordian knot to pieces, Faust un-
tied it. He is prouder than Rolla, and more energetic.

Superman

No long exposition is necessary as to the importance for us of *Faust*, Volume I and Volume II. The second is for us the more important: How did Faust finish his life struggle, and should I follow him? In all? In what?

The literary and aesthetic side of *Faust* is for me subordinate and, to speak sincerely, of little interest. There is only one thing I should like to say here. The second volume of *Faust* presents great difficulties to commentators. I add to this, that to me this second volume is not a bit more mysterious than the first. To me it is clear and transparent. True, there are various details of a symbolical, allegorical and even literary character as to the meaning of which I should not like to swear, but the meaning of the whole and the principal idea cannot, I believe, be mistaken—that is, to anyone who wants to see clearly.

The balance of the first volume of *Faust* can be summarized in the statement that knowledge for the sake of knowledge, knowledge too theoretical, too hair-splitting, knowledge which keeps a man apart from the healthy necessities of everyday life, is a great absurdity and, with its results, is necessarily hostile to life. But even that famous life is against life, if we comprehend it as Faust did.

Let us deal at once with the problem of Marguerite's tragedy and then we shall soon have done with scholasticism.

Life! Life comprehended and lived one-sidedly must end with the same fiasco as a one-sided philosophy. Faust sins against life in that he makes a be-all and end-all of love, his love. And in love Faust is where Rolla is, and therefore comes to the same end, even though he does not sink so deep as his Parisian twin-brother.

Does Faust not sink so deep? Is not Marguerite an ideal being, whereas Rolla ruins himself for love of a prostitute?

That unhappy, that ideal Marguerite! " . . . The purest and most beautiful of virgins," we read in the newest and most modern work about Goethe.[2]

I shall not quarrel with anyone who sees in Marguerite an ideal woman, but I should expect at least mention of the fact that Goethe purposely drew Marguerite thus so that he could demonstrate his thesis concerning the insatiability of love.

The corollary to this statement will not, I am afraid, meet with approval. For it is that Goethe, in writing of Marguerite, said what he had to say of women in general, or in plain words: Goethe had nothing better to say about women.

All Goethe's female characters are Marguerites. From the study of Goethe I acquire the conviction that only Ottilie in *Wahlverwandschaften*, with her deep love and lofty sacrifice, is an approach towards the real woman. Almost all the rest of the women figures are puppets. Goethe sees woman's beauty only in her body, and love for him is only the uniting of two bodies; about the betrothal, the marriage of souls he has not the least idea.

Goethe cannot conceive an independent woman, or the love and marriage of two beings loving, but also thinking and working together. He did not like that energetic

[2] Richard M. Meyer: *Goethe*, 1895, 2. In truth there is nothing ideal about Marguerite. On the contrary much that is not ideal. Everything!

thinking woman, Madame de Staël, he was actually frightened by her and ran away from her—the Titanic superman can only tolerate woman as a subman, because of whom he feels himself most vividly a superman.

That a woman might want to be a superman and even a Titan, Goethe did not deduce from classical mythology, though in Greek mythology he might well have found it. But what Goethe saw in Greek mythology was the woman-slave, and so his *Ifigenie* with its ideal of a humble, worshipping, devoted woman was born. This woman feels her weakness, but accepts it without objecting. The historical Iphigenia was supposed to have been sacrificed by her own father, this according with the moral code of the classical barbarians. Goethe's Iphigenia saves, in her womanly weakness, her Titanic race of the Tantalides from a bloody fate. It is remarkable that Goethe overcomes his Titanism so soon—his Iphigenia was born in 1779— and just with the character of a very woman.

Goethe's type of woman corresponds with the ideals of the contemporary German bourgeoisie. The German woman (*Hausfrau*) can always be certain that she will get to the heart of a man most surely through his stomach; it is not only the German woman that is just beginning to rise above this ideal! . . . after all, as regards this, we are but super-German. . . . On the other hand Goethe looks upon woman as ready at any moment to respond to the advances of a lover.

Love with Marguerite ends in the usual way. Faust did not yet need a cook *à la* Vulpius, and so the whole relation of the lovers to one another is comprised in a few philosophical phrases, and ends with brutal Don Juanerie.

Goethe's Faust:

Did not Faust sink as low as Rolla, or perhaps even lower? Is he not more inhuman? . . .

It will be objected that Faust's relation to Marguerite was only an episode, that in it Goethe described a bit of his own youth, and so on. Nevertheless I hold to my own opinion. *Faust* is the gospel of egoism, and his relations with Marguerite inexorably reveal his egoism.

Just read over the text carefully and notice especially the agreement between Faust and Mephisto: and it is just this agreement that gives us the key to the whole of *Faust* and also gives the tragedy of Marguerite its proper significance—a terrible one:

Werd ich beruhigt je mich auf ein Faulbett legen,
so sei es gleich um mich gethan!
Kannst du mich schmeichelnd je belügen
dass ich mir selbst gefallen mag,
kannst du mich mit Genuss betrügen:
das sei fümich der letzte Tag!

Mephisto does not immediately understand Faust, as we see from the further explanatory dialogue:

Das Sterben meiner ganzen Kraft
ist grade das, was ich verspreche.
Ich habe mich zu hoch gebläht;
in deinen Rang gehör ich nur.
Der grosse Geist hat mich verschmäht
vor mir verschliesst sich die Natur.
Des Denkens Faden ist zerrissen.
mir ekelt lange vor allen Wissen.
Lass in den Tiefen der Sinnlichkeit
uns gluhende Leidenschaften stillen!

262

Superman

In undurchdrungnen Zauberhüllen
sei jedes Wunder gleich bereit!
Stürzen wir uns in das Rauschen der Zeit,
ins Rollen der Begebenheit!
Da mag denn Schmerz und Genuss,
Gelingen und Verfruss
mit einander wechseln, wie es kann;
nur rastlos bethätigt sich der Mann.

MEPHISTOPHELES:

Euch ist kein Mass und Ziel gesetzt
Beliebt's Euch überall zu naschen,
im Fliehen etwas zu erhaschen,
bekomm Euch wohl, was Ruch ergötzt!
nur greift mir zu und seid nicht blöde!

FAUST:

Du hörest ja von Freud ist nicht die Rede.
Dem Taumel weih ich mich, dem schmerzlichsten Genuss,
verliebten Has, erquickendem Verdruss.
Mein Busen der vom Missensdrang geheilt ist,
soll keinem Schmerz künftig sich verschliessen,
und was der ganzen Menscheit zugetheilt ist,
will ich in meinem selbst geniessen,
mit meinem Geist das Höchst und Tiefste greifen,
ihr Wohl und Weh auf meinen Busen haufen,
und so mein eigen Selbst zu igren Selbst erweitern
und, wie sie selbst, am End auch ich zerscheitern. . . .

We see, then, that Faust makes quite consciously his contract with Mephisto and is not in doubt as to its far-reaching importance. Having become acquainted with Marguerite, he did not forget about his philosophy, he did not become a Rousseau, a child of nature—giving himself up to life, he did not destroy his reason, he merely stifled it in order to test it. Just as Faust experimented in his laboratory so he experimented in life, with life itself.

Faust is not capable of becoming so infatuated as Rolla. Faust in love is not so passive, nor can he be simple. Apriori he does not believe in the possibility of his finding satisfaction, he does not believe in the possibility of happiness, he does not even believe in real love— Marguerite is for him notning but one of his experiments subjected to his emotions and sensuality, while at the same time he keeps his reason cold and clear.

Faust's egoism is of a quite deliberate, completely rational type, it is a philosophical egoism, a terrible egoism.

Between Part I and Part II of *Faust* the commentator may, if he wishes, insert the period in which Faust repented for his guilt toward Marguerite. It was not, however, deep repentance, for Faust acts just as egoistically in the second as in the first part. Upon me the scene with Philemon and Baucis always made a sad impression. How ruthlessly Faust gets rid of them! Just as the first volume ends with several murders, and in the first instance with that of Valentine, Marguerite's brother, so in the second volume Faust burdens his conscience with the death of the old couple. The blame is the greater because there is no longer the excuse of passion.

Faust is consequently and continually an egoist from beginning to end.

When he and Wagner (at the very beginning of the first volume) mix with the people before the town, he is delighted by the cheerfulness of the crowd and rejoices with them:

> Hier bin ich Mensch, hier darf ich's sein . . .

but that humanity of his consists only of a brushing away of the dust from books. After he has ruined Marguerite he reproaches himself:

> Der Unmensch, ohne Zweck und Ruh . . .

The Faustian superman is not really a man.

Faust conquers Mephisto by the reason, and only by the reason—there is no place whatsoever for love in Faust.

Faust, of course, knows and feels that mere reason will not save him, and, therefore, in the end he turns to his fellow-men. But how! We read that he wants to embrace all mankind, but his embrace is not the embrace of love, but of philosophical pride. How he feels towards his fellow-man we see continually in Part II: he came very soon into the emperor's court and he gave advice and help in all circumstances; but finally he wanted to be—the ruler himself. He needed his fellow-men, but only in order to rule them. The superman remained, consequent to the very end.

And he would be a ruler absolutely, in accordance with the old aristocratic régime—an absolutist, and, of course, an augur, concealing from his people his (supposedly godlike) plans. Faust is a despot—in Nietzsche's words, *eine Herrennatur*:

> Wer befehlen soll,
> muss im Befehlen Seligkeit empfinden,
> Ihm ist die Brust von hohem Willen voll,

Goethe's Faust:

Doch was er will, es darf's kein Mensch ergründen.
Was er den Treusten in das Ohr geraunt,
es ist gethan, und alle Welt erstaunt.
So wird er stets der Allerhöchste sein,
der würdigste . . .

Quite in the spirit of the enlightened absolutism of the eighteenth century! Just notice all these potentates great and small whom Goethe describes, not only in *Faust*, but also in his other works: aristocratic good-for-nothings, and nothing more. On the other hand, what a difference we find between these and Tolstoy's and Dostoyevski's heroes, who look for people in order to work for them, and to deserve their love! Faust does not even know about the people. In not one of Goethe's many works do we find a poor man or anything about a poor man's life.[3]

"Nature, education, environment and habit kept me apart from all that was rough, and although I often came in contact with the lower classes, no closer relation resulted from it."

[3] "Natur, Erziehung, Umbegung, Gewohnheit hielten mich von allem Rohem abgesondert, und ob ich gleich mit den untern Volksclassen, besonders mit den Handwerken, öfters in Berührung kam, so enstand doch daraus kein näheres Verhältniss."—*Wahrheit und Dichtung*, I.5 book. This does not contradict what he once wrote to Madame von Stein: "But how greatly, on this dark road [of life] have I come, to love that class which men call the lower, but which for God is, without doubt, the highest. In it we find all the virtues together— moderation, content, simplicity, joy, faithfulness, patience, endurance in . . ." ["Wie sehr ich wieder, auf diesem dunkeln zug, Liebe zu der Classe von Menschen gelriegt habe! die man die niedere nennt, die aber gewiss für Gott die höchste ist. Da sind doch alle Tugenden deisammen, Beschranktheit, Genugsamkeit. Grader Sinn, Freude, Treue, uber das leidlichste Gute, Harmlosigkeit, Dulden — Dulden —Ausharren in . . ."] Written December 4, 1777.

Superman

Faust is continually concerned with activity, with energy; causes and results are for him secondary; he even says:

Die That ist alles, nicht's der Ruhm. . . .

and he characterizes this restless endeavour of his in the words:

Ich fuhle Kraft zu Kuhnem Fleiss. . . .

That is why he wants Titanically to tear away land from the sea—it never even occurs to him that he might work on the old land.

Faust is a romantic of action. Goethe once wrote that the idea of death in bed at home is disgusting to him (*Hausvaterod*)—this phrase enables us to fathom Faust's soul. Dostoyevski once said something against German *Vaters* and no doubt Goethe perceived the strange, narrow, wretched, philistine, shopkeeper egoism that hides behind the honourable mask of "family happiness" and similar moral phrases, which really comes to nothing more than cold calculation. But Faust breaks up the form only—he keeps to the same point of view; he satisfies egoism by different means, but he does not conquer it.

The Titan does not know and does not want to know old age—even when in the end he becomes blind he rejoices in the one thought that a bright inner light will begin to shine for him, and he hastens to complete his work as a ruler.

Professors of literary history in their simple admiration

Goethe's Faust:

(mingled somewhat with the jealousy of the educated proletariat) describe Goethe as a man who was happy and blissful in the extreme. But Goethe thinks differently from them about happiness; or rather, about this as about everything else, he has revealed to us his opinion with that rather daring sincerity which is, generally speaking, a splendid characteristic of his.

At the end of his journey Faust gives this account of his life:

OLD AGE:
Hast du die Sorge nie gekannt?

FAUST:
Ich bin nur durch die Welt gerannt;
ein jed: Gelüst ergriff ich bei den Haaren,
was nicht genügte, liess ich ziehn.
Ich habe nur begehrt und nur vollbracht,
und abermalls gewünscht, und so mit Macht
mein Leben durchgesürmt; erst gross und mächtig.
nun aber geht es weisse, geht bedächtig.—
Der Erdenkreis ist mir genug bekannt,
nach drüben ist die Aussicht uns verrannt,
Thor, wer dorthin die Augen blinzelnd richtet,
sich über Wolken seines Gleichen dichtet!
Er stehe fest und sehe hier sich um!
Dem Tüchtigen ist diese Welt nicht stumm.
Was braucht er in die Ewigkeit zu schweifen!
Was er ekennt, lässt sich ergriefen.
Er wandle so den Erdentag entlang;
wenn Geister spuchen, geh er Qual und Glück,
er, unbefriedigt jeden Augenblick!

Like Lessing, who did not want to have the complete

truth, satisfying himself with seeking it, Goethe renounces satisfaction. Faust knows that he is without a steadfast aim and without peace, but in the end in his Titanic pride he proclaims dissatisfaction as his rightful lot.

Perhaps here Faust pretends to be honest to a certain extent out of necessity, still, we believe him that he is capable of differentiating happiness from satisfaction, as he himself expresses it.

As with the progress of the times the old castes and classes with their settled views were broken up, even philosophy lost its enjoyment of the calm of a dead absolutism. Faust in this respect is a modern man; continual seeking, dissatisfaction, a kind of nervous endeavour, activity—these characterize this unsettled, unfinished period of new people.

Faust has in him a considerable amount of ethical dilettantism.

Modern man is not able to explain to himself so smoothly and simply the origin of evil as was pre-revolutionary man; our fathers always knew how to judge sin, and above all how to pass sentence on it. They liked to punish. We today no longer punish so much, and we conceive the origin of evil differently.

In this Goethe is quite modern. In *Faust*, in the very prologue, he formulates the question of the origin of evil and the freedom of the will in the manner of the older metaphysicians and of the Book of Job. But the answer to the old question sounds different; the poet makes the Lord Himself put into words on the spot the whole psychology of Faust's course of action:

Goethe's Faust:

Ein guter Mensch in seinem dunkeln Drange
ist sich des rechten Weges wohl bewusst. . . .

For Faust intention, endeavouring, longing and striving are enough. But at the end of his journey the proud Titan does not scorn all mercy from above:

Wer immer strebend sich bemüht,
den können wir erlösen;
und hat an ihm die Liebe gar
von oben Theil genommen,
begegnet ihm die selige Schaar
mit herzlichem Willkommen.

We must not then wonder even at the closing words of the first volume, words so often quoted, and still more frequently misused:

Das Ewig-Weibliche
zieht uns hinan. . . .

In what strong contrast are these words with Faust's conception of love and with Marguerite's too.

Goethe divides man just as incorrectly as Musset into sensual and spiritual parts; a more perfect harmony cannot be attained, and in the war between the two principles sensuality often secures absolute autonomy. This autonomy is not counterbalanced by the occasional autonomy of the ideal spiritual being. Faust remains divided, Faust-Mephisto.

Goethe has analysed the basic conception of Mephisto in numerous passages of *Faust* besides the already proverbial *curriculum vitae* which Mephisto himself gives:

Superman

        Ein Theil von jener Kraft,
die stets das Böse will und stets das Gute schafft.
Ich bin der Geist, der stets verneint!

    .   .   .   .   .

. . . Alles, was ihr Sünde,
Zerstörung, kurz das Böse nennt,
mein eigentliches Element.

Mephisto is described for us in many places:

O, dass dem Menschen nichts Vollkommes wird,
empfind ich nun. Du gabst zu dieser Wonne,
die mich den Göttern nah und näher bringt,
mir den Gefährten, den ich schon nicht mehr
entbehren kann, wenn er gleich kalt und frech,
mich vor mir selbst erniedrigt und zu nichts.
mit einen Worthauch, deine Gaben randelt,
Er facht in meiner Brust ein wildes Feuer
nach jenem schönen Bild geschäftig an.
So tauml ich von Begierde zu Genuss,
und im Genuss verschmacht ich nach Begierde.

Mephisto is cynical absolute depravity, he is a sceptic,
a blasphemer, a keen and bitter satirist, he is contradictious,
but he knows not in his argument milder irony or even
humour, a vulgar spitfire, impure and covetous, and
above all a sensualist. . . .

Marguerite summarizes this in the words:

Kommt er einmal zur Thür herein,
sieht er immer so spöttisch drein
und halb ergrimmt;
man sieht, dass er an nichts keinen Antheil nimmt;
es steht ihm an der Stirn geschrieben,

271

dass er nicht mag eine Seele lieben . . .
Mir wird's so wohl in deinem arm,
so frei, so hingegeben warm,
und seine Gegenwart schnürt mir das Innre zu.
. . . Das übermannt mich so sehr,
dass wo er nur mag zu uns treten,
mein ich sogar, ich liebte dich nicht mehr.
Auch wenn er da ist, könnt ich nimmer beten . . .

But on the other hand Goethe gives his devil other and higher tasks. Attention was long ago called to the fact that Mephisto has not a sufficiently unified character. He is not only a tempter, but he urges Faust on to activity and himself creates ("*Der reizt und wirkt und muss, als Teufel, schaffen*"), but most important of all, evil becomes the cause and the father of good. In Goethe the older dualistic view mingles with his pantheistic monism; hence on the one hand Mephisto is a mere negation and the opposite of good, on the other, again, a higher and more useful power is assigned to him. Once we hear that he has but limited power over the vital and creative powers of nature, elsewhere again he appears like a lower degree of nature spirit.

Goethe continually wavers between the metaphysical and the ethical conception of Mephisto. We get the absolutely cosmological definitions in which ancient chaos is mentioned:

Ich bin ein Theil des Theils, der Anfangs Alles war,
ein Theil der Finsterniss, die sich das Licht gebar,
das stolze Licht, das nur der Mutter Nacht
den alten rang, den Raum ihr streitig macht;
und doch gelingt's ihm nicht, das es, so viel es strebt.

Superman

Verhaftet an den Körpern klebt
und mit den Körpern wird's zu Grunde gehn . . .

but on the whole the ethical conception of Mephisto has the upper hand. To a certain extent this wavering is caused by the fact that Goethe personified and dramatized Mephisto. In Dostoyevski's *Brothers Karamazov* Mephisto plays a different part, an ethical and psychological part alone; of course, for the modern devil the novel is a better stage than the old theatre.

In view of this uncertainty it is no wonder that Mephisto is not conquered by Faust. Faust after death gets to heaven by reason of the fact that Mephisto, gazing upon an angel and being sensually enraptured, forgets all about Faust's soul. In place of a moral victory we have a metaphysical trick. Neither is Mephisto subdued by art. We read, though, that Mephisto has no power over the classical world, but that only means that the devil is basically a Christian, a later conception; it would be an open question as to whether art would have power over him. The chance saving of Faust at the end of Part II shows that Faust's ethics as well as his aesthetics were too weak to overcome Mephisto.

Let us leave Mephisto alone and consider how Goethe in *Faust* stated his own attitude toward the philosophical and religious problem of his day. The kernel of this problem Goethe himself crystallized in these fine words: "The real, the only and the deepest matter in the world and in human history, to which all others are subjected, remains the conflict between belief and unbelief." Where, then, does Goethe stand in the world war, where is his place and on whose side? On the side of faith? And what kind? . . .

Goethe in his whole view of the world is fundamentally a man of the eighteenth century. In his thought and emotion Goethe did not elevate himself above the eighteenth century and its problems and—errors. Goethe is less original than might be thought at first sight. I am convinced that that applies to him as a poet too. Men like Lessing and Herder are unjustly overshadowed by Goethe. True, very few are capable of writing like Goethe, and his spontaneous lyricism is a great and unusual gift.

Goethe in Part II of his *Faust*, instead of leading us ahead takes us back to the old classical past. This, if it only signified that Goethe was a classicist in art, would have nothing strange about it. But what is strange is that he is concerned to solve not only an artistic, but a vital contemporary problem, and for this a return to Hellas is inadequate. It was, as has been said, very comprehensible in the age of Winckleman, Lessing, Voltaire, but what broader significance can it have?

It is a matter of course that a return to Hellas is factually impossible; that is, the man of the eighteenth century can no longer make all the thought and emotion of the Greek his own.

Classicism cannot get rid of the content given by historical evolution and education—for Faust there remains of Helen only her dress and her form. And even Goethe's classicism is permeated with Christianity and with the newer philosophy, and it serves the dominant idea of humanism as preached at that period. In this

274

respect Goethe agrees with Lessing, Herder and Schiller, and with the whole period in general. But if we want to know how Goethe worked out the idea of humanity, what there is in it of his own, we must analyse the content of the idea and observe how its principal elements are synthesized. In the first place we may say that Goethe's humanism is, out of all proportion, more aesthetic than ethical. This subjection of ethics to aesthetics, this subordination of ethics to aesthetics, this identification of good social morals and beauty, went well with the salons of the falling nobility and the rising bourgeoisie; the provincial court of Weimar was a concrete synthesis of these two elements. But this synthesis was not a right one, and it was not that which the people of the eighteenth century sought in the Revolution, which they sought after the revolution.

My view is as follows: I have nothing to say against Goethe laying upon art and upon its importance for life an emphasis, and an emphasis so great that it raises it to the level of science and philosophy; but I do not agree with his making, in a word, a religion out of art. It is true that this belongs to the period, it is one of the characteristics of the man of the new age. It is, nevertheless, a vain attempt.

Goethe's humanism on its scientific and the philosophical side is rationalism. Rationalism is to philosophy and religion what classicism is to poetry. Faust-Goethe is a rationalist, that is, he believes in reason and in its almightiness, he would like to rationalize the whole of life:

Goethe's Faust:

Vernunft und Wissenschaft,
des Menschen allerhöchste Kraft. . . .

But Faust, even though he is on a level with his period,
cannot rid himself of scholasticism. Faust knows and feels
this, and, therefore, scholasticism is for him a target for
constant mockery. From homunculus, even though
he sets him in the pillory, he derives a kind of
joy.

Faust is not yet inspired with the modern scientific
spirit. He still delights in scholastic mystery. He declaims,
it is true, against anthropomorphism, and wants to adopt
positivism, but poetry, and especially its dramatic form,
makes anthropomorphism far too easy for him. In a prose
aphorism he writes: "Superstition is the poetry of life, so
it does not harm the poet to be superstitious." And so
Faust is full of mystery, Christian and pagan, he has
plenty of mysticism and superstition. He tries hard, of
course, to let charms and witches, these spirits and semi-
spirits, all that pagan and Christian mythology, be as little
as possible antagonistic to reason; at that time, too, the
rationalistic theologians "rationally" and "naturally"
explained the miracles which were contrary to all reason
and nature. In passing, for instance, he explains to us that
Faust can quite naturally be rejuvenated (if, à la Rousseau,
he works in the fields and so forth), but that he has a pre-
ference for trying to compound elixirs; in another place he
explains quite rationalistically how Marguerite, who is
still alive, can reveal herself to him as an "image" (Gr.
εἰδολον). Magic is for him nothing more than philosophical and cultural unnaturalness, bondage:

276

Superman

Noch hab'ich mich ins Freie night gekämpft.
Konnt ich Magie von meinem Pfad entfernen,
die Zauberspruche ganz und gar verlernen,
stand ich, Natur! vor dir ein Mann allein,
da wärs der Mühe werth ein Mensch sein.
Das war ich sonst, eh ich's im Düstern suchte—

but what is fatal is that he seeks out magic and devotes
himself to it; in one place even Mephisto reveals to us his
rationalistic creed:

Verachte nur Vernunft und Wissenschaft,
des Menschen allerhöchste Kraft. . . .
Lass nur in Blend—und Zauberwerken
dich von dem Lügengeist bestärken—
so hab ich Dich schon unbedingt . . .

but Faust again and again resorts to Mephisto's art.

Magic has, of course, not only a rational significance,
but also an ethical one, for it is a moral unnaturalness too
—an instrument of egoism. With charms Faust serves his
egoism alone; even when he uses them for others he uses
them only for his own good; you see it almost painfully
in the prison scene: Faust flies about with Mephisto at
will—to take his unhappy sweetheart out of jail on
Mephisto's cloak never occurs to him. That he (Mephisto)
brought him to her, that he gathered for him precious
treasures to give to her . . . all that he considered as a
matter of course.

That mysticism in *Faust* merges into philosophy and
poetry. Goethe, here as everywhere, formulated his
theory:

Goethe's Faust:

Poesie deutet auf die Geheimnisse der Natur und sucht sie durche's Bild zu lösen. Philosophie deutet auf die Geheimnisse der Vernunft und sucht sie durch's Wort zu lösen. Mystik deutet auf die Geheimnisse der Natur und Vernunft und sucht sie durch Wort und Bild zu lösen.

Faust's religion, too, is in agreement with this point of view.

Though Goethe is a rationalist and his mysticism has the character of philosophical gnosis, he reduces all religion to emotion:

> Nenn's Gluck! Herz! Liebe! Gott!
> Ich habe keinen Namen
> dafur! Gefühl ist Alles . . .

in this poetic phrase we find, as elsewhere, Goethe's aesthetic pantheism.

Faust also feels religious horror at the secrets of nature and of life (*"Das Schaudern ist der Menscheit bestes Theil"*). Should anyone say that this is a return to the natural religion of the Hellenes (and that thus Goethe did not accept from classicism merely its form, as I said above) I would protest: Goethe's pleasure in nature and in the natural sciences corresponds to the contemporary blossoming of the natural sciences and to delight in naturalistic romanticism.

In one who adopts this attitude there is not much of Christianity left. Faust, when the recollection of his childhood saves his life, sadly regrets it: *"Die Botschaft hör ich wohl, allein mir fehlt der Glaube."* Even in this we perceive the mood of the times. At that time Jacobi uttered the well-known words that he was a pagan by reason and a Christian by heart (*Gemüth*)—Goethe was, with some justification, called a pagan by his contemporaries, even though he himself at the close of his life claimed the title of a Christian.[4]

Goethe, so much is evident, amid the great struggle of his times, was satisfied on the whole with the rationalism of the times, avoiding a more precise formulation.

Will Niemand sein Gefuhl und seine Kirche rauben

sounds like Lessing's Nathan, but Goethe's undecidedness is implicit in that sentence too.

Goethe's Faust is a Protestant. I do not mean by that only that in questions of love he behaves himself otherwise than the Catholic Octave or Rolla. Certainly he is not so nervously agitated, the ascetic ideal no longer troubles him, and in general he is sexually more natural even though sometimes, perhaps, coaser. (Mephisto goes as far as cynicism.) Goethe, too, has written some poems praising sensuality quite in a "pagan manner," but on the whole he was always capable of controlling himself. Perhaps this also was due to egoism.

The whole Faustian idea is Protestant, and especially the fact that Faust relies entirely upon himself. In Faust there is a bit of the Cromwellian independent; he does not fear even the devil, and he makes his way up to the throne of the Highest—by philosophy, without prayer; prayer is for him only awe before unpenetrated secrets. The

---

[4] April 7, 1830, he said to Müller: "Sie wissen, wie ich das Christenthum achte, oder Sie wissen es vielliecht auch nicht: wer ist denn noch heut zu Tage ein Christ, wie Christus ihn haben wollte? Ich allein veilleichte, ob ihr mich gleich fur einen Heiden haltet."

Catholic Faust for all his resistance feels weaker, he relies either on mercy or he despairs.[5]

That Goethe borrows Catholic drapery does not matter. For many Protestants, from the very beginning, their own cult has not sufficed. More particularly the second part of *Faust* was written during a strong romantic movement, with a reversion to Catholicism, even among Protestants. Goethe, as in other matters, so in this succumbs to the strong influences of the time.

Protestantism manifests itself also in the form and manner of the Faustian revolution. The German revolution was contemporary with the Reformation, so that in the eighteenth century the Germans were quieter and, therefore, relatively more conservative than the radical French. The Revocation of the latter by the Edict of Nantes suppressed the Reformation, and, therefore, prepared the way for the Encyclopaedists and the Jacobins. German

---

[5] The Protestant origin of the Faustian idea was again proved in an interesting manner by G. Milchsack: *Historia D. Johannis Fausti des Zauberers*, Theil I, 1892–7. (I would not accept all Milchsack's deductions.) Goethe himself quite consciously prefers Protestantism to Catholicism. In Protestantism he sees pure Christianity, in Catholicism he sees, in the first instance, the Church endeavouring to gain power over the masses. The Church is not going to educate its masses, else they would drop away from it, and therefore it is the task of Protestanism to forestall the Catholics with noble efforts to develop, and thus to work even for the Catholics. For the Catholics will not be able to resist enlightenment and through enlightenment they will approach Protestantism, which again through the same enlightenment will free itself from its sectarianism, so that in the end there will be unity and harmony: there will be Christianity of thought and action, people will feel free and elevated by right humanity, differences of external cult will lose their importance. (Goethe to Eckermann, April 11, 1832.)

revolutionary feeling was in the eighteenth century rather literary, philosophical and theological, less political, and political revolutionary feeling was of a milder type. Protestants already believe more in reform than in revolution. (*"Ohne Rast, aber ohne Hast."*) So also Faust carries out his revolution philosophically; he is also much more positive than his French twin. He does not reject all the old, but joins it to the new. This synthesis he tries to construct positively; pure negation, hopeless negation no longer tempts him. In politics, too, he likes to attach himself to established things. So strong is this conservatism in revolutionary Faust that he becomes a reactionary in many respects. The French Revolution satisfied itself often only with exterior politics. The Faustian revolution penetrates more deeply, to the very foundations. Hence the exterior does not bother Faust, rather, at least, it does not excite him so much. The creator of Faust was certainly rather bored at the duke's court, but he tolerated it, nevertheless, and not even Faust forgot the macrobians, and judging from the age to which he lived took care to have a good digestion. Goethe at least devoted a considerable amount of thought to the kitchen.

Faust and the Faustian idea haunted me for a very long time. Already on the form in school I learned *Faust* by heart, but I soon felt that I could not get enthusiastic about it. I studied Goethe a great deal, and it was just on his *Faust* that I concentrated.

For years and years these studies continued, for years and years I compared all the Faustian creations of world literature and tried to understand them in connection with the whole development of culture.

Today I have no doubt about *Faust* and Goethe.

There is not enough unity in Goethe. He is a Spinozian, but what he preaches in his *Faust* is the gospel of dualism, and of an unnatural dualism. He is sometimes enthusiastic about old metaphysics, but at the same time he forces himself into Kantian criticism and empiricism. This empiricism, often conceived in the spirit of modern positivism and realism, he unites again with a strange gnostic mysticism and scholasticism. A Spinozian and at the same time a Kantian, he claims to be considered a Christian; he is a Protestant, but he finds a certain amount of pleasure in Catholic romanticism; he is a Christian, but at the same time a classic pagan and humanist. . . .

All these elements are no doubt united by a strong personality. But I do not see that the synthesis is critical enough, really unified or harmonious—only the person gives it unity, and the lack of real harmony is made up for by the powerful fancy of the poet. Goethe is a very giant of dilettantism. We can see that in *Faust.*[6] It is no matter that Goethe borrowed the almost complete idea of *Faust*, but it is important that on *Faust* he worked all his life without being able to bring about the longed-for unity. It is not a matter here, of course, of literary unity only, and of the individual disparities which we see in both volumes and in their differing plans; it is a matter here of

[6] I see in *Faust*, then, even more incoherence than, e.g. Kuno Fischer (*Goethe's Faust*, 2 vols., 1893), and Baumgart's work (*Goethes Faust als einheitliche Dichtung erlautert*, I, 1893), which contradicts Fischer, does not convince me.

the very noetical and philosophical foundations. And in view of this I summarize my opinion of Goethe by saying that he is a dilettante—a giant among dilettantes.

Goethe's dilettantism is the best proof that he did not overcome scepticism.[7]

For Goethe the worldly man remains the ethical ideal. This is the practical side of dilettantism. But dilettantism is a shallow thing whatever side you look at it from. Actually, Goethe is for me a very vivid demonstration how a tremendous mind, a great genius, taking part in the spiritual struggle of several generations, could be satisfied to leave his life's secrets unsolved. That he always candidly points out that he does so is his greatest greatness.

The Faustian problem is a very serious one for me, so I cannot be satisfied with less than a most careful analysis of Goethe's *Faust*. Let the reader, therefore, not wonder that I set forth once more here the chief philosophical elements of *Faust*. I just want to realize more particularly what it is in *Faust* that I object to. I am concerned to get to understand Faustian dilettantism. I have lately spoken fairly frequently of dilettantism, and I have reproached not only the elder, but even some of the younger literati and politicians with it. Now suddenly I declare that Goethe is a dilettante—will not this create confusion?

Not at all. Dilettantism is a modern synthesis of various and extremely different cultural elements. There is hence a difference between dilettantism and dilettantism according to the elements which it contains, and there is a

_____

[7] He himself wrote: "Eigentlich weiss man nur, wenn man wenig weiss; mit dem wissen wachst der Zweifel." (I do not believe that.)

difference as to how they are blended in it and with what philosophical depths.

Goethe in the fight between belief and unbelief constructs his great artistic-philosophic-religious synthesis against scepticism. It is a comprehensive synthesis—it comprises special aspects of humanity and man as a whole.

In the first instance this synthesis is characterized by a predominance of aesthetic elements over ethical elements. Faustian ethics, considered from the practical point of view, are nothing more than egoism. Mankind (we read continually in Eckerman) is a community of dunces and idiots, the material for outstanding men to work with. Love is reduced to sexual, sensual love. Goethe in all his creative work does not deal with children (what he says of his own childhood makes no difference here)—and yet so many words above love! How is it possible to love and not to love the little ones?

Just as aesthetics preponderate over world ethics, so Goethe replaces too much religion by metaphysics. And his metaphysics has a rather strong scholastic element. In the intellect the struggle between science and myth, belief and superstition, magic and philosophy is overcome. Goethe flees from science and philosophy like Musset, like Comte and the romantics. Faust is more rational than Rolla, Faust is a Protestant, but so much the more do we feel in him that disparity between reason and fancy, the present and the past.

Goethe conceives religion both rationalistically and romantically. He sees metaphysics in religion, but he also sees in it emotion. These elements are not reconciled and united in Goethe. The Church, despite its domineering spirit and imperfections, Goethe accepts as the leader of the weak and imperfect. Too often religion is compensated for by art. There is a strong artistic element in Goethe's love towards nature; through this love his religion becomes not so much pantheistic as mainly naturalistic.[8]

Goethe, by means of this subjectivism of his, evades naturalism, but in doing so he at once loses the ethical element in his religion. Goethe's ethics is wholly naturalistic—natural and inborn powers are for him moral. Christianity and paganism stand in sharp contrast to one another.

Faust does not, through his synthesis, find peace for his soul. His soul is fatally divided and at variance with itself. In this restlessness, in this dissatisfaction, in order not to despair there is finally nothing left for him but practical activity; but even here he keeps himself going by constantly hastening from one action to another. This activity, this restless endeavour is the real character of Faust and the lot of modern man; its counterpart is at best resignation, delighting in its woes and sufferings. (*"Ich bin ein Mensch gewesen und das heisst ein Kampfer sein."*)

Faust is a real Titan, a superman. But he did not fight his fight out. Despite all his strength he was not victorious. Faust's head burns, but his heart remains too cold. Like Comte, Goethe laid much more stress upon new teaching than upon his new life. He is a Titan of the

[8] Read the last conversation with Eckermann (March 11, 1892); there is in it the essence of Goethe's religious philosophy; I would here call your attention to how Goethe kept on invoking Christ and the sun.

reason, but a weakling at heart. He is a strange mixture of revolutionary philosophy and reactionary life.

Goethe is strong, very strong, but Shakespeare had already gone farther, much farther.

That is how I understand Goethe's dilettantism. It is a different dilettantism from Renan's, and it cannot and must not be compared with Vrehlicky's type of mechanical syncretism. Renan was a dilettante in art and philosophy, Goethe was not a dilettante in art. It was just from art that Renan made a Jesuitism of the heart. Goethe as an artist is absolutely genuine, he is himself and complete, and knows not such compromises as Renan's. Goethe, too, philosophizes much more genuinely and much more deeply than Renan. Renan sees his principal opponent in Jesuitism, but in his fear of the devil he uses Beelzebub to chase him out. Working against scepticism and unbelief, Renan overfills the brain with individual ideas, artificially, but cleverly joined together; he has not a coherent whole, or even a great unity. Renan's dilettantism is a philosophical aestheticizing daintiness, it is modernized scholasticism; Goethe tried to make a new creative synthesis with art, just as Kant tried to make it with philosophy—hence Goethe differs from Renan not only in degree, but in quality.

Chapter IV

German Faustism

I THINK that the development of post-Goethe German literature is not at variance with my opinion.

In modern German literary circles a "return to Goethe" has often been talked of. This is comprehensible, for Goethe is to it what Kant is to German philosophy, and in a similar manner a "return to Kant" was advocated. I think that such returns are impossible. Besides, the difficulties of the most recent German literature have their source either directly or indirectly in Goethe and his ideas.

There are, therefore, voices to which Goethe no longer makes any response.[1]

Here I should like to determine Goethe's historical place in German literature, though only in a general way.

I will not discuss here how the idea of Faust had been worked out before Goethe's time, how much Goethe accepted from his various predecessors, which of his con-

---

[1] The latest is R. M. Meyer: *Goethe*, 1895, who tried to judge Goethe from the modern point of view. But Meyer's arguments, which are rather literary-aesthetic, are not my arguments; not even Vischer's older criticism of the second volume of *Faust* ("ein mechanisches Product, nicht geworden, sondern gemacht, fabriziert, geschustert"), although I realize Vischer's social motive, expressed later in his satirical *Faust, Part III: Faust, Der Tragoedie dritter Theil. Treu im Geist des Goetheschen Faust gedichtet, von Deutobold Symboliʒetti Allegarawitsch Mystifinʒinski* (Fr. von Vischer), 4 ed., 1896.—Duhring (*Die Grossen der modernen Literatur*, 1893). It is not deep enough, and besides, the author has adopted Duhring's manner.

temporaries worked on Faust (Scherer brings in Lessing's fragment, Müller, Wiedmann, Schreiber, Klinger, Soden, Schink), nor will I dilate upon Goethe's influence upon the new age, or even *Faust's*. Enough has been written on these subjects.

I see Faust in his contemporary setting.

Faust with his philosophy, his rationalistic humanism, and his classicism is the child of the eighteenth century. I do not say that in a derogatory sense, but the ideas of our time are almost all from the last century. Nevertheless, the conception and execution of *Faust* is antiquated to us. *Faust* is based on German philosophical idealism. For German literature Goethe is a standard of pure art. Goethe did not write so much about Kant as about Schiller; and still Goethe is closer to Kant, both in his intellect, in his tendencies, and in his method. They have in common extreme intellectuality, the endeavour to overcome both scepticism and tradition by reason. Even ethics are, for both, mainly rational. But that applies only to formal principles: materially Kant's ethics differ fundamentally from those of Goethe—true, Kant's anti-egoistic imperative leads to quite aristocratic conclusions. If *Faust* was compared with the *Critique* there would be found even in particulars a marked agreement (for example in the matter of anthropomorphism—I have given an excerpt from *Faust*). There is, however, a difference, and a marked difference, between the two: Kant is a rigorist, Goethe is a dilettante. There is a difference also in philosophical depth: Kant is not satisfied with the superficial.

Faust can also be compared with Hegel's philosophy. Hegel is, of course, more historical, and thus the dualism

German Faustism

Faust-Mephisto becomes for him a historical dualism. To Hegel, the Faust-Mephisto story is the story of one and the same person. As far as dualism and its unification are concerned, Fichte, for instance, and post-Kantian German philosophy as a whole form a background for *Faust*. The German idealists made a god out of the individual—Stirner in his *Individual* sounds as if he were writing a commentary on Faust's egoism.

Schopenhauer lays greater emphasis on the mysterious side of life, the intellect is for him already subjugated, will and emotion take the first place. Goethe does not so much yield to emotion as place life-force above reason. This psychological romanticism shows itself very strongly in *Faust*. Schopenhauer, with his pessimism, continues in the mode of Faust after he had ruined Marguerite. Pessimism is the logical result if blind force governs an individual and his life. And to blind force Faust, too, trusted very greatly.

Nietzsche, under the influence of Schopenhauer, made this element but a component part of his superman. The baptismal certificate of the latter comes direct from *Faust*. Nietzsche is more subjective than Goethe, and, in his subjectivism, consciously more consequent. Goethe's subjectivism was shipwrecked on egoism and sought a compromise with objectivism. But Nietzsche derives his subjectivism as modern people in general do, more from emotion than from the intellect; in the end he surrenders completely to blind will and Darwin's instinctive struggle for existence. The Faustian superman degenerates from the conscious Titan into the blind wrestler, the philosophical Promethian surrenders at discretion to the selective chances of evolution. The Titan-superman reduces himself *ad absurdum*. The revolt of Nietzsche's superman is no longer a sign of strength, but of weakness, out of the superman there came only an anti-man of pure negation. Zarathrustra, who was to become a superman, nay, a super-Christ, degenerated into a mere antichrist.

Nietzsche's followers of the type of Panizza became in the end caricatures of Faust—a superman in the light of sad reality cannot but be comical.

In such failures we can see, as if under a microscope, the mistakes of *Faust*. The Faustian superman is an incarnation of egoism and sceptical subjectivism.

In the imaginative literature of the nineteenth century the Faustian idea rules not only among the Germans, but in world literature in general. We have learned what Musset's relation to Goethe is; Goethe himself defined his relation to Byron—the rest of Faust's influence we shall fathom in succeeding essays. Here we are concerned only with German Faustism.

The nineteenth century carries on the revolution of the eighteenth century, changing, for the most part, merely its weapons: we carry on our revolution by means of emotion, whereas Faust's contemporaries made use of reason. The nineteenth century is romantic, sentimental.

To be exact, it is only *mere romantic*. For romanticism, too, had ripened in the previous century. Goethe himself paid his tribute to it with his Wertherism.

Faust is harder. The relation of *Werther* to *Faust* is well characterized by the poet's attitude, in each, to suicide. In his youth Goethe, of course, only romantically played with suicide. ("*Grille des Selbstmordes*"; as in *Wahrheit und Dichtung* he says himself.) In *Faust* the problem is not only emotional, but rational, metaphysical. However, even in *Faust* there is still a good deal of sentimental romanticism. Goethe in Volume II philosophizes about his romanticism, making Byron his son and Helen of Troy's, and it is noteworthy that of the younger generation he chose Byron and Byron only.

From romanticism, if we consider the main movements only, there developed among the Germans a decadence various in form and degree, and in that decadence, and with it, what is called modernity. Of modernity I say, that it grew out of the decadence and with it: for modernity is the child of the decadence and at the same time an attempt to get rid of the decadence.[2]

Romanticism—decadence—modernity prevail over post-Goethe Faustism too. So powerful, so authoritative, and so contemporaneous is Goethe's idea that the problem of *Faust* is still being solved and worked out.

Immediately after publishing Volume I of *Faust* the Epigoni begin to appear. I name only Grabbe (he combined Faust with Don Juan purposely, as if that association were not already in Goethe) and Holteye. (Scherer brings in the following names from the preceding period: K. Schöne, Klingemann, Julius v. Voss, C. C. L. Schöne, J. D. Hollmann.) The following from German literature seem to me to be more typical and significant:

[2] The reader will infer that for me German and French realism and naturalism are not so dramatically opposed to romanticism as is usually asserted. Realism is a matter of method, romanticism of the prevailing mood; they may exclude each other, but they need not. (More about this matter in the study on Zola.)

German Faustism

Heine, Lenau, Richard Wagner, and finally among the most recent writers, Hauptmann.

I begin my remarks with Heine. (Really only remarks, no literary history!) I could not say that one work of Heine's satisfies me more than another, but as a whole they have considerable significance.

I do not mean only his literary revolt against bourgeois philistinism, but his whole world-view, and still more his Mephistophelian temperament, breaking out in a strange mixture of Voltairian classicism, redolent of the aridity of Talmudian sophistry, of sentimental Byronism, rising by degrees to cynicism, and of decadent anarchism.

Like Faust, Heine leaves the heights of idealism and throws himself into the lowlands of sensualism—sensualism not only out-philosophized, but instinctively racial, Semitic. In Heine we can study the man of the new age, how step by step he becomes disillusioned—in love and in art, in politics and finally in philosophy. His heart betrays him first, his head follows—what, anyhow, would the head be without the heart for the modern man? Heine, like many others, also rejected all culture in the end. ("*Vizli-Puzli*.")

Hegelianism made of Heine not only a Titan, but a god. As a god he behaved like Goethe's god in the poem, *God and bayadère*, but very soon there was no money or health for that. The godliness wore off (the reader will see that I am keeping to Heine's self-analysis), until it finally perished. Heine was cured of apotheosic illusion and even of liberal atheism.

als der Atheismus anfing, sehr stark, nach Käse, Brantwein

uі¹d Teback zu stinken: da gingen mir plötzlich die Augen auf, und was ich nicht durch meinen Verstand begriff, ich jetzt durch den Geruchssinn, durch das Missbehagen des Ekels, und mit meinem Atheismus hatte es, Gottlob! ein Ende.

Titanic aristocracism is really very hard to get rid of. Heine in his strange hostile-friendly relation to Goethe did not fall in with Faust on this matter. To repent during illness and from fear is not to solve the problem. I do not know whether, having become a Christian in his own old way even on his death-bed, that strange delight (*Wollust*) in suffering troubled him—I, at least despite all his literary repugnance towards romanticism, do not believe that that repentance was very deep, even though it was to blood. The poor fellow became a Lazarus (*Laʒarus*), but still without real, strengthening hope. And so his Faustian-Byronic revolutionism, despite all its intensity of feeling, did not contribute to the solution of the problem of the times. Heine was not altogether genuine.[3]

About Faust's convictions there can be no doubt. Heine's revolutionary sentiment was always more negative; for positive reform he lacked heart and real faith— his insensitivity to Boern (to a certain extent even toward Platen) clearly shows that he could talk about the period of action which was to follow philosophizing, but that he was not capable of being a safe leader of it. But he comprehended the social movement of the age, and Saint Simon had quite a marked influence upon him, but not a

---

[3] Compare: *Der Doktor Faust, ein Tanʒpoem; nebst kuriosen Berichten über Teufel, Heʒen und Schwarʒkunst,* 1847. Mephistopheles is exchanged for Madame Mephistopheles.

deep one. Lassalle seemed to him to be the expected Messiah of the nineteenth century! That is characteristic of Heine and it is not contradicted by his later idealization of Judaism and his delight in Rothschild. And, in the Jewish way, Heine never forgot all the humiliations and woes which in his youth he had to suffer both from Christians and from Jews. That hatred, breaking the shackles of prejudices thousands of years old, spoke a language comprehensible to all the oppressed and humiliated—but it was not the language of love, but of violence. . . .

Heine journalized Titanism—in this was his strength but also his weakness.

Hardly had Goethe finished his *Faust* when Lenau created a new Faust (1833–1835). A really new one even though under the influence of Goethe's great work; but Lenau's attempt is the more interesting in that he was able to work out the given material independently. Independence I mean, of course, in some of the leading ideas, not in the details.

As all Titans so also Lenau's Faust loses the faith of his youth and sinks into scepticism—and Lenau's turning from religion is the more painful in that belief had a great influence upon him in his youth, and in that he was deeply pious. Goethe's Faust never felt the loss of faith as did Lenau's Faust—Lenau's Faust is a Catholic, and, therefore, the rejection of faith leaves an emptiness greater and deeper than in the Protestant Faust. Lenau's Faust feels in this the same as Musset's Octave and Rolla.

With scepticism the fear of death necessarily associates itself—the consciousness of one's own weakness and insignificance. But the sceptic wants to be a god, he wants to forget that he is a created being and that modesty befits a creature—pride leads him to the illusion that he is a god. Of course, that is only an illusion and a self-deception.

Könnt' ich vergessen, dass ich Creatur . . .

In this self-deception the Titan step by step breaks all the ties that bind him to life. Having lost faith—faith in Christ—he falls away from nature until there is nothing left for him but his own ego. But it is his own ego that he cannot bear: like a scorpion he destroys himself and ends up by despairing and suicide.

Lenau analysed very precisely and typically this pathological development of his Faust. It will be of value to us in further studies if we comprehend and get a thorough understanding of this matter and what we have already discussed will gain in cohesion. We meet with much the same kind of thing in Dostoyevski.

In academic terminology: in Lenau's Faust, as in every Faust and Titan, a struggle takes place between objectivism and subjectivism; in other words, Lenau's Faust loses his position in the external world and limits himself ever more and more to his own subjective world, and this he, like everyone else, cannot bear—he begins, as Lenau says, to gnaw at himself until he destroys himself. And of this process, Faust's gradual concentration upon his ego, the manner in which this subjectivism leads to an illusion of equality with the divine, how the individual worships himself and how he destroys himself by his pantheism (*"Dich, Welt und Gott in Eins zusammen-schweissen"*),Lenau becomes aware with inexorable clarity.

German Faustism

Faith gives a man an object to live for, and thus binds him to life. If faith is no longer sufficient, nature helps. Lenau's Faust knows this, but he loses not only faith but also love towards the world, towards nature. He feels that the objective world is beginning to disappear from his head and his heart, and, therefore, in his longing for objectivization he throws himself into the whirl of sensual love. He knows that love would save him and bind him to a being outside himself and by this means to the world and to life, but love is for him, as for Rolla, and for Goethe's Faust, only sensuality, and this cannot save him. Amid this whirl of passion pure love touches him, but only touches him, and for a moment only; instead of saving him it destroys him. Love towards Mary makes a murderer of him—he kills Mary's betrothed, and by this means kills himself.

Lenau in an unusual dramatic poem, *Don Juan*, analyses the significance and the result of sensuality. Don Juan wants to get by sensuality what Faust tries to get by metaphysics:

> Es heisst mich meiner Manneskraft vertrauen,
> und sprengen Kühn des Edens feste Thüren,
> den Cherub an der Pforte niederhauen.

By means of sensuality Don Juan escapes from himself and attaches himself to the world:

> Die Selbsvertiefung wollte nie behagen,
> statt in mich selbst zu graben, zog ich vor
> keck in die Welt ein derbes Loch zu schlagen.

But sensuality in the end only makes one dull, makes

an animal out of man; he longs for the "incarnation of women" as Lenau himself says of his Don Juan. Despite this, however (seeking this embodiment of womanhood is of course in vain, and in the end nothing but an illusion veiling licentiousness), in the end Don Juanism necessarily ends in disgust—and Don Juan, like the philosophizing Faust, is forfeited to the devil. The only difference is that Don Juan does not cause his own death, remaining objective to the very end:

> Der Todesstoss muss mich von aussen treffen,
> Krankheit, Gewalt—nur sei's gegenüber—

whereas Faust having lost his objectivity ends in subjectivist suicidal delirium.

De facto, for Faust the objectivist, the Don Juan stage soon ends on the one hand in disgust and boredom; and on the other hand, it is brought to an end by subjectivism, eclipsism.

There is yet another stage between Don Juan boredom and extreme subjectivism, namely hatred. Sensual love changes into hatred: of course this love is not really love, hence when it turns to boredom it causes hatred toward men and toward the world. This hatred is still objectivistic, but reaching in suicide its culminating point, its crisis, it becomes hatred towards its own ego—and murderous hate ends in self-murder.

Goethe describes the same process, but Goethe's Faust does not suffer so acutely from the disease of the century as Lenau's Faust or Musset's Rolla and Octave. Goethe's Faust, too, is led by sensuality to murder and to desperation, but despite this he is stronger, or if you wish he has less sensitive nerves, and thus the balance between the world and himself is not lost. Lenau's Faust has weaker nerves, his disease in every stage is more acute, and therefore also it ends differently from the disease of his predecessors.

From Lenau's *Faust* we can, therefore, judge better what the transition from faith to scepticism and to subjectivistic pantheism means, and what the transition from objectivism to subjectivism means in general, what the oscillation of a Titan's life between sensuality and hatred of the world and of himself means, and that terrible Titanic dualism of murder and self-murder.

As has already been mentioned, we find this kind of analysis in Dostoyevski too; and we have it already in Lenau. Lenau's Faust is the authoritative type of a Catholic Faust, and that is why I have discussed it at greater length.

I maintain that my explanation is correct, as the reader will easily see if he reads carefully just that one scene where Mephistopheles relates his and Faust's devilish plan:

> Am Menschen ist's ein mir beliebter Zug,
> dass, wenn's Geschick ihm eine Wunde schlug,
> wenn ein Verdruss die Seele ihm erreicht,
> der Sinnenreiz viel freier ihn beschleicht;
> als wären als dann seine Tugendwächter,
> —die doch am Ende nur gedungne Fechter—
> vom Schmerz berauscht, verschlafen an der Pforte.
> Gewaltig packten ihn des Grafen Worte;[4]

[4] Count Isenburg, a friend of Faust in youth, visits him and persuades him to depart from his ways. . . .

nun steht's mit meinem Faust am rechten Sprunge,
ganz durchgeweicht ist mir der arme Junge.
wogegen er sich lange mochte sträuben,
dem wird er nin sich rasch entgegenstürzen,
im Drang sich zu zerstreuen, zu betäuben,
die Tage des Verdrusses abzukürzen.
frisch zu versehren seine Lebenskraft
im Todestaumel süsser Leidenschaft,
Von Christus ist er los; noch hab ich nur
zu lösen meinen Faust von der natur.
Gelingen wird's, ich had' es mir durchdacht!
Tief in die Lust, hervor die Lieb erwacht!
Mit Weibern zärtlich rohes Spiel getrieben!
Manch Kind gezeugtm—So wird der grade Stand
sich zwischen Faust und der Natur verschieben
und er im Unmuth Sturmen an dem Rand.
Dann fasst die Liebe ihn am steilen Bord
und stürzt hinab ihn jählings in den Mord,
und schlug er der Natur darum manche Wunde
so lässt sein Stolz ihn nicht Versohnung suchen;
nein! weil er sie gekränkt wird er ihr fluchen
und los sich reissen wild aus ihrem Bunde.[5]
Ist mir der Bruch gelungen zwischen beiden,
von jeder Friedensmacht ihn abzuschneiden,
dann setzt er sich mit seinem Ich allein,
und in den Kreis spring ich dann mit hinein.
Dann lass ich rings um ihn mein Feuer brennen,
er wird im Glutring hierhin, dorthin rennen,
ein Skorpion sein eignes Ich erstechen.—

---

[5] The reader should read over more carefully the scene: *Der Abendgang*—how Faust by hatred, by murder estranged himself from nature. In short, Lenau's idea can be expressed thus: nature is life itself, every flower says, Do not kill!

German Faustism

So wird mein Schmerz am Göttlichen sich rachen,
so will Verstossner ich mein Leiden kühlen,
verdenband mich als Gegenschöpfer fuhlen.

Just a few more remarks and mainly about the
Catholicism of Lenau's Faust.

Altogether we have in Lenau as in the French (see his
Faust and in *Don Juan*) that peculiar, restless sensuality;
Mephisto says of it in one place:

schwankt noch immer zwischen Lust und Scheue . . .

Lenau looks upon science and philosophy quite differently from Goethe. He sees in them sin and a decisive
incompatible opposition to faith; he would fain teach
truth through crime. Like Goethe's Faust he does not
trust in himself, and he is not able to save himself: he
despairs and ends in suicide. Lenau's Faust is a Titan,
but a weakling—he wants to crush the Highest by negation, spite and blasphemy—Lenau's Mephisto, we have
read, is only an anti-Creator, and his own creative power
he reveals by hatred, destruction, death.

Lenau himself at one time thought of becoming a
Protestant; and he acquired an intimate acquaintance with
the ideals of the Reformation (see his works: *The Albigenses*
and others), but he did not get the better of his scepticism
or his pessimism either religiously or philosophically.
He sank completely into sentimental romanticism and by
it his sublime spirit was destroyed. . . .

Lenau's Faust is more modern than Goethe's Faust.
His pessimistic romanticism is a continuation, not only
a result, of rationalistic Faustism.

German Faustism

Literary historians have already called attention to the similarity of Eschenbach's *Parsifal* and Goethe's *Faust*—Richard Wagner's *Parsifal* is definitely a solution of the Faustian problem. Despite, however, considerable similarity a glance suffices to show that there are also obvious differences, and in general Richard Wagner's mood and point of view are quite different from Goethe's. Wagner is a full-blooded decadent, and in this he differs from Goethe in whom the decadence is still incipient. Wagner is, one might rather say, a decadent romantic—in him romanticism, over-ripe, degenerated into decadence.[6]

The Faustian problem is solved by Wagner religiously and not only metaphysically, and already in this *Parsifal* differs most fundamentally from *Faust*: the Titan-sinner awaits salvation and a saviour, and, of course, he must be his own saviour:

> Höchsten Heiles Wunder:
> Erlosung dem Erlöser!

Despite this Protestant individualism, sin in Wagner, like salvation, is collective. The sin of modern man is civilization, from it modern man must save himself—thus Wagner outdoes Rousseau's religious rationalism. The real importance of civilization lies in the fact that nature, while yet uninjured by it, perceives its own strength,

---

[6] I would call the reader's attention to the fact that recent composers have been attracted by the theme of Faust: Mozart (*Don Juan*), Berlioz (*La Damnation de Faust*), Chopin (*Don Juan fantasie*), Gounod (*Faust*), Schumann (*Overture to Faust—Manfred*), Wagner wrote an overture to *Faust*, Liszt (*Faust Symphony—Episodes from Lenau's* Faust), adaptation for the piano of Berlioz's *Damnation de Faust*; Rubinstein (*Demon—Faust*), Smetana (*Demon*).

perceives the unbearableness of civilization and rids itself of it once and for all by revolution: revolution gives man strength, art gives him beauty, for the Wagnerian Titan must be a strong and beautiful man.

The revolution of salvation, as a collective act, will be carried out by the nation as a whole, by the German nation; of course the saviour will be an individual too, but he will only fulfil his task if he can subordinate and sacrifice himself to the whole, and if he gives real expression to that by which the whole lives. And this individual saviour will fulfil his task only if he is enraptured by that sacred illusion (*Wahn*) which will strengthen him in voluntary abandonment and suffering, in his self-sacrifice.

Of this divine illusion is born the most sublime and the purest artistic work. This takes the form more particularly of genuine (Wagnerian) music: music differs from other arts in being the absolute incarnation of the world substance, the very essence of the world itself—music (we can no longer get along using Schopenhauer's words) is the melody to the text which is called the world. In music the world speaks to us directly in its own language. Music replaces language and overcomes language: languages are a means to civilization and, like civilization, mistaken—the very fact that in modern times music has such a great influence is a proof that modern man is trying to escape civilization. To modern civilization music is what Christianity was to the over-ripe ancient civilization; music is, too, the only real Christian art. At the same time it is a mainly German art—music is the art in which, maybe, the artistic achievement of the future is progressing towards maturity. In it the higher synthesis of poetry, myth, of all art and philosophy, will be brought to completion. Richard Wagner in his *Parsifal* (or even in the *Ring der Nibelungen*) supplied the germ, nay, more than the germ, of this work of the future: on to the Wagnerian stage created by architect and painter there steps an actor, creating by mimicry, song and word. Music and poetry complete the artistic whole. The real artist of the future, however, is the nation. In artistic work man finds real satisfaction, which he longs for because of the triviality and the misery of life and the world.

Artistic work is, hence, religion. Religion in its very essence is nothing but the knowledge that the world is an evil, an illusion, a dream: religion is that vast desire for salvation from that illusion, and we shall attain salvation only by resignation, by sacrifice, by belief. Art (genuine art) is the imaginative creation of mythical religious symbols, not for dogmatic ends, but in order to lead to the understanding of the real meaning of religion.

Music, and with it artistic work as a whole, is, then, like St. John the Baptist to the expected Saviour, it is in a sense that Saviour Himself, in so far as it is identified with religion.

I do not know whether I have been successful in drawing the reader's attention to the main problems of Wagnerian metaphysics which have their roots in Schopenhauer's pessimism; the doctrine of blind will, of the *substance* of the world, of salvation, the denial and the destruction of that will are Schopenhauerian, as is also the philosophy of music and art in general. The reader must, of course, endeavour to understand this, and he must as much as possible live himself into Wagner's mystical mood—for it is, after all, evident that we are moving in a mystical and mythical realm.

The Faustian problem acquired with Wagner a new metaphysical and religious meaning: the world and the life of each one of us is in itself an evil and a sin, and that is why, again, this world and life consist of nothing but the desire to overcome this world and life: that overcoming cannot come about through reason and philosophy, but through life itself; in the depths of our consciousness the miracle must happen, and it will happen only if we feel the deepest sympathy with the misery of the world, sympathy towards our fellow-men with whom, as with the whole world, we feel ourselves to be one and the same being. Pantheism, which forced Lenau's Faust into despair, forces the Wagnerian-Schopenhauerian Parsifal into sympathy. Lenau's Faust still believes in the possibility of happiness, and he chases it—Parsifal came to know that this happiness is not and cannot be, and then he finds satisfaction in sympathy. By sympathy he conquers the world.

Historically speaking, evil is synonymous with what we call civilization and culture. In particular, the State, as an organ of civilization, must be overcome and replaced by pure religion: language, we are told, is overcome by music. Civilization will be broken by nature; civilization being reason, will be done away with by instinct. The natural power is the nation—not that nation which is recognized by law, and by the State, that is to say, not a nation of the selfish intelligentsia and educated people, without bourgeoisie, without the peasant mob; to the

German Faustism

nation belongs only he who out of his mere human nature draws the strength for revolution against the unnatural pressure of civilization. A nation is a synthesis of all those who feel the common misery. The real artist creates the heroic figures that man in his misery longs for.

From the moral point of view, culture appears as corruption due to surfeit—as sexual perversion. To overcome this perversion means to become natural, naïve, and, of course, mainly, not to become unnatural, to keep one's purity and simplicity. In *Parsifal* Wagner describes for us Amforta's fall and his recovery through the uncontaminated Parsifal. Parsifal defies temptation by Kundry because he recollects in time Amfort's error. Amfort succumbed to the temptation of that same Kundry, and Parsifal has deep sympathy for him.

> Durch Mitleid wissend
> der reine Thor . . .

Parsifal is and remains simple, pure, but still he has recognized his danger of falling, he has come to know the "turbid glow," but has quenched it through sympathy. By this sacrifice, by this suppression of egoism, Parsifal attains two things: Amfort is saved and his fall undone, and Parsifal himself is saved.

Musset, longing so much for purification, would hardly be satisfied with that solution—how can Amfort be saved by someone else's sacrifice? And is he saved purely passively? Or are we to think that his ruin is also retrieved by his illness?

After Goethe, Wagner is one of the greatest and most genuine of dilettantes. His dilettantism has all the faults of dilettantism, the chief of which is uncritical synthesis, the joining, the tying together of elements incompatible with one another. The unity is artificial, forced. Wagner combines Catholic and Protestant Christianity with Buddhism and Brahmanism; at the same time, however, he opposes Christianity, though his opposition takes the form of antisemitism; likewise, although he is a German nationalist, his uncritical culling of not only various elements of old German culture but even of Roman and Celtic ones does not matter to him; Goethe, Kant, but most of all, of course, Schopenhauer, adopt this synthesis, the concrete form of which is to be *Gesammtkunstwerk* (co-operation of the arts). I fully admit that Wagner with that idea of his did a great deal for art, nay, I admit that the idea itself is in certain respects a right one, but what is wrong with it is that dilettantist synthesis.

That inorganic forcible combination and identification of elements which cannot be identified (religion can never be art, or even music: science and philosophy cannot be brought into consonance with ancient myth), the harmony and calm which Wagner tried so much to find, cannot be attained by the means he proposed. Wagner's religion is a *salto mortale* to pure superstition; his mysticism and mysteriousness cannot satisfy a man who has been through Kant and Hume and has lost his Christianity; Wagner, with his symbols, snatches scraps of faith to which lifeless exotic myths and ceremonies cannot give life. In the end Wagnerian symbolism as a whole is nothing but scholastic materialism acting upon the senses much more than upon the soul; the visible Grail, the bleeding lance, and quite in the spirit of naturalistic decadence, bleeding Ámfortas, the corpse of Titurel, and yet again a sensuous feasting of the eyes upon fantastic figures and stage sets, the masterly sensuous, enervating music and finally that tickling of the nerves and of the senses by a devil-woman like Kundry and by the witch-maidens—in short, decadence to the highest degree. The doctor himself is attacked by the illness which he is fighting. That is why decadence has, in his works such an outstanding place, and it has a greater effect than his medicine—the medicine itself is, of course, decadent.

Wagner's system cannot stand against even comparatively severe criticism. Take his philosophy of religion: the idea of religion merges, as has already been said, into the ideal of art, into myths, and in the end you will find in Wagner statements which signify that religion is really nothing more than a social manifestation of the sex instinct and the like.[7]

Wagner's *proton pseudos*, like Goethe's before him, is the identification of life with sensuality, only that Wagner exceeded Goethe in decadence. Woman is, for Wagner, a principle, unconscious of itself and absolutely simple— a man giving himself to a woman performs, by means of his love, Rousseau's decivilizing miracle, but Wagner

[7] "Die gemeinsame menschliche Natur wird am stärksten von dem Individuum, als seine eigene und individuelle Natur, empfunden, wie sie sich in ihm als Labensund Leibestrieb kundgibt; die Befriedigung dieses Triebes ist es, was den Einzelnen zur Gesellschaft drängt, in welcher er eben dadurch, dass er ihn nur in Gesellschaft befriedigen kann, ganz von selbst zu den Bewusstsein gelangtdas als ein religioses d.h. gemeinsames, seine Natur rechtfertigt."—*Gesammelte Schriften und Dichtungen*, IV, 91.

forgot that, in man, he is setting instinct above reason, and just that instinct alone by which his philosophy of woman is seriously shaken. *De facto* Wagner worships and adores the sexual instinct in general. In *Parsifal* he shows us in the figure of Kundry just simply a woman-Mephistopheles (a woman-Mephistopheles is as characteristic for Wagner as for Heine), he forgot real woman, although the Grail Kings are married. It is quite characteristic of a decadent cleverly to describe disease and to take a delight in sexual excitement. True, Wagner continually speaks about the strength of love—but in such a manner that he only stresses its impotence. The weakling Nietzsche too continually prattles about superman.

Wagner tells us that through Elsa in *Löhengrin* he became conscious of the real essence of the woman of the future and of true love. Through her jealousy, he says, he comprehended the fulness of love; I, on the contrary, see in *Löhengrin* that he requires of woman a blind, a slavish love—Löhengrin in his part as an aristocratic augur does not even reveal to Elsa who he is—what kind of *love* is possible here? Is it love, is it *friendship* of which Wagner sometimes speaks? No, Elsa is only a decadent edition of Marguerite, to whom Faust did not and could not reveal who he really was and what he wanted because she would not have understood.

I have no mind to belittle Wagner. No, I reject only his religion and his philosophy. But, of course, Wagner and Schopenhaeur are the best possible examples of how a great genius can get things into a tangle, and how just because of his doing so he is liked by the people of our age. That is, indeed, a *signum temporis*!

German Faustism

Our age likes mysticism and occultism in all its forms, hence so much the more must Wagner be applauded; even the chauvinistic French themselves accepted his mysticism. Wagner, ultra-romantically, believes only in emotion and in the blind instincts, reason is for him only a form or manifestation of emotion—psychology of this kind is very popular today ("*Im Drama sollen wirewissend werden durch das Gefuhl.*") Belittling the reason opens the door wide to superstition—and superstition is popular. A superstitious person does not criticize and accepts all the contradictions of the decadent synthesis: he swallows, without hesitating, any number of definitions of religion and each one different, he rejoices when his master praises now power, now German pugnacity, but at the same time he likes the fact that he is to sacrifice himself in the Christian manner, and he likes this the more because that bloody sacrifice is taking place—on the stage. The decadent philistine likes to play the part of are volutionary, and he is full of delight that he will wipe out hated civilization at one blow and that he will become a strong man, a man. . . . In this revolutionary mood not even the labourer is hateful to the Wagnerian aristocrat, for he knows that only the labourer can carry out the revolution, he is the genius, the genuine artist and the prophet of the future—socialism, finally, is a quite artistic background for the superman-Titan who unites in himself all cultural forces and powers (Wagner accepts "culture," but not "civilization"!); the Wagnerian Titan is a founder of religion, a philosopher, a mythologist, an artist, a spokesman of pure humanity and of the nation and so on, the saviour of the world and at the same time of himself.

309

German Faustism

On Richard Wagner's face we see the sardonic grin of the decadent Mephistopheles. Compared with this, old Faust was rather strong. From him this composite Titanic elixir derives.

Our Smetana had already done it better in music.[8]

The youngest Faust is Hauptmann's master bell-founder Heinrich in *Versunkene Glocke*. From the *Sunken Bell* Wagner, Nietzsche, Goethe speak to us, each so clearly in his own words and thoughts that we see at once that we have a feeble piece of work before us. Besides, the drama is in itself somewhat lethargic (this applies to all of Hauptmann's dramas). The poet, as if he did not dare to speak openly and definitely, does not dare to think definitely and strongly—where you expect a serious, manly word, you meet with philosophic diplomacy. There is something Jesuistic here, I would almost say, at any rate a strange old-world mixture of subtlety and weakness.

Hauptmann's Faust is taking to the mountain a bell for a little chapel, but a household god in the forest overturns his cart and the bell falls down into a lake. The bell-founder dives after his work—though he had been dissatisfied with it. Half-dead after his sousing he reaches the house of Wittichen the witch, and here he is cured by the fairy Rautendelein (the name is an anagram on *Edelnatur*?). In her voice the master recognizes the tones which had sounded within him, but which he had tried in vain to breathe into his bells. The priest with some friends comes for the bell-founder, and the witch whose

[8] This is Smetana, the Czech musician, not Smetana the philosopher.

house he is living in gives him up. Now it is Rautendelein's turn—she comes down from her mountains to the
people and to the master's house—the fairy cures him at
home (his faithful wife has not been able to do it) and,
having receovered, he slips away into the mountains after
his fairy. There he wants to build his church and to cast
a new bell. He is full of life and determination—but
again the priest and the wrathful people come: he is not
afraid of the people, but there is within him a penitent
pain and mistrust; and then he hears that his wife lies
deep in the lake with the bell, and when she rings it
loudly, Faust returns, broken, to his former community.
But he no longer finds peace or a home there—again he
returns to the woods. Rautendelein in the meantime has
married the old god in the well—the witch once more
bewitches her for a moment and in her arms the bell-
founder dies just before sunrise.

Master Heinrich (Goethe's Faust was also Heinrich)
as everyone can see, is a type of the incompleteness and
fragmentariness of the times. Hauptmann's Faust continually wavers between the old and the new world and
is not able to make a manly decision; it is more by accident
than by anything else that he gets into the mountains, it
is not by his own will, and just because of this, then,
he constantly makes pilgrimages from the mountains to
the valley, from the valley to the mountains.

And what does he want in those mountains?

All we see is that Master Heinrich wants to leave the
old church and its religion, but all his symbolism can tell
us nothing definite or new about what he wants except
that he is dissatisfied with the old life and wants a new

one. But the life in the mountains is an old life—the realm of Pan, the nymphs, the fairies and the other spirits is older than the life he is abandoning. So much having been already written about Titans, Hauptmann might have known this already.

All we hear about the new bells that are to sound in the new church is:

> . . . Mit wetternder Posaunen Laut
> mach es verstummen aller Kirchen Glocken
> und künde, sich in Jauchzen überschlagend,
> die Neugeburt des Lichtes in die Welt.
> . . . Und nun erklingt mein Wunderglockenspiel
> in süssen, brunstig süssen, Lockelauten,
> dass jede Brust erschluchzt vor roeher Lust:
> es singt ein Lied, verloren und vergessen,
> ein Heimatlied, ein Kinderliebeslied,
> aus Märchenbrunnentiefen aufgeschöpft,
> gekannt von jedem, dennoch unerhört
> und wie es anhebt, heimlich, zehrend-bang,
> bald Nachtigallenschmerzbald Taubenlachen—
> da bricht das Eisin jeder Menschenbrust,
> und Hass und Groll und Wuth und Qual und Pein
> zerschmiltzt in heissen, heissen, heissen Thränen.
> So aber treten alle wir and Kreuz
> und, noch in Thränen, jubeln wir hinan,
> wo endlich, durch der sonne Kraft erlost,
> der todte Heiland seine Glieder regt
> und strahlend, lachend, eröger Jugend voll,
> ein Jüngling, in den Maien niedersteigt . . .

Rejuvenation, then—we know that Goethe's Faust desired that; power—this Wagner promises; happiness—that Nietzsche preaches. But how and by what is rejuvenation to be attained? how can we instil strength into degenerated nerves and veins, and what is there to look forward to and to enjoy? . . . Oh! if only these modern men would but realize how empty and even monotonous those programmes of theirs are!

What does Rautendelein represent? The primitive world *à la* Rousseau? The Germanic world (or as Nietzsche calls it, the Hellenic)? And what, in the dialect of the authors, do these mythical beings signify? The people, the nation? Hauptmann in his *Weavers*, like other moderns, placed himself on the side of the people, but it does not seem to me that he did so from complete conviction (in the introduction to the *Weavers* he flirts with his weaver ancestry). I do not say that he did not appreciate the seriousness of the problem of the times; on the one side the individual—on the other the masses; but Heine already felt that, Wagner felt it, we all feel it. But in Hauptmann there is a "lonely man," an aristocrat, he does not feel with the people. We can feel this in all his work, and having said so much we have said all.

I will philosophize no longer as to what may be deduced from the fairytale form of the work (*Die Versunkene Glocke: ein deutsches Märchendrama*): as to its simplicity, mythical content and so forth—these ingredients are already familiar; but why did not Hauptmann, like a decent merchant, at least weigh them; so much of this, so much of that!—but no, the buyer has to do the weighing himself. The decline from Goethe's Faust is evident and great! Except for one incident (Hauptmann's Faust is married, but not much is made of that—Marguerite has become a respectable German housewife and mother) the *Sunken Bell* does not give us anything new, nor does it even show us the old more forcefully.

In German literature since Goethe there has been no writer talented enough to excel Goethe's *Faust*, or even to present to us his problem in a more modern form, such efforts as *Faust der That*, or more bluntly: *Kampf um Gott*, are one as weak as the other.

There are rather spirits who, leaving Faust for the time being, set out on a more passable way. Among the most talented of these I reckon Otta Ludwig and Gottfried Keller. Otta Ludwig, impelled to return to the past, became a disciple of Shakespeare. He did well, Otto Ludwig, too, understood the soul of the people better than did Hauptmann, and loved it better (*Zwischen Himmel und Erde.*)

Gottfried Keller is, too, more "popular" than many of his great predecessors, and more "popular" than many moderns, even though he ostentatiously claims to be a social democrat. Gottfried Keller sincerely loves his people (*Die Leute von Seldwylla*), and that counts for much more than the socialistic programme of Arne Holz (*Buch der Zeit—Leider eines Modernen*).

The Faustian problem was conceived by Keller, I should say, more intimately, more nationally (*Der grune Heinrich*) than by the numerous modern Titans in miniature. His religious and philosophical *credo* has already been formulated in his recently published memoirs. Taking his cue from Feuerbach he requires atheism and the conviction of mortality not only as a man, but as an artist: " . . . I am firmly convinced that no artist who does not fully and exclusively feel the desire to be a mortal man, has a future," he says, in his summary of atheistic humanism, the significance of which lies precisely in his strength of conviction and faith. We pass in Keller from Wagner's dilettante man of the mist to sunny clearness and certainty.

Finally, I must not forget to mention Hebbel. The creator of the new drama in Germany in his finer works has dealt, of course, with the life of the proletarian people. There has long been a prevailing tendency in literature thus to pour oil on troubled (social) waves. But a good deal of oil would have to be poured upon the troubled waters of the Faust problem before they were calmed—and the oil would have to be of good quality. There is not very much of this oil in Hebbel, at least we moderns look for it in vain.

INDEX

316

Index

317

Index

Index

Index